500
W I L D
Game & Fish
Recipes

500
W I L D
Game & Fish
Recipes

• •

From the readers of Game & Fish Publications

Edited and with an introduction and commentary by Galen Winter

WILLOW CREEK PRESS

Minocqua, Wisconsin

Previous ISBN 0-932558-27-5

ISBN 1-57223-008-8

Published by WILLOW CREEK PRESS
an imprint of Outlook Publishing
P.O. Box 147
Minocqua, WI 54548

For information on other Willow Creek titles, write or call 1-800-850-WILD.

For *Game & Fish Publications* subscription information, write to Game & Fish Publications, 2250 Newmarket Parkway, Marietta, GA 30067, or call 404-953-9222.

Printed in the U.S.A.

Acknowledgements

This book was made possible by the contributions of people who know and love fish and game. We asked readers of *Game & Fish Publications* to send us their favorite original recipes that featured species of North American fish and game. The response was overwhelming. These original recipes joined those from an earlier publication, *101 Wisconsin Recipes*, to make what we feel is the most complete cookbook of its type ever aimed at outdoors people.

Besides the payment our contributors received, we have recognized them by showing their names at the end of each recipe they contributed, and we'd like to recognize them again here. To these people we say thanks, and to those who will use this book for years to come we say, simply, enjoy!

Alma E. Morton
A. J. Bahls
Robert Blair
Bonnie Japuntich
Robert Niehaus
Beverly Rychter
Todd Schauer
Mrs. James Pierce
Elsbeth C. Davison
Mrs. Walter Passehl
Ray Charles
Ray Lardinois
A. H. Ludwig
Eugene N. Russell
Mrs. Emil Pagel
Howard Kohlhepp
Mrs. John Allen
Andy Weber
Donald Welch
Donald Kender
Ron Sarauer
Larry Bolchen
Kenneth Mallak
C. Bison
Judy Debriun
Ted Janot
Mrs. Phyllis Harder
Margie Kmetz
Jim Bruckner
Larry Hitchcock
Bruce Gunther
Terry Baumgartner
Greg Allen
Karle E. Tonn

C. W. Gray
Mrs. Len Johnson
Eric A. Lewis
Virginia Kraegenbrink
Mrs. Richard Miller
Jean Harris
Mrs. Cliff Rauscher
Mrs. Rhea Sasse
Mrs. Hilary Loabieck
"Jimmie" Garnett
Bill Gloeckler
Robert Weiss
Mrs. Loren Lane
Curtis Heise
Richard Kuhman
Mrs. Al Zierden
David Brower
Louis A. Loboda
Ed Schulmpf
Dave Johnson
Carol Bach
Peter Konopacky
Mary L. Olson
Craig Parks
Mrs. Elaine Olson
Jeanne Urban
Ellen Rosborough
Donna Gilbert
Henry & Mary VanKerkvoorde
Helen Tschida
Mrs. Lucille Fenske
Ted Urban
Yvonne Boelter
Mark Holzmann

G. D. Winter
Mrs. Mabel Schroeder
Nancy Huennekens
Darla Arndt
John Schultz
Mrs. Charles Reichert
L. F. Krueger
Paul Merfeld
Marilyn Lemke
Mrs. D. J. Kutcher
Berneice Dombek
Chris Dorsey
David Manson
Donna & Jim St. Laurent
Jan Jacobson
Terry Collard
Mrs. Richard Strauman
Deb Schroeder
Larraine Overturs
Marjorie Hausen
Sue Ziegler
Mrs. Charles Miller
Mike Berger
Jim Tilkens
Dean Dashner
Carol Nushart
Anley Christianson
T. A. Danowski
Tom Goddard
Jerry Ringwelski
Heidi Scheinert
Mike Hinz
Al Dawydiuk
Laverne Wubben

Ray Barczyk
Mrs. Joseph Vross
Cathy Fehrenbach
Mrs. C. N. Atkinson
Shane Clarke
Christina Syverson
Mrs. Charles Booth
Mrs. Elaine Heiar
Lloyd Recore
Dan Danczyk
Donald Dorner
Karen Schmidt
Margie Homer
Mona Bouressa
Penny Hickman
Dick Baumgartner, Jr.
Spencer Anderson
Florence Burhans
Lori Kramer
Mrs. George Mass
Mrs. Anne Danowski
Mrs. Lyle Kothbauer
Judy Dixon
Mrs. Char Schroll
Sue Hartzell, Cornell
Sharon Prochaska
Deb Heusi
Mrs. Francis Lardinois
Marlene Eder
Ray Kreuzer
Bob Thorpe
Dr. Karl Johnson
John Milani
Floyd Plank

Mrs. Ken Radke
Jane Gosvold
Esther Heath
Rick Peterson
Robin G. Nelson
Mrs. Don Koch
Shirley Peterson
Fred Hoekstra
Janine Zeutschel
Herb Behnke
L. F. Holzworth
Ken Tomaszewski
T. W. Poulette
Marie Jorgensen
Gary Kraszewski
Pollie Richelman
Jill Delforge
Mary DeLong
Brad Peotter
Harry Grayske
George Mauthei
John Renard
Mrs. Jeff Van Caster
Betty Miller
Mary Lynn Schroeder
Mrs. Edward Zinniel
Steve Windett
Carol Vanooyen
Gerald Lahner
Shirley Dyrud
Cathy Fehrenback
Brenda & Paul Ross
Gib Dutton
Iris Faude

Kevin Voigt
Kathryn Cowdery
Tracy Johnson
Dennis Mayer
Mrs. Paul Marty
Paul Codette
Alice Wilker
Harold Knudtson
Shelley & David Hraychuck
Gretchen Larson
Emma Olson
Darlis Wilfer
G. A. Seefeldt
Bob Vosen
Marilyn Benish
Mrs. Jan Teachout
Keith Reda
Bret Roddenback
Jean Bradtke
Debbie Hoppe
Susan Stray
David Post
Gail Nigbor
Velma Bray
Mrs. Robert Brown
Mary Scott
Jerry Wick
John C. Wessel
C. Benson
Jim Schoneman
Charlotte Larson
Dan Hirchert
Mrs. Pat Arnston
Mrs. Maureen Steele

The editors wish to thank Susan Scheinert and Sue Smith for their assistance in the review and selection of the recipes contained in this book.

Contents

....

Introduction

Back in the days when *Homo Erectus* made his appearance on the earth, mankind had a pretty tough time of it in the edible meat department. Few were brave enough to challenge a black bear for the salmon it had knocked out of the stream, and man didn't hunt most of the animals; it was the other way around. As a result, the only flesh he was able to get consisted of the dead bodies he found. And sometimes they had been dead for quite a spell before he found them. I think our early ancestors initiated the practice of throwing meat on the fire not for the effect on the taste buds but for the purposes of eliminating the smell.

As time passed, our ancient progenitors became accustomed to and developed a taste for burned meat, preferring it over grass, dried roots, stones, and the bark of trees. (The burning of meat on coals is still ceremoniously observed by campers—who, apparently, don't mind grass, dried roots, stones, and the bark of trees mixed in with their hamburger.) It was our prehistoric ancestors' burning of meat which signaled the beginning of wild game cookery and marked the first halting steps of mankind towards civilization.

As a direct result of this early game cooking, the population of the earth increased. After an evening meal, folks would hang around the cave fire telling lies and, thus, did not freeze to death during those cold prehistoric Februaries. Moreover, saber-toothed tigers didn't want to have anything to do with fire, so they often went hungry. Some of them completely discontinued the practice of eating people and evolved into pussycats. Mankind's lifespan began to increase and soon there were a lot more mouths to feed. In no time at all, there weren't enough dead bodies to go around. It was in this atmosphere of crisis that man's second great leap forward occurred.

An unsung hero invented the snare, the trapper appeared on the scene and more meat became available for the campfire. Trapping was reasonably effective with smaller animals, like rodents,* but history contains no record of a snare ever catching a trout, a turkey, an elk, or a mule deer. You can't really blame the primitive if he longed for a venison chop, a roast mallard, or a charcoal-broiled walleye. (A diet of mole, wild leek, and acorn—day after day—can be boring.) The trapper wasn't able to provide the supply of meat the growing population demanded of him.

Then one day, a primeval genius said to himself, "What if I mix up some carbon with sulfur and nitrate of potassium and then pour it down a pipe—the interior diameter of which is such that twelve lead balls fitting into the pipe will weigh one pound—and then, what if I shove one of those lead balls down on top of the powder, aim the pipe at a moose and then ignite the mixture??? Oh, to hell with it. It's too complicated." So instead he invented the spear, the bow and arrow, and the split bamboo fly rod, and fish and fowl as well as the larger animals made their appearance on mankind's table.

And with the advent of those new foodstuffs, there came the requirement for the development of new methods of food preparation. If the hunter had not come back to the cave with a mallard, the cave woman would never have invented duck á la orange. Without duck á la orange, there would have been no need to invent the orange. And without the orange, Central Florida would still be a wasteland. No orange groves. No Disney World. Perhaps

---

* The cooking of rats and mice is evidently a lost art, because not a single such recipe was sent to us for inclusion in this cookbook.

not even a Mickey Mouse.

Not only do the culinary and entertainment worlds owe a debt to the game cook, the arts and sciences are similarly obligated. Numbers and the basics of mathematics were a by-product of the cooking of game. The standardization of recipes had been impossible until some early cook produced a system for giving a uniform and universally understood answer to the question, "How many gourds full of bay leaves do you add to the Hairy Mammoth Stew?" And after spending years and years to arrive at the proper ingredients and proportions for the Bearnaise sauce, the caveman deer camp cook didn't want to forget it. He marked it down on a piece of birchbark and the rudiments of writing were discovered.

History abounds with similar examples. Few know that Brunhilde Gutenberg was a terrible cook. Her schnitzel was too salty and there wasn't enough hassen in her hassenpfeffer. And it was all because her handwriting was atrocious. No one could read her recipes, not even Brunhilde herself. Finally, in desperation, her husband invented the printing press and thereafter, Brunhilde Gutenberg was able to read her cooking notes, became an excellent game cook, and the Age of Enlightenment overtook the Dark Ages.

And so went the progress of the human kind—onward and upward—seemingly linked to the progress of the culinary arts. During the past century, however, it has not been all beer and skittles for either the well-being of society or for the state of game cookery.

Today, the younger generation has been weaned away from bear, bluebill, beaver, and bullhead in favor of chemical-laced junk foods. The art of preparing meals is dependent upon an electric can opener and a microwave oven capable of quickly defrosting TV dinners. Artificial coloring is added to everything to convince us it is palatable and soy beans are used to make ersatz hot dogs as well as steering wheels.

(One tastes about like the other.) We put so many chemicals in the hamburger, we are approaching the time when the label will say: "Meat has been added for historic reasons."

Last week I picked up a box of mashed potato flakes and found it contained: dried potatoes (so far, so good) and vegetable monoglyceride (I have no idea just what that is—and I suspect I'd rather not know). Then I was informed the "quality" was "preserved with sodium acid pyrophosphate, sodium bisulfite, citric acid and BHA." BHA is a puzzler. The only thing I could come up with was Baked Hungarian Aardvark—but I don't suppose that's right. Most of us will go to our graves never knowing what BHA is. "Citric acid" is easy enough to understand. But why would anyone want to add lemon, orange, or grapefruit juice to the mashed potatoes? It's a discomforting thought and apt to make one a bit uneasy.

This mild distress turned to anxiety when I looked up "sodium" in the dictionary. It was sandwiched in between "sodden" and "Sodomite"—which is not a good start. The definition was: "A metallic, alkaline element, only found in combination, as saltpeter, etc." Well, right there I said to myself, "This stuff is not for me."

If there is any doubt in your mind, the "pyrophosphate" additive should remove it. "Pyro," as anyone in the arson squad will tell you, comes from the Greek and means fire—as in "pyromaniac." And you all know that phosphate is something you put on the grass to make it grow greener. Pyrophosphate. Pyro-phosphate. You know, I believe someone has been burning horse manure and adding it to the potato flakes. That's one hell of a way to preserve quality.

While the character of our food has been rocketing downhill, what has been happening to the texture of our lives? It's gone to pot, friends, that's what's happened to it. Bach, Beethoven, and Frank Sinatra have been replaced by punk rock and a mindless electronically generated clatter, produced at a decibel level that would shatter the composure of a garden slug. Crime is on the rise. Our elected representatives molest children, take cocaine, and support gay rights. The fire ant moves farther north each year, and I can't get the parsley to grow worth beans.

Though we live in such a time of frightening crisis and moral decay, don't fret, become morose and head for the medicine cabinet for a double handful of sleeping pills or valium. Help is on the way. Humanity runs a risk of being saved. And it all happened this way.

Last fall, a handful of woodcock and grouse hunters were sitting around a camp in Central Wisconsin. They had finished a meal of snow goose breast, baked in the earth under the embers of a cook fire. The meal had been topped off with a Mouton Cadet Bordeaux. If I recall correctly, a drop or two of potent libation had been dispensed. The cares of the day and the condition of the world were discussed.

With a unanimity rarely attained in the group, it was agreed that the progress of mankind from the ancient bogs to the age of the computer had been not only accompanied by, but also occasioned by, the advancement of its ability to prepare wild game. Next, it was established that the recent alarming deterioration in the quality of life has been not only accompanied by, but also occasioned by a similar *deterioration* in mankind's ability to prepare wild game. It was the considered opinion of the group that, if civilization was to be saved, people had damn well better learn how to cook game.

Broadsides were printed, runners were sent out, and letters were written. A number of accomplished game cooks, willing to share their favorite recipes, joined together to reverse the downward spiraling of man's state in the universe. The result is this cookbook.

Out-of-doors chefs and camp cooks sent their favorite recipes—ones which have withstood the tests of time, critical wives, acerbic husbands, and the members of hunting and fishing camps. A number of them show that their authors have clearly attained gourmet chef status. (This should come as no surprise since a gourmet cook is nothing more than a good camp cook who has been housebroken.)

The group of hunters who started it all prefer to remain anonymous and ask that any public subscriptions to raise funds for the building of a suitable monument to them be, instead, donated to the DU and TU people. They are satisfied with the simple knowledge that they have saved civilization and need no further public accolade.

And even if life, in general, continues to go to hell, you, at least, will be able to face approaching havoc and cataclysm secure in the knowledge that you are an island of sanity, able to prepare savory meals of not only such conventional game viands as duck, pheasant, venison, trout, and squirrel, but also, if need be, of more esoteric substance, such as porcupine, eel, and skunk (a comforting thought, to be sure).

Given such a supply of quality instructions for the preparation of game, you need only secure the appropriate foodstuffs. You can still find meat from animals not fed with chemicals, fowl that haven't spent their whole existence from egg to supermarket suspended above the earth in wire cages, and fish that have managed to pass their entire lives in natural streams, rivers, or lakes.

There are four ways to establish a supply of game. There is the primeval method of looking around for dead bodies. This system may appeal to the hard core "back to nature" folk, but it is not recommended to those of you who have not yet been committed. You can pick up a fly rod, scatter gun, tip-up, cane pole, or what-have-you and have the fun and the added dimension of producing your own supply. Of course, the problem is resolved if you already hunt or fish. Finally, if none of the above suits you, hang around hunters and fishers, say nice things and they'll be sure you receive ample stores of wild meats.

A word of warning to the uninitiated: The stocking of the freezer without intent to cook is a dangerous game. Over the course of a single season, a large volume of provision can be built up. If you simply dump it into the garbage, one fine day your spouse will ask for a rabbit stew and you will have to (A) explain why there are no rabbits in the freezer; (B) run down to the market, search the meat section for some domestic bunny and hope the difference will not be noted (it will); or (C) sell your body to the nearest rabbit hunter.

If the third alternative appeals to you, be sure your spouse doesn't fish eel and occasionally ask for an eel dinner. While rabbit hunters, by and large, are youngish and good looking, eel fishers are not. They are usually old, crumbly, and regularly smell of dank, swampy places. (It should also be noted that judges in most of the civilized areas of the republic refuse to order alimony payments if the inability to cook game is listed as the cause for divorce.)

With a supply of wild game and a good cookbook (this one) you are prepared to fight the forces of evil and save humanity. However, if you are satisfied with the domesticated junk you eat and have no interest in game cookery, give this book to the warden and ask him to return it to the library from which you stole it. Read no further. You're wasting your time and can be more profitably engaged in the making of license plates.

If you are an accomplished camp cook, read on. We hope you'll find some new recipes and expand your repertoire.

If you aren't a game cook but have the vague suspicion that the entirely natural foods represented by the wild fowl, fish, and game meats are superior to the packaged junk in the super market, you've come to the right place.

—*Galen Winter*

FISH
Chapter One

Organizing a cookbook is not a simple task, free from worry and frustration. It would be if you were allowed to do everything alphabetically. (If you wanted to find the forward, you'd look between FISH and GOOSE.) But simply because such a system has never been done before, the alphabetic program was rejected.

Due to an unfortunate incident in high school over 40 years ago — involving formaldehyde, the school's tropical fish collection, poison ivy, and the biology department's terrarium — the school biologists and I are not on good terms. They sure do hold a grudge over there. (I've forgiven them.)

In any event, I've been unable to get order, family, and species information from them. If they had cooperated, the recipes for *aythya affinis* could easily be separated from those of the *aythya merila*. But we must play with the cards we are dealt.

This cookbook is organized by the number of legs on the foodstuff. To make things easy for you, the 5, 3, and 1-footed creatures have been eliminated. If you want a recipe for one of them, write to the editor (don't bother me).

I thought the organization problem was solved and then someone sent in a recipe for crayfish. I don't know how many legs one has, but I'm almost certain it's more than four. I suppose I could have overlooked a few extra feet, called it four, and put it in with moose and woodchuck.

Then came the frogs. They should be bunched in with the ducks and geese, if you count only hind legs, or else, if you count front legs, they too would join the crayfish with the rabbits. This is the sort of thing that leads to sleepless nights.

Well, the crayfish and the frogs, the eel and the turtles have all been declared to be fish and appear in this section of the book. If you don't like it, return the book to the publisher and try to get your money back. Just try.

CABIN WHITE BASS

MAKE DIP OF EGG and evaporated milk, roll fish in either cornmeal, bread crumbs or cornflake crumbs.

Fry fish in butter or margarine and sprinkle with parsley flakes or paprika. Serve with butter beans.

Bob Vosen, Fond du Lac

Bass
1 egg
1/3 cup evaporated milk
Cornmeal, bread crumbs or cornflake crumbs

BASS WITH HAM IN CREAM SAUCE

PLACE FISH IN A POT with water, salt and lemon juice. Cover and bring to boil. Simmer for about 10 minutes until fish flakes with a fork.

Remove fish from pot, cool and break into small chunks. Combine condensed mushroom soup and milk in a saucepan and heat slowly. When mixture is about to bubble, add ham, fish and pimento, and stir gently until hot. Add a dash of cooking sherry to flavor, and spoon mixture over rice or noodles. Serves 4-6.

Mrs. Char Schroll, New Richmond

2 whole white bass
(1½-2 pounds each)
1 cup diced ham
1 cup water
1 teaspoon salt
1 teaspoon lemon juice
1 can condensed mushroom soup
1 can sweet milk
½ teaspoon pimento, chopped
Dash of cooking sherry

BEER BATTER SMALLMOUTH

FILLET FISH, WASH and pat dry. Place fish in medium sized mixing bowl and break both eggs over them. Rub fillets in egg and let stand for a few minutes.

Mix flour and baking powder in large mixing bowl. Add beer and stir until mixture obtains a smooth, thick and creamy texture (add more beer for lighter batter).

Take fillets from egg bowl and, while still wet, shake them in a plastic bag with 1 cup of seasoned bread crumbs until thoroughly coated.

Take breaded fillets and dip in batter mixture, then carefully place in hot oil (may use skillet or large deep fat fryer). Oil should be tested for proper temperature by placing a drop of batter in it. If batter sizzles immediately, oil is proper temperature.

Cook until a light golden brown. If using skillet, fillets must be turned.
Serves 4.

Jim Schoneman, Appleton

1 cup flour
1 bottle beer
1 teaspoon baking powder
1-2 cups seasoned bread crumbs (store bought)
2 eggs
Cooking oil
4   12-14 " smallmouth bass

BEST BASS CASSEROLE

COOK FISH, DRAIN, combine milk, soup and pour over diced meat. Add onions and pour into 1½ qt. casserole dish. Bake at 350° for 20 minutes. Garnish with onion rings or parsley and oranges.

Christina Syverson, Tomah

2 lbs. diced bass meat
3/4 cup milk
1 can condensed mushroom soup
2 tablespoons diced pimento
½ or 1 cup onions
Salt and pepper

PLANKED BASS

THIS ONE IS FOR CAMPER OR SHORE LUNCHES. Tack fillets or whole fish (skin side down) to flat board large enough to hold fish. Use wood like hickory, maple or apple. Prop up board with fish attached near hot coals and brush fish with bacon fat or whole pieces of bacon, as it broils. Drip lemon juice and shake on salt and pepper as fish begin to brown. When meat is flaky, remove.

IMPORTANT: Do not use pine, cedar, walnut or oak for a board as they give too strong a flavor.
Karle E. Tonn, Fredonia

Large fillets of bass, or whole split bass.
Bacon fat or whole strips
Lemon
Salt & pepper

BEER BATTER — for fish and vegetables

COMBINE DRY ingredients. Reserve ½ cup to roll fish, and/or vegetables such as eggplant, zucchini, okra, green tomatoes, mushrooms, and cauliflower. Add liquids to other ½ cup of dry ingredients. Roll food items in dry mixture. Dip in moistened mixture. Deep fat fry at 350° for 3-4 minutes or until tender.

Marilyn Benish, Yuba

1 cup flour
1½ teaspoons baking powder
½ teaspoon baking soda
½ cup beer
¼ cup lemon juice

SMELT BATTER

MIX DRY INGREDIENTS. Add oil and beer to mixture to make batter like heavy syrup. Let stand 1 hour. Just before dipping, add more beer until batter is at heavy syrup stage again. Dip fish and fry in hot oil.

1 cup buttermilk pancake mix
½ cup instant mashed potatoes
2 tablespoons oil
2 tablespoons parsley flakes
2 tablespoons minced onion (dried)
1 teaspoon salt
½ teaspoon pepper
Beer

BEER BATTER

MIX INGREDIENTS together. Also good for chicken and onion rings.

Mrs. Laurence Harder, Ripon

1 egg beaten
1 teaspoon salt
1 teaspoon sugar
1 teaspoon baking powder
1 scant cup flour
1 cup beer not cold (room temperature)
1 cup milk may be used in place of beer

FISH BATTER

MIX INGREDIENTS TOGETHER. Add stale beer to mixture (so it has the consistency you prefer but thick enough to coat fish). Fry fish in hot shortening until done. This batter can also be used for onion rings.
Mrs. Walter Passehl, Wausau

1/3 cup pancake flour
1/3 cup white flour
2 eggs
Salt & pepper (to taste)
Stale beer

[16]

FISH BATTER

MIX ALL INGREDIENTS and add water slowly while stirring at slow speed with electric mixer until batter is creamy.

Dip fish in and fry. Also works well on chicken.

Bob Vosen, Fond du Lac

2/3 cup corn starch
2/3 cup corn meal
1/3 cup flour
2 teaspoons salt
4 teaspoons baking powder

QUICK BATTER FRIED-FISH FILLETS

BEAT MILK AND EGGS. Dip fish in mixture. Roll in Bisquick which has been mixed with salt and pepper. Fry in hot oil. You may add butter during the last minute of frying if desired.

Dan Danczyk, Stevens Point

1 cup Bisquick
½ cup milk
1 egg

MUSTARD SPECIAL FISH BATTER

DIP PAN FISH OR BASS in mixture. Then dip in mashed potato flakes. Fry in oil until done. (Use filleted fish).

Shirley Dyrud, Janesville

2 eggs beaten
2 teaspoons French's Yellow Mustard

BEER BATTER FISH

CUT FISH INTO serving portions. Dip fish pieces into batter, drain. Fry 2-3 minutes in hot fat, lard, or oil.

Donald Dorner, Luxemburg

4 lbs. fresh fish fillets
2 eggs slightly beaten
½ teaspoon tobasco
½ teaspoon salt
2/3 cup beer
1 cup flour
2 tablespoons oil

CAMPER'S BEER BATTERED FISH

STIR IN BEER to consistency of thin pancake mix. Dip fillets in, mix with fork and deep fry to a light golden brown.

Spencer Anderson, Baraboo

1 cup complete pancake mix
½ teaspoon salt
1 can beer

BEER BATTER FISH

POUR ALL INGREDIENTS into plastic bag and mix. Put 1 piece of fish in at a time. Cover well with flour. Set on paper bag until all fish are done.

Heat oil, dip flour-covered fish into your beer and flour mixture. Tap on side of bowl and then set into hot oil, take out when golden brown.

Cathy M. Fehrenbach, Milwaukee

1/8 tablespoon pepper
1 tablespoon salt
1½ cups flour

1 cup flour
1 can beer
(mix beer and flour together with mixer)

EASY BEER BATTER

BEAT TOGETHER BISCUIT MIX, beer, egg and salt. Pat fish or meat dry. Dip in batter to coat both sides. Fry in hot cooking oil for 10 minutes on each side or till golden brown and done.
   Yield: 4 servings.
Virginia Kraegenbrink, Menomonee Falls

Fish, pheasant, grouse, etc.
1¼ cups packaged biscuit mix
3/4 cup beer
1 egg
¼ teaspoon salt
Cooking oil

BEER BATTER

BEAT EGG YOLKS until light and lemon colored. Stir in beer and tobasco sauce. Add sifted flour, salt and paprika until well blended. Beat egg whites until stiff and fold into batter. Dip your fish, then fry.
A. H. Ludwig, Oshkosh

2 eggs separated
2/3 cup of beer
5 drops of tobasco sauce
1 cup sifted flour
½ teaspoon salt
½ teaspoon paprika
2 tablespoons melted butter

INSTANT BEER BATTER

MIX INGREDIENTS IN A BOWL. Dip salted fish in batter and fry in deep fryer until brown.
Eric A. Lewis, Oshkosh

1 cup "Jiffy" mix
1 egg
About ½ bottle of beer

SOUFFLE STUFFED CATFISH

BRUSH BOTH SIDES of fish with melted butter. Roll in cracker crumbs. Cut frozen spinach souffle crosswise into 6 equal pieces. Place 1 piece of souffle crosswise in center of fish fillet, fold ends of fish over souffle. Pour salad dressing over bottom of 12x8x2" baking dish. Place fillets seam side down. Bake at 375° for 35-40 minutes.
   Spoon lemon cheese sauce on serving platter. Arrange fillets over sauce, garnish with watercress and lemon wedges.

Karen Schmidt, Racine

6 fillets of catfish (2-2½ pounds)
2 tablespoons butter, melted
3/4 cup cheese flavored
   cracker crumbs
1 pkg. (12 oz.) frozen spinach souffle
½ cup buttermilk salad dressing
Lemon-cheese Sauce
Lemon wedges
Watercress

LEMON-CHEESE SAUCE

IN PAN COMBINE lemon juice, cream cheese, beaten egg, sugar, mustard, and tarragon. Cook over low heat until cream cheese is melted. Stir in salad dressing and parmesan cheese. Heat until hot enough to serve. Makes 1 1/3 cups.

Karen Schmidt, Racine

2 tablespoons lemon juice
1 pkg. (8 oz.) cream cheese
cut in cubes
1 egg beaten
1 teaspoon sugar
½ teaspoon dried leaf tarragon
¼ cup creamy buttermilk salad
dressing
¼ cup parmesan grated cheese

FRIED EEL*

REMOVE HEAD, LOOSEN skin and with a strong jerk, pull skin over entire body. Cut eel open and wash thoroughly and cut into 3" lengths: Dry, dip into slightly beaten egg and roll in bread crumbs or cornmeal. Fry in hot fat 375-380° until done.

Drain, and serve with cucumber sauce or tartar sauce.

Gib Dutton, Rochester, MN

Eel
1 egg
Fine bread crumbs or cornmeal

SAVORY FISH CHOWDER

IN DUTCH OVEN, fry bacon until crisp, remove and crumble. In the drippings cook celery, onion and garlic until tender. Stir in the flour, gradually add the water and bouillon. Bring to a boil, add the potatoes, reduce heat, cover and cook 10 minutes.

While that cooks, take small pan and about 3 cups water, and boil fish fillets until they break into pieces. Drain.

Add to other kettle, put in lemon juice and cook 15 minutes. Add half and half and pimento. Heat. Garnish with parsley and crumbled bacon pieces. Serve hot. Makes about 2½ quarts.

Iris Faude, Medford

4 slices bacon
½ cup chopped celery
½ cup chopped onion
1 clove garlic
½ cup flour
6 cups water
8 teaspoons bouillon or 8 cubes
1½ cups diced potatoes
1 lb. fish fillets
½ cup lemon juice
2 cups half and half milk
3 tablespoons chopped pimento
Parsley

FABULOUS FISH SOUP

CUT ONE LARGE FISH into small serving pieces. Boil fish and chopped onions until tender. Remove fish and strain stock. Beat egg and add sour cream, then add to strained stock. Season to taste. Reheat but do not allow to boil.

Ray Lardinois, Algoma

Any type large fish
1 small onion, chopped
Salt & pepper
1 egg
1 cup sour cream
Parsley (optional)

FISH CHOWDER

BONE AND SKIN any fresh water fish of about one pound. Fry out ½ pound salt pork or extra thick bacon. Trim off fat.

Combine the fish and pork, add 1 cup water and cook until tender (about 10 minutes). Add the potatoes, onions, green peppers, tomato soup and 1 cup water. Salt to taste.

Cook slowly for about 1½ hours covered, stirring occasionally. If desired, add Beaumond season, oregano or bay leaves.

Robert Blair, Beaver Dam

1 lb. fresh water fish
½ lb. thick bacon or salt pork
2 cups water
2 cups thinly sliced potatoes
½ cup chopped green peppers
1 - 10 oz. can tomato soup
Salt

---

* EEL FOOTNOTE: If I were to prepare eel, my kitchen utensils would include a hemostat attached to the end of an eleven-foot pole. (I wouldn't touch an eel with a ten foot pole.)

GRANDMA'S FISH CHOWDER

COMBINE IN LARGE KETTLE:
8 medium potatoes, sliced; 3 medium onions, sliced; 1 quart tomatoes; 1 lb. boned fish cubes. (panfish of any kind are good). Salt, pepper and whole allspice to personal taste.

Cook ingredients over medium heat until well done. Be sure to stir well and watch carefully to prevent scorching. Add water to mixture if needed. Before serving, add ¾ cup margarine or butter and ½ pint half and half. Serve hot. Sprinkle with grated cheese if desired. Hot bread and a crisp salad complete the menu.

This chowder is good the first day but fantastic when reheated the next day!
Bonnie Japuntich, Hayward

1 lb. boned fish cubes (panfish of any kind)
8 medium potatoes, sliced
3 medium onions, sliced
1 quart tomatoes
Salt, pepper and whole allspice to taste
¾ cup margarine or butter
½ pint half & half

FISH CHOWDER

IN SAUCEPAN, COOK ONIONS with garlic and pepper in butter until tender. Blend in soup, cream cheese, and milk; add fish and corn. Bring to boil; reduce heat. Cover; simmer 10 minutes or until done. Makes about 7 cups.
(Your own recipe of homemade potato soup makes this main-dish chowder even more tasty.)

Marilyn Benish, Yuba

¼ cup chopped green onions
1 small clove garlic, minced
1/8 tablespoon cayenne pepper
1 tablespoon butter or margarine
2 cans (10 3/4 oz.) cream of potato soup
1 pkg. (3 oz.) cream cheese, softened
1½ soup cans milk
2 cups fish (any type boned fish; canned tuna, salmon or shrimp may be substituted or combined with the fish
1 can (8 oz.) whole kernel corn (undrained)

FISH CHOWDER

BROWN BACON IN LARGE kettle, remove bits, reserve. Add onions to bacon fat and cook till tender. Add potatoes, salt, pepper and water.

Place fish, cut into medium-sized pieces, on top, cover, simmer 25 minutes or until potatoes are tender. Remove any skin from fish.

Add milk, evaporated milk, butter, diced bacon; heat. Makes 6 servings.

Mona Bouressa, Neenah

¼ lb. bacon, diced
3 sliced medium onions
5 diced pared medium potatoes
4 teaspoons salt
¼ teaspoon pepper
3 cups boiling water
1½ lb. white bass (or the catch of the day)
1 qt. milk, scalded
1 cup undiluted evaporated milk
3 tablespoons butter or margarine

FISH CHOWDER

COVER POTATOES AND ONIONS with water and boil until soft, mash with masher, do not drain.

Add fish fillets, boil until fish flakes and is soft.

Add tomato juice or whole canned tomatoes, and break into chunks.

Add the rest of the ingredients. (Do not boil).

Mrs. Rhea V. Sasse, Fremont

6 cups raw potatoes, sliced or diced
1 cup chopped onion
1 tablespoon salt
5 cups boned, skinned, fish fillets (any kind)
2 cups tomato juice or whole canned tomatoes
1 cup half and half
½ cup butter
Dash of pepper

CAVIAR MEAT LOAF

STEAM THE EGG SACKS for 15 minutes until they appear grey/white. (Use about 1½ lbs.) Cool until they are easy to handle and then peel the protective lining away. Combine fish eggs with cracker crumbs, egg, milk and salt and pepper to taste. Add remaining ingredients and bake at 350° until bubbles cease and slight crust forms on top. Sprinkle grated Swiss cheese on top and serve with tartar sauce or French Onion dip.

Brenda and Paul Ross, Fremont

1½ lbs. egg sacks
1 cup cracker crumbs
1 beaten egg
¼ cup milk
Salt & pepper
2 tablespoons pickle relish
2 tablespoons chopped onion
1 tablespoon Realemon
Grated Swiss cheese

CABLE CAVIAR

FOR THIS GOURMET CANAPE, you can use the roe from northern, walleye or perch. The roe must be strictly fresh or frozen fresh in water and used when barely thawed.

Bring enough water to completely cover the roe to a boil. The water may be lightly salted. Remove what membrane you can from roe but do not break up. Gently put roe into boiling water and cook for 10 minutes.

Drain cooked roe thoroughly and mix in rest of ingredients with a fork. Chill thoroughly.

Serve on crackers, toast points, cocktail rye.

Margie Homer, Cable

2 cups roe
3 tablespoons olive oil
3 tablespoons lemon juice
1 teaspoon onion salt
½ teaspoon garlic salt
1 heaping tablespoon mayonnaise
1 heaping tablespoon fine bread crumbs

1 tablespoon worcestershire sauce
½ teaspoon dill weed
½ teaspoon oregano
Black & red pepper
Dash of tobasco
Salt to taste

WOODSMAN LOBSTER

BRING A KETTLE OF SALTED water (½ cup salt to 1 gallon water) to a rolling boil. Pop in the crawfish and simmer until they turn a deep red. Break off the tails. Serve like shrimp and let each one shuck out his own meat. Serve with melted butter flavored with lemon juice.

Dan Hirchert, Platteville

2 dozen or more crawfish
Salt
Butter

FISH COCKTAILS

CLEAN, SKIN, AND FILLET any small fish — crappies, sunfish, perch. Cut in small pieces (bite size). Cook in boiling salt water, just until tender.

Remove carefully from water and let cool.

Add your favorite cocktail sauce to fish — refrigerate about 4-6 hours.

Serve cold as Hors d'oeuvres.

Mrs. Jan Teachout, Waupun

Fish fillets
Cocktail sauce

BOILED CRAWFISH

CUT OFF HEAD LIKE a shrimp. Wash in cold water. Drop into rapidly boiling water, salted with sprigs of dill. Be sure you use dill in cooking crawfish.

Cook 15-20 minutes or until shells turn pink. Drain. Cover with cold water to chill, then drain and remove shell and legs and intestinal vein (the black line along the back).

Crawfish are from clean, cold, unpolluted waters, and are sweeter than shrimp.

Gib Dutton, Rochester, MN

Crawfish
Dill sprigs

SEAFOOD DRESSING

MELT BUTTER, ADD VEGETABLES, and saute until tender. Add all the remaining ingredients except the bread crumbs to the vegetables and cook over low heat for 10 minutes. Add this mixture to the bread crumbs and mix thoroughly.

Marilyn Benish, Yuba

6 tablespoons butter
¼ cup celery, finely chopped
½ cup onion, finely chopped
¼ cup green pepper, finely chopped
½ pound shrimp, cooked and diced
1 teaspoon parsley, chopped
1 teaspoon pimento, finely chopped
½ teaspoon paprika
1 teaspoon worcestershire sauce
½ teaspoon seafood seasoning salt to taste
1/8 teaspoon cayenne pepper
¼ cup dry sherry
1½ cups bread crumbs

RECIPE

LAY FISH OUT and dry with paper towel. Crack 4 eggs and beat and put in bowl. Then take Waverly crackers and smoosh till fine. Then take the dried fish and put into the egg yolk and then cover with Waverly crackers. Put oil in pan and put fish in and let fish cook until lightly brown. Then eat.

Keith Reda, age 12, Madison

Fish
4 eggs
Waverly Crackers

FROG LEGS

SLIP SKIN OFF HIND quarter of frog. Wash frog legs thoroughly. Dry. Salt and pepper. Dip in egg. Roll in bread crumbs. Fry in deep fat at 385° until brown.

Dan Hirchert, Platteville

Frog legs
Salt, pepper
1 egg, slightly beaten
Fine bread crumbs
Cooking oil

FROG LEGS

THE HIND LEGS OF FROGS are the only part that is eaten. Cut legs from body. Wash and turn down the skin and pull off like a glove. Wash and clean. Marinate legs in mixture of salt, pepper, and lemon juice about 1 hour. Dip quickly in egg, roll in crumbs or cornmeal. Fry in hot fat at 385° until brown and done. Serve with a tart sauce.

Gib Dutton, Rochester, MN

Frog legs
Salt, pepper
Lemon juice
1 egg
Bread crumbs or cornmeal

FRIED FISH

DIP FISH IN WORCESTERSHIRE sauce. Sprinkle with seasoned salt. Dip in flour mixture. Fry at 300° until golden brown.

Bret Roddenbach, Beloit

Fish
Worcestershire sauce
Pancake flour
1 tablespoon dry mustard
Salt and pepper
4 tablespoons butter
1/8 cup water

ALMONDINE FISH

BAKE FISH IN OVEN until done, at 325°. Then melt 1 stick of butter or margarine, add 4 oz. sliced almonds. Cook in a small kettle on stovetop slowly until you can smell the almonds. Add ¼ cup lemon juice. Pour over fish and serve immediately.

Recipe good with walleye, bluegills, perch or bass.

Mrs. Maureen Steele, Fond du Lac

Fish
1 stick butter or margarine
4 oz. sliced almonds
¼ cup lemon juice

FISH PATTIES

SKIN AND FILLET a northern pike or any large fish. Cut in pieces and grind in a grinder two times.

Add egg, cracker crumbs and milk to fish so it will hold together. Add salt and pepper to taste. Form into flat patties and fry in hot butter or shortening until golden brown on both sides.

Mrs. Jan Teachout, Waupun

Large fish
1 egg
Cracker crumbs
Milk

FISH SANDWICH

FILLET PAN FISH (no skin on). Sprinkle "season all" seasoned salt on both sides of fillet — dip in flour and egg. No milk added. Then roll in soda cracker crumbs, or Ritz crackers. Fry in deep fat until golden brown. Put on toast with lettuce and tartar sauce.

Mrs. Pat Arntson, Webster

Fillet pan fish
Seasoned salt
Flour
1 egg
Cracker crumbs

Tartar Sauce
1 cup salad dressing
1 teaspoon sweet pickle or dill relish

FISH FLAKED FRITTERS

BOIL TWO CUPS OF FISH and flake.
Add egg, milk, worcestershire sauce, onion, salt and pepper to flaked fish. Thicken slowly with about ½ cup pancake mix until mixture can be formed into patties. Fry in ½ inch of peanut oil.

Charlotte Larson, Cornell

2 cups fish, flaked
1 egg, beaten
1 tablespoon milk
1 tablespoon worcestershire sauce
1 onion, diced
Salt and pepper to taste
½ cup biscuit or pancake mix
Peanut oil

FISHY STUFFED ZUCCHINI

ADD COOKED ZUCCHINI to stuffing mix along with butter, lemon juice and fish. Mix well. Begin adding water and moisten to desired consistency.

Place stuffing mixture in zucchini shells. Pour diluted mushroom soup over top; if preferred, other types of creamed soups may be used.

Place in shallow baking pan with ¼ inch water in bottom to prevent shells from sticking. Bake at 350° for 30 minutes. Garnish with chives, parsley, or paprika.

Marilyn Benish, Yuba

6 zucchini — 1½ by 8 in. cut in half and boiled in salted water
4 cups packaged herb-seasoned stuffing
1½ cups cubed raw fish (your choice)
2 cups water
¼ cup lemon juice
1/3 cup butter
1 can mushroom soup slightly diluted with water or milk

FLAKED FISH CASSEROLE

MIX EGG YOLKS AND MILK together slowly in pan. Add tapioca, salt, pepper, celery, onion and mix well. Cook and stir until mixture comes to a boil. Remove from heat. Add fish and parsley. Mix well. Beat egg whites until stiff peaks form. Gradually fold into fish mixture. Spoon into greased 1½ quart casserole. Sprinkle with crushed potato chips. Bake at 350° for 50 minutes or until firm and brown. Serves 4.

Karen Schmidt, Racine

2 egg yolks
2 cups of milk
2 tablespoons quick-cooking tapioca
1½ teaspoon salt
Dash of pepper
½ cup chopped celery
1½ teaspoon chopped onion
2 cups flaked fish (salmon, lake trout)
2 tablespoons parsley
2 egg whites
½ cup crushed potato chips

FISH MONTEREY

MELT BUTTER IN LARGE skillet. Add lemon juice and sherry. Arrange fish in skillet and cover with thin slices of the cheese. Cover and simmer 15 minutes.

Gretchen Larson, West Salem

6 tablespoons butter
1 tablespoon lemon juice
2 tablespoons cooking sherry
4 ounces Monterey Jack cheese
1½ lbs. fish fillets (crappie, bass, northern, walleye)

FISH AND SPINACH SALAD

POACH OR STEAM FISH — prepare ginger dressing by pouring all ingredients in jar and shaking well. Makes ¾ cup dressing.

Break fish into bite-size pieces. Pour dressing over fish, cover and refrigerate for at least 1 hour. Toss with remaining ingredients.

Karen Schmidt, Racine

1 pound fish fillets (walleye, perch, northern pike)
Ginger dressing (see below)
6 ounces fresh spinach torn into bite-size pieces
1 can (16 oz.) chilled and drained bean sprouts
1 stalk celery, cut diagonally
4 large green onions sliced
12 cherry tomatoes

Ginger dressing
¼ cup salad oil
3 tablespoons white vinegar
2 teaspoons sugar
1½ teaspoon salt
1 teaspoon soy sauce
½ teaspoon ground ginger
1/8 teaspoon pepper

OVEN BAKED FISH

MELT OLEO. Dip fillets in oleo, then in crumb mixture. Bake at 350° for 25-30 minutes.

Shelley and David Hraychuck, Sayner

½ cup oleo
2/3 cup cereal (cornflakes, Wheaties, etc.)
¼ cup parmesan cheese
½ teaspoon basil
½ teaspoon oregano
½ teaspoon salt
¼ teaspoon garlic powder
1 lb. panfish fillets

FISH BURGERS

GRIND FISH, POTATOES and onions together. Add flour, salt and pepper. Mix well. Form patties and fry in oil in a skillet until nicely browned on both sides.

Velma Bray, Fennimore

2 lbs. fish (any kind, filleted and bones removed)
1 lb. raw potatoes
¼ - ½ lb. onions
Salt and pepper
Flour to thicken

SAVORY OUTDOOR BAKED FISH

PLACE FISH ON INDIVIDUAL sheets of heavy-duty aluminum foil. Salt and pepper. Top each fillet with the onion, tomato, and parsley. Spoon the salad dressing over the fillets reserving a small amount to heat and serve on baked fish.

Bring foil up over fish and seal with double fold. Seal ends. Place on grill over medium hot coals.

After 10 minutes, test. If the fish flakes easily, remove from heat. Juices from bottom of packages may be added to reserved dressing mix when served.

Marilyn Benish, Yuba

1½ pounds fish fillets (perch or bass)
3 tablespoons each of minced onion, chopped tomato, and minced fresh parsley
1 pkg. dry Italian-flavored salad dressing mix. (Prepare salad dressing as directed except substitute ½ of required oil with butter and ½ of vinegar with lemon juice)
Salt and pepper to taste

HOMEMADE FISH FRY

RINSE AND PAT DRY fillets, sprinkle with lemon juice. Combine flour and garlic salt. Blend egg and milk.

Combine bread crumbs, parmesan cheese, parsley, and seasoned salt. Coat fillets with flour and dip in egg mixture, then in crumb mixture. Place in refrigerator for 1 hour.

Fry in oil until brown on each side — about 10 minutes each side. Serve with tartar sauce.

Mrs. Robert Brown, Schofield

Fish fillets (1 lb. of your choice)
¼ cup flour
¼ teaspoon garlic salt
2 eggs beaten
¼ cup milk
1 cup fine bread crumbs
2½ tablespoons parmesan cheese
1½ tablespoon parsley
1 tablespoon seasoned salt
Lemon juice
Oil

Tartar sauce

1 cup mayonnaise
2 carrots grated
1 medium onion grated
3 tablespoons sweet pickle relish
(Combine all ingredients and refrigerate for at least 2 hours.)

OVEN FRIED FISH

CUT FILLETS IN SERVING pieces. Dip in milk and roll in bread crumbs. Place in well greased baking pan, sprinkle with salt and pepper. Drizzle melted butter over fish and bake at 500° for 10-12 minutes or till fish flakes easily with fork. Makes 3-4 servings.

Bret Roddenboch, Beloit

1 pound fish fillets or steaks
½ cup milk
½ cup fine dry bread crumbs
2 tablespoons melted butter
Dash salt and pepper

FISH STICKS

DIP EACH FILLET into beaten egg and then roll it well in cornmeal and flour mixed together. Fry in hot pan; season to taste.

Mary Scott, Manawa

3 lbs. of any type fish fillets
1 cup yellow cornmeal
1 egg well beaten
1 cup flour

BAKED FISH FILLETS

CUT FILLETS IN SERVING PIECES. Place in greased shallow baking dish. Sprinkle with lemon juice, paprika, salt, and pepper.

In saucepan, melt butter, blend in flour, dash salt, and dash pepper, and a dash of Accent seasoning salt. Add milk, cook and stir till thick and bubbly. Pour sauce over fillets.

Sprinkle with crumbs. Bake at 350° for 35 minutes. Trim with parsley. Makes 3-4 servings.

Bret Roddenboch, Beloit

1 pound fish fillets
1 tablespoon lemon juice
1/8 teaspoon paprika
1 tablespoon butter
1 tablespoon all purpose flour
Salt, pepper, and Accent seasoned salt
½ cup milk
¼ cup buttered bread crumbs
1 tablespoon snipped parsley

BUTTER BROWNED FISH

PLACE LAYER OF FILLET pan fish on butter greased cookie sheet. Brush butter or margarine, salt and pepper on fish.

Put under broiler approximately 5 minutes on each side.

Remove from cookie sheet and put on platter. Garnish with parsley and lemon wedges.

Shirley Dyrud, Janesville

Pan fish fillets
Butter
Salt and pepper

FISH CAKES SUPREME

DROP FISH FILLETS in lightly salted, boiling water. Reduce heat and simmer 3-5 minutes depending on thickness of fillets. Do not boil as this toughens fish. Drain well, cool and flake.

Mix celery seed, mustard, mayonnaise or salad dressing, worcestershire sauce and egg. Add cubed bread and mix thoroughly. Add flaked fish and mix gently. Pat into cakes and fry in shortening until golden brown.

Emma C. Olson, Boyceville

1 lb. flaked fish fillets
1 teaspoon celery seed
1 teaspoon prepared mustard
1 teaspoon worcestershire sauce
½ cup mayonnaise or salad dressing
1 egg
4 slices soft bread, cubed

FISH FLORENTINE

MAKE SAUCE BY MELTING butter in sauce pan, add flour and salt, stirring constantly. Add milk, stirring until thick.

Next, place fish in buttered baking dish. Pour sauce over fish. Sprinkle with paprika. Bake at 325° for 20 minutes.

Penny Hickman, Gordon

1 lb. fish fillets
1 cup white sauce
½ cup sliced pimento-stuffed olives
½ cup shredded cheddar cheese

White Sauce

3 tablespoons butter
3 tablespoons flour
½ teaspoon salt
1 cup milk

FISH SURPRISE

PUT FISH FILLETS in 13x9x2 in. baking pan, salt and pepper and put lemon juice on them. Make cracker topping in a medium bowl. Spoon cracker topping over fish fillets. Arrange bacon slices diagonally over top. Bake at 400°, basting every 10 minutes with pan juices, 30-35 minutes or until fish flakes easily when tested with fork. Garnish with parsley and lemon wedges, if desired.

Mary Scott, Manawa

3½ lbs. any type fish fillets
Salt and pepper
2 tablespoons lemon juice

Cracker topping

½ cup crushed crackers
½ cup mushrooms
¼ cup chopped onions
2 tablespoons chopped parsley
1½ teaspoon salt
1/8 teaspoon pepper
¼ cup butter melted
2 tablespoons lemon juice
6 slices bacon

FISH ROYALE

DROP FISH FILLETS in lightly salted, boiling water. Reduce heat and simmer 3-5 minutes depending on thickness of fillets. Do not boil as this toughens fish. Drain well, cool, and flake.

Mix well all ingredients except fish. Add flaked fish and mix gently.

Put into 1 qt. casserole and bake at 325° about 25 minutes. Remove from oven and add topping. Return to oven until topping is hot and bubbly.

Emma C. Olson, Boyceville

1 lb. fish fillets, flaked
½ cup mayonnaise or salad dressing
1 teaspoon worcestershire sauce
¼ teaspoon celery salt
¼ teaspoon salt
Dash of pepper
1 pimento, chopped fine
¼ teaspoon dry mustard
1 tablespoon parsley flakes
1 egg, slightly beaten
2 slices bread, cubed small

Topping

3 egg yolks
2 tablespoons lemon juice
½ cup butter or margarine, melted
(Place egg yolks and lemon juice in bowl. Beat 1 minute. Pour melted butter or margarine into mix slowly. Beat on high speed until thick.)

STUFFED FISH

STUFFING FOR 4 POUND FISH

Wash and salt and pepper fish inside and out. Cook celery in water for 5 minutes with butter. Pour over rest of ingredients and mix. Stuff fish, place on cabbage leaves. Bake at 500° for 10 minutes, then 400° for 30 minutes. (about 10 minutes a pound)

Jerry Wick, Milwaukee

1 cup chopped celery
½ cup water

6 tablespoons butter or oleo
4 cups bread crumbs
3 tablespoons chopped onion
1½ teaspoon sugar
¼ teaspoon sage
3/4 teaspoon salt
½ teaspoon pepper
Small can mushrooms
½ cup coarsely cut cucumbers
Cabbage leaves

BAKED MUSKIE WITH DRESSING

SOAK BREAD CUBES in warm water and squeeze out.
Add all ingredients. Mix well, add hot water if more
moisture is needed.

Fill cavity of muskie and tie to keep dressing inside.
Salt fish and pat with butter. Place on shallow pan and
bake at 375° for 1 hour or so depending on size of fish.
Serve with french fries and warm applesauce.

Darlis Wilfer, Phelps

1 pkg. bread cubes
1 onion, chopped
2 stalks celery, chopped
1 apple chopped
2 eggs
1 tablespoon vegetable oil
Salt and pepper

BAKED MUSKIE

SKIN AND CLEAN MUSKIE. Cut as far up to the head
as possible. Lay fish in tin foil. Salt and pepper inside
of fish. Add sliced onions inside of fish until filled.
Put bacon strips over and around fish. Now partly
fold up the tin foil and add water to about ½ inch in
bottom. Lay on cookie sheet.

Seal and bake for 1 hour at 425°, then open foil
and bake for ½ hour or longer at 350° until brown.

Mrs. Richard A. Miller, Plymouth

Muskie
Onions
Bacon strips
Salt & pepper

SWEET AND SOUR MUSKIE

BRING INGREDIENTS TO A boil in a pan for 5
minutes. Add fillets and cook slowly until fish flakes.
Remove fish and place in casserole dish.

Thicken juice with cornstarch and cream. Mix and
pour over muskie fillets. Serve hot.

Darlis Wilfer, Pehlps

2 cups water
½ cup vinegar
1 teaspoon salt
1 tablespoon sugar
2 onions
Allspice
1 tablespoon cornstarch
½ cup cream

WEBER MUSKIE

MAKE TRAY OF FOIL for grill, with chips if wished.
Put 3-4 oz. of beer on tray. Place fish on tray. Season
with onion, garlic, parsley, and butter.

Cook 30 minutes. Add the rest of the beer on and
around the fillet and cook for 30 more minutes.

John Wessell, Milwaukee

Any size fillet or side of muskie
1 12 oz. bottle of beer
Onion salt, garlic salt, parsley flakes
1 stick butter
Wood chips (optional)

BUTTER SAUCE FOR BAKED TROUT OR MUSKIE

MELT TOGETHER. Use as a sauce over broiled or
baked trout or muskie.

Darlis Wilfer, Phelps

1½ sticks butter or oleo
¼ teaspoon turmeric powder
1/8 teaspoon curry powder
¼ teaspoon dry mustard
2 tablespoons lemon juice
Few drops of tobasco sauce
1 teaspoon salt
Dash of worcestershire sauce

BAKED MUSKIE

CLEAN, SCALE, AND REMOVE head of fish. Stuff body with wild rice, and wrap in foil shell. Place in Weber grill for 1 hour.

Baste every 20 minutes with a lemon, butter, and dry vermouth sauce.

G. A. Seefeldt, Winter

1 muskie

Sauce
¼ stick butter (melted)
Juice of 1 lemon
¼ cup dry vermouth

NORTHERN LOAF

COMBINE BREAD AND CRACKER crumbs, mix eggs, milk and butter together and pour over bread and cracker crumbs. Let stand till soft (about 15 minutes). Add remaining ingredients and mix well. Place in greased loaf pan and bake at 350° for 50-55 minutes or until set. Serve with cheese potatoes, vegetables and tartar sauce.

C. Bison, Appleton

2 eggs
½ cup milk
3 tablespoons melted butter or oleo
½ cup soft bread crumbs
3/4 cup crushed saltine crackers
1 pint canned northern, drained, boned, flaked
½ teaspoon salt
¼ teaspoon pepper
¼ cup minced onion
1 tablespoon lemon juice

NORTHERN PIKE FISH PATTIES

FILLET NORTHERNS. Grind the fish through the fine blade of a food grinder. Several grindings may be necessary to reduce the rib bones to pieces that will not be noticed when the fish is cooked.

Drain the fish thoroughly. Add egg, salt and pepper, and spices and flour to hold the patties together. Shape them into patties, roll in flour, then in beaten egg and seasoned cracker crumbs. Sprinkle them with paprika, lay on a buttered cookie sheet, and bake at 375° until they are golden brown.

They make good fish sandwiches to serve on buns.

Mrs. C. Atkinson, Cable

Northerns
1 egg
Salt, pepper
Chopped parsley or chervil
Flour
Seasoned cracker crumbs
Paprika

BETTY'S MUSTARD SNACKS

SALT BOTH SIDES of fillets and let set overnight in the refrigerator.

Lay the fillets on paper towels and dry fish well. Grease a 9x13 glass baking dish with Mazola Oil so there's ample amount all over the dish. Bring mixture to boil, then spread over the fillets. Cover dish with foil and bake at 350° for 45 minutes. When done, remove as many bones as possible.

Pack in a jar and store in the refrigerator. Tasty treat on soda crackers.

Betty Miller, Luck

2 lbs. northern fillets
6 tablespoons Mazola Oil
6 tablespoons parsley flakes
2 tablespoons chopped onions
1 clove minced garlic
6 tablespoons prepared mustard

POOR MAN'S LOBSTER

DEBONE 2-3 NORTHERNS and cut in 1 inch chunks. Boil in water with 2 tablespoons salt and 2 tablespoons caraway seed for 5 minutes. Pour off water and dip in 1 cup of melted butter or margarine. (lemon juice optional)

G. A. Seefeldt, Winter

2-3 northerns
2 tablespoons salt
2 tablespoons caraway seed

MARINATED NORTHERN BROIL

MARINATE FOR AT LEAST 1 day (can be several days) northern fillets by covering them with a mixture of 1 part Kikkoman sauce, 1 part dry white wine, 1 part lemon juice, pepper to taste. A little water may be used, and 1 sliced onion.

When ready to broil, melt enough butter or margarine to cover bottom of flat baking pan that will hold your amount of pieces laid side by side. Lift fillets out of marinade and arrange one layer in pan. Put a generous dab of butter or margarine on each piece and place under broiler.

Broiling time depends on thickness of fish. May be turned once with pancake turner. Should be cooked through, but do not over-broil.

Margie Homer, Cable

Northern fillets
1 part Kikkoman sauce
1 part dry white wine
1 part lemon juice
Pepper
1 sliced onion

BAKED PERCH

BUTTER A 1½ QT. BAKING DISH. Cover bottom of dish with the parsley. Place seasoned perch in dish and top fish with 2 tablespoons chopped parsley and 2 tablespoons chopped fresh dill. Pour hot water around fish and bake at 350° for 20-25 minutes, or until fish flakes.

Transfer perch to a warm serving platter and garnish with sprigs of parsley, dill, and lemon wedges. Serves 4.

Shane Clarke, Palmyra

8 medium-sized perch, dressed
1 teaspoon salt
½ teaspoon pepper
¼ cup finely chopped parsley
¼ cup hot water

BLUEGILL NIBBLES

CUT FILLETS INTO THIN, bite-sized pieces. Pour the beer into a saucepan and bring to a boil. Add a few bluegill at a time. Bring to a boil and cook for 3 minutes. Remove the fish carefully. Serve immediately with a sauce of catsup and horseradish.

Mary Lynn Schroeder, Green Bay

Bluegill fillets
1 bottle beer
½ cup catsup
1 tablespoon horseradish

CRAPPIE & CHEESE DELIGHT

COMBINE ALL INGREDIENTS and mix well. Pour into baking dish. Bake at 350° for 45-50 minutes.

Christina Syverson, Tomah

½ cup chopped onion cooked until tender in 1 tablespoon butter
2 cups diced fish
3 eggs slightly beaten
1½ cup milk
2/3 cup finely crushed crackers
1 cup sharp processed American cheese
Pepper to taste

FISH SALAD

SKIN AND BONE FISH. Simmer until just done in salted water with lemon juice in it. Cool and cut into cube sized pieces.

Add lemon juice, Hellman's mayonaise and chopped chives. Chill. (Add horseradish if you like.)

Robert Blair, Beaver Dam

Whitefish, sturgeon or any fresh water fish.
Lemon juice
Hellman's mayonaise
Chopped chives
Horseradish (optional)

FISH DUGLERE

SEASON FISH FILLETS with salt and pepper. Melt butter in a skillet, add onion and garlic. Cook until soft.

Place fillets in pan. Arrange tomatoes and parsley over fish. Add wine and water to fish, cover with waxed paper, making a hole in center of the paper. Cover tightly and simmer for 8 minutes or until fish flakes easily with a fork.

Remove fish to hot platter.

Cook liquid down some, remove garlic. Mix flour and butter and stir into boiling liquid. Cook until thickened. Pour sauce over fish and serve at once. Nice with boiled rice.

Elsbeth C. Davison, West Allis

4 fish fillets
1 tablespoon salt
Dash pepper
3 tablespoons butter
1 medium onion, cut fine
1 clove garlic
¼ cup cooking wine
4 ripe tomatoes, peeled & chopped
1 teaspoon chopped parsley
¼ cup water
1 tablespoon flour
2 tablespoons butter (second stage)

BAKED FISH WITH WINE

MIX BREAD CRUMBS, herbs, salt and pepper. Spread this mixture over the fish fillets in a greased shallow baking dish pouring the wine and tomato sauce in the dish. Set in a moderate oven (375° F.) to bake, uncovered, for 25 to 30 minutes. Baste fish at regular intervals with liquid in the pan.

Beverly Rychter, Gleason

4 fillets of fish
1 cup tomato sauce
1 slice lemon
1 teaspoon parsley, minced
½ teaspoon salt
¼ teaspoon black pepper
½ teaspoon mixed powdered mace & marj
3/4 cup bread crumbs
1 cup wine

FRENCH FRIED FILLETED PERCH

FIRST SHAKE PERCH in a bag of flour seasoned with salt and pepper.

Dip fillets into above mixture after adding egg and milk. Remove from mixture and roll into bread crumbs and dip fry until golden brown and crispy.

Mrs. Cliff Rauscher, Green Bay

2 lbs. perch fillets
2 eggs whipped
¼ cup canned milk
Flour
Salt and pepper
Bread crumbs

HERB BAKED FISH

PLACE FROZEN FISH FILLETS in 10 x 6 x 1½ inch baking dish. Dot with butter and sprinkle with seasonings. Add bay leaf, arrange onion rings over top of fish. Pour cream over all. Bake uncovered in moderate oven (300°) about 30 to 40 minutes, until internal temperature of fish is 140°. If not frozen, bake as little as 10 or 15 minutes. Check the thermometer often. Serves 4.

Alma E. Morton, Madison

1 lb. fresh water fish fillets
1 tablespoon butter
1 teaspoon salt
Dash pepper
1 small bay leaf
½ teaspoon garlic salt
¼ teaspoon oregano
¼ teaspoon thyme
½ cup thinly sliced onion, seperated in rings.
1/2 to 3/4 cup light cream

POTTED BULLHEADS

CLEAN BULLHEADS and place 8 to 10 or more in a casserole dish. Season with salt and pepper. Slice 2 or 3 onions over top. Make a mixture ½ to ½ of vinegar and peanut oil. Pour over fish, cover with a muslin cloth.

Set casserole in a pan of water and bake 2½ to 3 hours at 275° oven. Cool and place in refrigerator for 5 days. When you take them out of the refrigerator, let stand at room temperature for an hour to liquify the oil.

Virginia Kraegenbrink, Menomonee Falls

8 - 12 clean bullheads
Salt & pepper
3 onions
Vinegar
Peanut oil

FISH AND BROCCOLI ROLLS

COOK 3/4 LB. BROCCOLI until tender. Drain well. Beat 1 egg slightly. Add 2 tablespoons milk, salt and pepper 1 lb. fish fillet. Combine ½ cup fine bread crumbs and 1/8 cup parmasean cheese. Dip each fillet in egg. Dip in crumbs. Wrap each fillet around small bunch of broccoli. Fasten with toothpick. Set in buttered baking dish. Dot with butter, pour tomato juice over all and bake at 400° for 30 minutes.

Alma E. Morton, Madison

1 lb. fish fillet
3/4 lb. broccoli
1 egg
2 tablespoons milk
Salt & pepper
½ cup fine bread crumbs
1/8 cup parmasean cheese
Butter
Tomato juice

GRILLED WHOLE FISH

THIS RECIPE WILL WORK FOR ANY FISH from smelt to salmon - as big as your grill will accomodate. If the fish has a skin which is rich in fat, basting will not be necessary. For large fish keep a more moderate fire.

Sprinkle the inside of the fish with salt & pepper and lemon juice. Put fish on a well greased grill or in a greased hinged broiler and brown carefully on both sides. Baste if you wish with equal parts of melted butter and white wine.

Fish will be ready when the flesh flakes easily with a fork or toothpick. Remove the bones before serving if you wish, but be sure to give each guest some crisp, charcoal flavored skin. Serve with lemon juice and parsley butter.

Greg Allen, Chippewa Falls

Fish of any size and variety
Salt & pepper
Lemon juice
Butter
White wine (optional)
Parsley

FISH FILLET ALA ORANGE

SPRINKLE FILLETS with salt and pepper. Slice orange very, very thin for garnish, set aside. Cut peelings off orange and cook in boiling water for 2 minutes. Drain, set aside.

Melt butter in skillet and cook onion, do not brown. Lift out.

Put fish in skillet, add orange and lemon juice with water. Sprinkle onion over fish along with the boiled orange rind.

Cover with oiled waxed paper with hole in the center of the paper. Simmer for 7 minutes.

Remove fish to hot platter. Cook liquid down to ½ cup.

Cream second butter on list and flour, add to liquid. Cook until thickened. Season to taste.

Arrange orange slices over fish and pour sauce over all. Serve at once. A nice orange flavor.

Elsbeth C. Davison, West Allis

Fish fillets, any kind, not too thick
2 oranges
3 tablespoons of butter
½ of a medium onion
Juice of 1 lemon and 1 orange. Cut rind off orange first, very thin.
¼ cup water
1 tablespoon butter (second stage)
1 tablespoon flour

POOR MAN'S LOBSTER

CLEAN AND CUT in 2 or 3 inch slices any large fish - northern, bass, walleye, trout and even carp.

Boil 2 quarts of water, add 3 tablespoons vinegar and 1/3 cup salt. Add slices of fish, simmer just until the flesh is white and starting to flake. Remove fish from water carefully, place on broiler pan lined with foil (place about 4 inches from heat).

Sprinkle fish with salt, pepper, paprika, lemon juice and butter. Turn over and broil. Take from broiler and serve on hot platter. Dip fish in parsley, melted butter or margarine and serve with lemon slices while hot.

Yield: serves 3 to 4.

Virginia Kraegenbrink, Menomonee Falls

1 large game fish
2 quarts water
3 tablespoons vinegar
1/3 cup salt
Pepper
Paprika
Lemon juice & slices
Butter
Parsley

BROILED PERCH IN FRENCH DRESSING

MARINATE FISH in French dressing for 1 to 2 hours in refrigerator.

Place marinated fish fillets on flat, shallow pan.

Place fish 3 inches from broiler. Broil 7 to 8 minutes. Baste several times with French dressing.

Serves 4 people nicely.

Elsbeth C. Davison, West Allis

4 jumbo perch
¼ bottle of French dressing

FILLETS ELEGANTE

PLACE FILLETS IN 9" pie plate. Dash with pepper and dot with butter. Spread soup over fillets; sprinkle with cheese and paprika. Bake in hot oven (400°) for 25 minutes. Serve with lemon slices.

The above recipe can be made with any type of fresh water fillets.

Yield: 4 servings.

Ray Charles, Kimberly

1 lb. fish fillets (fresh or frozen)
2 tablespoons butter
1 10oz. can frozen condensed cream of shrimp soup, thawed
¼ cup grated parmesan cheese
Paprika

SOUP BAKED FISH

ARRANGE FISH IN SHALLOW PAN, spread with melted butter. Sprinkle pepper over fish.

Bake in hot oven at 500° about 25 minutes. If fish slices are thicker, bake longer.

Spoon soup over fish along with chopped parsley, sprinkle cheese over top. Return to oven 5 to 10 minutes more. Garnish with cuke slices and serve at once.

Makes 6 servings.

Elsbeth C. Davison, West Allis

1 package fish fillets (breaded)
2 tablespoon butter
Dash of pepper
1 can condensed tomato soup
2 tablespoons chopped parsley
½ cup shredded cheddar cheese
Thin cucumber slices (garnish)

STUFFED FISH MUFFINS

GREASE 8 2½ IN. MUFFIN CUPS — set aside. Cook bacon till crisp, drain, reserving drippings. Crumble, set aside. Measure drippings, add enough melted butter or oleo to equal ¼ cup.

Prepare stuffing mix according to package directions, using dripping mixture instead of butter. Stir in bacon and onion.

Wrap one fish fillet inside each muffin cup, pressing it against sides. Spoon about 1/3 cup stuffing mixture into center of each roll. Brush with additional melted oleo. Bake at 375° for 30 minutes. Serve with sauce.

Mrs. Edward Zinniel, Fond du Lac

3 slices bacon
Oleo (melted)
1 6 oz. pkg. San Francisco style stuffing mix
¼ cup finely chopped onion
8 perch or pike fillets

Sauce

Either Bearnaise sauce or hot melted butter

PERCH, BLUEGILL, OR CRAPPIE FILLETS

DIP FILLETS FIRST INTO Realemon juice then into a beaten egg (with a little milk), then into flour.

Using only about 3-4 tablespoons of Crisco Oil, heat the oil in fry pan and then turn heat down to medium low. Fry fillets slowly until golden brown.

Season while frying with salt and pepper.

Darlis Wilfer, Phelps

Perch, bluegill or crappie fillets
Realemon juice
1 egg beaten
Milk and flour

BAKED SALMON WITH RICE AND OLIVES

WASH FISH AND DRY INSIDE and out with paper towels. Sprinkle inside with salt.

Mix all ingredients well and stuff fish. Place on oiled cookie sheet and baste fish with butter. Measure the thick part of fish and bake 10 minutes per inch or until fish flakes easily.

Mrs. Charles Booth, Waupaca

4-5 lbs. salmon
¾ cup chopped onion
¼ cup butter
1 1/3 cup cooked rice
1 cup chopped celery
1 cup sliced stuffed green olives
1 cup sliced seeded ripe olives
¼ teaspoon salt
¼ teaspoon pepper
½ teaspoon sage
¼ teaspoon thyme
3 tablespoons lemon juice

BOILED SALMON STEAKS

BRING 4-QT. POT OF WATER to boil and add lemon juice and crab-boil. Return to boil and place salmon in for 10 minutes. Remove with slotted spoon.

Mary Scott, Manawa

4 salmon steaks
2 teaspoons lemon juice
1 tablespoon shrimp or crab-boil spices

SALMON PARTY BALL

DRAIN AND FLAKE SALMON, combine salmon and cream cheese, lemon juice, onion, horseradish, salt, and liquid smoke. Mix. Chill several hours.

Combine pecans and parsley. Shape salmon into a ball. Roll in nut mixture. Chill well. Serve with crackers.

Steve Windett, Platteville

1 jar (2 cups) canned salmon
1 8 oz. pkg. softened cream cheese
1 tablespoon lemon juice
2 teaspoons grated onion
1 teaspoon prepared horseradish
¼ teaspoon salt
¼ teaspoon liquid smoke
½ cup chopped pecans
3 tablespoons parsley

FLAVOR CRAVER DIP

BEAT ALL INGREDIENTS together. Chill for several hours.

Serve with fresh vegetables and chips. (Smoked fish can be used in place of the canned salmon.)

Carol Vanooyen, East Troy

½ cup chili sauce
½ cup mayonnaise
8 oz. cream cheese, softened
2 teaspoons horseradish
¼ cup finely chopped onions
1 pt. salmon
Season salt to taste

SALMON IN PARCHMENT with SOUR CREAM SAUCE

PREPARE A STRIP OF aluminum foil large enough to envelop the fish completely. Lay the fish on the foil and sprinkle generously with the freshly ground pepper and salt. Pour over the lemon juice.

To make the sauce, add juice, salt, pepper and dill to sour cream and mix. Spread over salmon. Spread onion and parsley over sour cream mixture. Wrap fish and sauce in foil being sure to wrap securely so juice cannot get out.

Lay in a baking pan and bake in 425° oven for 40 minutes. Do not open the package during baking. Lay the salmon on a hot platter and pour over all the juices. Garnish with the lemon wedges and green pepper if you wish. Serves 4 to 6. If fish is boned, the skin will come off easily when fish is removed from the pan.

Mrs. Jesse Bytell, Grafton

1 (2 lb.) piece of coho salmon
Freshly ground pepper
1 teaspoon salt
¼ cup lemon juice
Lemon wedges & green pepper rings for garnish

SAUCE
1 tablespoon lemon juice
½ teaspoon dill seed (or fresh dill)
1 medium onion, thinly sliced
1 tablespoon chopped parsley
1 cup commercial sour cream
½ teaspoon salt
Freshly ground pepper

SALMON LOAF

COMBINE ALL INGREDIENTS. Bake in loaf pan at 325° for about 45 minutes. Serve with creamed peas.

Mrs. Elaine Heiar, Bloomington

1 qt. home canned salmon
1 cup sour cream
1 medium onion chopped fine
2 eggs
1 cup celery chopped fine
8 soda crackers rolled fine
Salt and pepper to taste

SALMON LOAF

COOK ONION AND CELERY in ¼ teaspoon butter until soft. Beat eggs, add all ingredients, and mix. Bake in greased pan 8¼x9½x2½ in a 350° oven about 55 minutes. Invert on platter.

Carol Vanooyen, East Troy

2 tablespoons minced onion
1/3 cup chopped celery
2 eggs
¼ teaspoon butter
½ can cream of celery soup
2 tablespoons Miracle Whip
½ cup milk
1 pt. salmon, drained and flaked
1 cup cooked rice

SALMON SPREAD

COMBINE ALL INGREDIENTS and beat until smooth. Let stand several hours.

Use as spread on crackers or bread. Good on party rye.

Carol Vanooyen, East Troy

1 pkg. 8 oz. cream cheese at room temperature
½ pt. salmon, drained
2 teaspoons lemon juice
1 teaspoon prepared mustard
1 teaspoon horseradish
Salt and pepper to taste
Dash of hot pepper sauce

CHEESY SALMON STRATA

TRIM BREAD CRUSTS, cut in half diagonally. Arrange half in 8x8x2" greased baking dish (2 qt. size). Sprinkle with cheese, salmon, and onions. Put on remaining bread triangles.

Combine soup, eggs, and milk, pour over casserole. Cover. Chill 6-24 hours.

Before serving, combine ¼ cup dry bread crumbs, 2 tablespoons melted margarine, ¼ teaspoon paprika. Sprinkle over top. Bake in 325° oven till set, about 1 hour.

Carol Vanooyen, East Troy

6 slices day old bread
4 oz. sharp or medium shredded cheese (1 cup)
1 pt. salmon, drained and flaked
1 10½ oz. can cream of mushroom soup
2 beaten eggs
1 cup milk
2 tablespoons finely chopped onions

MARINATED SALMON STEAKS

MIX ALL INGREDIENTS except salmon steaks in a shallow bowl. Place fish in plastic bag. Pour marinade over fish. Seal bag. Refrigerate 1½ hours turning bag over two or three times. Set oven to broil and/or 550°.

Grease broiler pan. Remove fish from marinade. Reserve marinade. Arrange fish on broiler pan; baste with marinade. Broil 4-5 inches from heat for 5 minutes. Turn, baste with marinade. Broil until fish flakes easily in center, about 5 minutes. Makes 4 servings.

Lloyd Recore, Valders

½ cup vegetable oil
½ cup white wine vinegar
1 teaspoon sugar
1 teaspoon dried parsley flakes
½ teaspoon dried Italian seasoning
¼ teaspoon garlic salt
¼ teaspoon onion salt
1/8 teaspoon paprika
1/8 teaspoon pepper
4 salmon steaks, about 1 in. thick

STUFFED BAKED COHO

SOAK SALMON IN GARLIC water for 30 minutes. Salt and pepper cavity and sprinkle with lemon juice. Put the wild game stuffing in cavity and lay fish on aluminum foil and sprinkle more lemon juice on fish. Lay chunks of butter around fish then seal foil and place in a roaster and bake at 350° for 1-1½ hours. Also delicious on the grill. Just ½ hour on each side. (Slit foil)

Mary Scott, Manawa

1 5-7 lb. coho salmon
Lemon juice
Salt and pepper
Wild game stuffing

BROILED SALMON

SPRINKLE SALMON STEAKS with garlic salt, pepper, and lemon juice. Brush melted butter or margarine over steaks. Broil in broiler or in outdoor grill on rack lined with foil for about 10 minutes on each side.

Before removing from grill, add 1 tablespoon sour cream to top of steaks and warm about 1 minute.

Gerald Lahner, Eau Claire

Salmon steaks
Garlic salt, pepper and lemon juice
Butter or margarine
Sour cream

STUFFED COHO ALA WEBER

MIX STUFFING BY HEATING 1¼ cups water in large saucepan. Stir in ½ of the butter until melted. Stir in crouton type stuffing mix until moisture is absorbed. Add tomato pieces. Fill cavity of fish, do not over-stuff as the stuffing expands. Tie the fish closed lightly with string along the length of fish to retain stuffing and ease of handling. Melt butter and lemon juice in small sauce pan. Use to baste fish periodically.

Use indirect method for cooking. Coals are placed to the sides of the Weber kettle with a drip pan in the middle. Place fish *directly* on the grill above the drip pan. This allows the grease and oils to escape from the meat during cooking. Grease and oils are source of what many people refer to as a "fishy" taste.

Roast approximately 10-15 minutes per pound until fish flakes. When over half of the total cooking time has elapsed, fish should be turned on the other side using two spatulas. Some of the skin will stick to the grill. Baste after turning.

Michael A. Hinz, Sheboygan

1 5-6 lb. Coho
8 oz. crouton type stuffing mix
¼ lb. stick of butter
Small onion, finely chopped
1 small tomato, cut in small pieces
1 tablespoon lemon juice

SMOKED FLAVORED SALMON

PACK FISH INTO ½ PINT JARS, add liquid smoke, and seal. Process 90 minutes at 10 lbs. in pressure cooker.

Serve as a spread on crackers by mixing ½ pt. salmon, 1 diced onion and 1 8 oz. pkg. cream cheese.

Mary DeLong, Chippewa Falls

Filleted salmon cut in 2 in. chunks
¼ teaspoon liquid smoke

JELLIED SALMON

COMBINE INGREDIENTS IN DOUBLE boiler, stirring until thick. Add 1 tablespoon gelatin dissolved in 2 tablespoons water, and 1 pint drained flaked salmon. Mold and chill until firm. Serve with a cucumber sauce. Kraft Creamy Cucumber salad dressing makes an excellent sauce.

Mary DeLong, Chippewa Falls

½ tablespoon sugar
½ tablespoon salt
1 tablespoon flour
1 teaspoon dry mustard
2 lightly beaten egg yolks
2 tablespoons melted butter
1 cup milk
¼ cup vinegar
Gelatin

HERB BROILED SALMON

FIRST CUT INTO 6 PIECES about 1 in. thick. Salt and pepper and put fish skin side up on broiler pan.

Mix butter, dillweed, thyme, and onion powder. Brush on fish and put under broiler for 5 minutes. Brush other side and cook for about 10 more minutes.

Al Dawydiuk, Milwaukee

filleted salmon
½ teaspoon salt
½ teaspoon pepper
2 tablespoons butter, melted
1/8 teaspoon dillweed
¼ teaspoon thyme
¼ teaspoon onion powder

SALMON CUBES OR STEAKS

FILLET AND BONE SALMON, cut into 2 in. cubes. Rinse and place into a bowl with eggs. Stir pieces till covered with egg. Place in refrigerator for 6-8 hours, stirring occasionally.

Take each cube or steak and roll in cracker crumbs. Fry in cast iron frying pan on medium heat with about 1 in. of shortening. Turn as brown, about 6 minutes. Serve with melted butter and lemon juice.
Note: Soaking salmon in egg helps to take away strong fish flavor.

Brad Peotter, Rhinelander

Salmon cubes or steaks
2 well beaten eggs
Cracker crumbs

WISCONSIN FISH BOIL

FILL A LARGE KETTLE two-thirds full of water. Boil onions, lemon, bay leaves, vinegar, salt and pepper for ¼ to ½ hour.

Drop in fish. Any good meated white fish in chunks or fillets can be used (Lake Michigan salmon is very good). Once it starts to boil hard again, permit it to keep boiling for 15 minutes. Serve with melted butter, boiled potatoes and rye bread.
Mrs. James Pierce, Pewaukee

1 salmon or several smaller game fish cut into chunks.
4 large white onions
¼ - ½ fresh lemon (sliced paper thin)
4 bay leaves
½ cup vinegar
Salt & pepper

SALMON STEAKS

TAKE 3-1 INCH SALMON STEAKS and place them in a shallow baking dish. In a seperate pan melt ¼ cup butter and add ½ teaspoon salt, ¼ teaspoon paprika, 2 tablespoons of barbecue sauce and 1 teaspoon Worcestershire sauce. Brush over salmon, then lightly sprinkle each salmon steak with lemon juice. Bake in moderate oven 375° about 20 - 25 minutes.

Yield: 3 servings
Bill Gloeckler, Milwaukee

3 - 1 inch salmon steaks
¼ cup butter
½ teaspoon salt
¼ teaspoon paprika
2 tablespoons barbecue sauce
1 teaspoon worcestershire sauce
Lemon juice

CANNED TROUT

SKIN AND REMOVE big bones. Cut fish into 1½ by 1½ inch pieces. Drain well. Fill pint jars 1 inch from the top. In each jar add:
½ teaspoon canning salt, 2 tablespoons catsup, 1 tablespoon white vinegar, 1 tablespoon oil.

Seal jars and place in a preheated oven at 250°F. Bake for 3 hours. Turn off the oven leaving the jars there until cooled, then remove. Canned trout can also be cold packed in boiling water bath for 4 hours.
Mrs. Hilary Loabieck, Neenah

Fresh trout
½ teaspoon canning salt
2 tablespoons catsup
1 tablespoon white vinegar
1 tablespoon oil

WISCONSIN SALMON CASSEROLE

COOK GREEN PEPPERS and onion in butter until soft. Remove from heat; add cream of chicken soup, stirring until smooth. Break salmon into pieces in the juice of the jar. Place half of noodles and salmon in layers in a buttered 1½ qt. casserole, add half of the soup mixture and then repeat layers. Sprinkle cereal on top. Bake for 30 minutes in a 325° preheated oven.

Velma Bray, Fennimore

2 tablespoons chopped green pepper
1 tablespoon butter
¼ cup milk
1 pt. jar of home canned Wisconsin salmon
1 tablespoon chopped onion
1 10½ oz. can cream of chicken soup
2 cups cooked noodles
1 teaspoon melted butter in
1 cup Rice Krispies

LEMON POACHED SALMON

IN LARGE SKILLET, combine water, onions, lemon juice, salt and pepper. Bring to boil and simmer 5 minutes to blend flavors. Add salmon steaks and simmer 7-10 minutes until salmon flakes easily. Lift salmon out of liquid onto platter. Sprinkle with dill weed and garnish with lemon wedges.

Gerald Lahner, Eau Claire

4 cups water
¼ cup sliced green onions
2 tablespoons lemon juice
½ teaspoon salt
1/8 teaspoon pepper
4 6 oz. salmon steaks
Lemon wedges and dill weed

GRILLED SALMON WITH FENNEL BUTTER

CUT FILLETS INTO 4 equal portions. Sprinkle with salt and pepper, and rub on oil to coat all sides.

Trim fennel and cut into ¼ in. cubes. There should be about 1½ cups. Put in pan, add water and 1 tablespoon butter. Cook 5 minutes.

Pour cooked mixture into blender and add 4 tablespoons butter. Blend as fine as possible. Pour into pan. Bring to boil, add salt, cayenne, and nutmeg. Simmer for 3 minutes.

Cook salmon for 4 minutes on one side. Turn and cook for 4 minutes on other side. Transfer fish to warm serving dish. Serve with hot fennel sauce spooned over fish, or on the side. Makes 4 servings.

Karen Schmidt, Racine

2 lbs. salmon fillets, boned and skinned
Salt and pepper to taste
2 tablespoons oil
1 head fennel (about ¾ lb.)
1/3 cup water
5 tablespoons butter
1/8 teaspoon cayenne pepper
1/8 teaspoon nutmeg

LAKE MICHIGAN SHORE LUNCH

MIX BISQUICK, FLOUR, corn meal, and garlic salt together. Cut the salmon fillets into 3 in. serving pieces. Dip each fillet into lemon juice, then coat each with the batter. Fry the fillets in very hot shortening or bacon grease to seal in the delicate flavor of the salmon.

This is a super recipe for our Great Lakes salmon.

Ray Baranczyk, Manitowoc

Boneless salmon fillets
1 cup Bisquick
½ cup flour
¼ cup cornmeal
½ teaspoon garlic salt
Lemon juice

SALMON FOIL BAKE ALA HARRY

RINSE THE SALMON fillets well and pat dry with paper towel.

Roll the fillets in the bread crumbs, and center them on a piece of foil large enough to be folded and completely sealed (can double wrap).

In layers, cover the fillets with the mushrooms, scallions, and salt and pepper. Add the layer of tomatoes, sprinkle on the dill weed, and the parmesan cheese.

Fold up the foil, and just before sealing the package, add the dry white wine.

Using the direct cooking method, place the foil-sealed fillets on covered grill over hot coals for 12-15 minutes per side. 30 minutes maximum.

Remove the fillets to a serving tray and garnish with parsley sprigs and sliced lemon. Serves 6-8.

(If a Weber or similar grill is not available, preheat oven to 375° and bake for 25 minutes, turning once.)

Harry Gryske, Pewaukee

2 medium sized salmon fillets (approximately 4 lbs.)
½ cup finely chopped scallions
1 large tomato, sliced thin
1 cup thinly-sliced mushrooms
4 tablespoons dry white wine
2 cups dry bread crumbs
2 tablespoons parmesan cheese
½ teaspoon dill weed
Salt and pepper

SMOKED SALMON

SPLIT FISH ALONG backbone. Remove head, tail, and small fins (large fish should be steaked). Scrub fish with G.I. brush on both sides. Rinse with cold water. Soak overnight in salt brine strong enough to float an egg.

Add 1 cup brown sugar to each 2 gallons of brine. Remove from brine and rinse with cold water. Dry with towel. Place on smoker back with skin side down. Sprinkle on garlic salt, pepper, hickory smoke salt, and 1/8 - ¼ in. thick brown sugar. Sprinkle liquid smoke on top of brown sugar. Put in smoker and smoke until it flakes, using fruit tree or hardwood chips.

When fish has cooled, remove from smoker racks and wrap in saran wrap. Will keep, if refrigerated, for 30 days.

Laverne C. Wubben, Hazel Green

Salmon
Salt brine
1 cup brown sugar
Garlic salt
Pepper
Hickory smoke salt
Brown sugar

FRENCH FRIED SMELT

POUR BEER IN BOWL (any brand, cold or at room temp). Add enough dry pancake mix to make a thin batter. Beat batter well to remove all the lumps.

Dip cleaned smelt into batter, and deep fry in hot oil for about 2 minutes, or until nicely browned.

Salt fish and drain on paper toweling — serve hot, with tartar sauce if desired.

Mrs. Jan Teachout, Waupun

Smelt
1 can beer
Dry pancake mix

DEEP FRY SMELT

SMELT HAVE A RICH, delicious flavor and are best when deep fried. A beer batter for smelt can be made with ¼ cup of cornstarch; ¼ cup of flour and two egg whites. Mix beer, cornstarch and flour together. Beat the egg whites until stiff, and fold into the flour mixture.

Dip dry smelt into batter and deep fry.

This recipe can be used on any fish fillets which are deep fried. It can not be used on pan fried fish because it will flatten. The batter gets its airy consistency from the egg whites - as soon as the batter covered fish hit the hot oil, the coating puffs.

"Jimmie" Garnett, Wisconsin Rapids

Enough smelt to feed 4 people
¼ cup cornstarch
¼ cup flour
2 egg whites
Beer

SMELT

SEASON FRESH OR frozen (thawed) smelt with onion salt.

Roll in flour and deep-fat fry until golden.

Simple and tasty.

Mrs. Joseph Vross, Two Rivers

Smelt
Onion salt
Flour

GLORIFIED SHEEPSHEAD

PLACE SHEEPSHEAD FILLETS in a pan with 1 tablespoon shrimp spice tied in a cheese cloth bag. Bring to boil, then simmer for 5 minutes.

Grease baking dish large enough to place fish single layer. Sprinkle fillets with 2-3 tablespoons lemon juice. Set aside.

Saute onion in ¼ cup margarine or butter. Add salt, basil, paprika, or seafood seasoning to taste.

To this mixture, add rest of ingredients. If not enough moisture, add 1-2 tablespoons water.

Spoon this mixture on the fillets and sprinkle with paprika.

Bake at 375° about 45 minutes. (Skin the sheepshead, and then fillet them.)

Alice and George Manthei, Janesville

10-12 Sheepshead fillets
1 tablespoon shrimp spice
1 onion sauteed in ¼ cup margarine or butter
Salt, basil, paprika, or seafood seasoning
2 well beaten eggs
1 cup bread crumbs
6½ oz. can minced crabmeat

POOR MAN'S LOBSTER WITH LAKE STURGEON

SKIN STURGEON, REMOVE head and spinal cord (sturgeon have no bones).

Cut fish into 2 in. square pieces. Boil chunks in water for 5 minutes. (Add 2 tablespoons salt and 2 tablespoons caraway seed to water).

After boiling, pour off water and dip chunks in butter or margarine. Lemon juice optional.

G. A. Seefeldt, Winter

Sturgeon
2 tablespoons salt
2 tablepoons caraway seed
Butter/margarine

SUCKER PATTIES

GRIND FISH, GARLIC, and onions. Then add eggs and seasoning, and mix.

Crush crackers and mix again. (Do not grind crackers with fish.)

Fry in skillet in about ¼ in. oil very slowly. (Do not deep fry.)

John Renard, Green Bay

5 lb. sucker
4 eggs
1 lb. crackers
2 lbs. onions
5 large cloves of garlic
2 tablespoons chili powder
1 tablespoon lemon juice
1 teaspoon tumeric
2 tablespoons salt

TARTAR SAUCE

MIX INGREDIENTS together and serve.

Cathy Fehrenbach, Milwaukee

1 cup mayonnaise
¼ cup pickles (use sweet relish)
1 tablespoon French dressing

STUFFED TROUT

STUFF TROUT AND PLACE in crock pot or slow cooker. Put 1 cup warm water in and lemon juice (you can also add 1 teaspoon of crab boil, if desired). Cook on low for 3-4 hours.

You can also do this without the stuffing, cook for 2-3 hours.

Mary Scott, Manawa

2-4 trout, rainbow, brookies, brown
Wild game stuffing
1 tablespoon lemon juice

Stuffing

10 slices bread, shredded
1 large onion
1 green pepper, chopped
Poultry seasoning
Water (to moisten, not soak)

BAKED TROUT WITH MUSHROOMS AND LEMON

CLEAN TROUT, WASH, and wipe dry. Place in glass baking dish. Melt butter. Add mushrooms, parsley, lemon juice, and spices. Arrange fish. Spoon butter and mushrooms over fish and bake at 350° for 25-30 minutes.

David and Shelley Hraychuck, Sayner

2 2-3 lb. trout or salmon
1 tablespoon parsley
1 cup fresh mushrooms sliced
1 cup butter
Dash grated nutmeg
Salt and paprika
Juice of 1 lemon

STUFFED TROUT

IN LARGE SAUCEPAN, melt butter. Add water and lemon juice. Stir. Add onion, celery and mushrooms, cooking till tender but transparent. Add salt and pepper to taste.

Stir in stuffing cubes and dill, moistening well. Remove from heat.

Stuff trout with mixture. Place on foil, baste with melted butter and lemon juice. Close foil up and bake at 350° until fish flakes with fork, about ½ hour.

This can also be cooked on a grill turning foil once or twice during cooking.

Mrs. Jeff Van Caster, Conover

3 lbs. trout, cleaned and scaled
2 cups herbed stuffing cubes
2/3 cup water
1/3 cup butter or margarine
¼ cup finely chopped onion
¼ cup finely chopped celery
¼ cup finely chopped fresh mushrooms
1 teaspoon dillweed
1 tablespoon lemon juice
Salt and pepper

GOURMET BAKE LAKE TROUT

PRE-HEAT OVEN TO 375°. Wash trout well and dry inside and outside. Rub inside cavity with lemon juice and salt.

Fry onions, celery, sage, and thyme in oil for 5 minutes. Add peanuts, rice, salt, and pepper. Mix well and spoon into trout. Secure opening with skewers or lace with string. Place in shallow baking dish (uncovered).

Mix wine and water and pour over fish. Bake 25-30 minutes or until done.

Mrs. Charles Booth, Waupaca

4-4½ lbs. lake trout
1 teaspoon salt
2 tablespoons lemon juice

Dressing

¾ cup chopped onions
½ cup chopped celery
½ teaspoon sage
½ teaspoon thyme
2 tablespoons oil
½ cup chopped peanuts
1½ cup cooked rice
½ teaspoon salt
¼ teaspoon pepper
½ cup white winte
¾ cup water

BAKE STUFFED LAKE TROUT

PREHEAT OVEN TO 375°. Grease shallow baking pan. Stuff trout or spread the seafood dressing over each fillet. Use toothpicks to secure dressing inside whole trout. Roll fillets and fasten with toothpicks.

Place fish in prepared baking pan, and season with salt, pepper, and lemon juice.

Sprinkle bread crumbs over fish. Melt butter and pour over fish. Bake at 375° for 25-30 minutes or until fork-tender.

Marilyn Benish, Yuba

Lake trout, whole or fillets (enough to serve 6)

Seafood Dressing

Salt and pepper to taste
3 tablespoons lemon juice
1 cup fine bread crumbs
1/3 lb. butter, melted

HEAVENLY STREAM TROUT

COMBINE BACON GREASE and Crisco in equal amounts, enough to cover half the trout while frying.

Dip fish in buckwheat flour and place in fry pan on medium high heat. Turn to wet each side first and then turn heat down to medium and fry, turning every 2-3 minutes until golden brown. The fish grease can be strained and reused many times (keep refrigerated).

Carol Nushart, Brillion

Trout
Buckwheat flour
Bacon grease
Crisco
Salt/pepper

WEBERED LAKE TROUT

START WEBER GRILL (good bed of coals.) Lay fillets on foil and spread butter, covering both fillets. Next sprinkle with lemon juice, salt, and pepper. Spread onions over fish and wrap with foil. Make sure you have tight seal to prevent leakage.

Place on grill for 45 minutes, turning intermittently.

Jim Bruckner, Chilton

2 lake trout fillets (trimmed)
2-3 onions, chopped
2 sticks butter
Lemon juice
Salt and pepper

GOLDEN FRIED RAINBOW TROUT

WASH TROUT AND PAT dry with paper towels. Fry bacon until crisp, remove from pan and add other oil or margarine to pan drippings. Combine milk, salt and pepper.

Combine flour, cornmeal, and paprika. Dip fish in milk mixture, then in flour mixture. Fry in pan with bacon drippings and oil (hot) for 4-5 minutes on each side until fish flakes easily with fork. Drain on paper towels and serve hot with bacon.

Mrs. Charles Booth, Waupaca

6 pan-ready rainbow trout
12 slices bacon
1/3 cup melted margarine or oil
¼ cup evaporated milk
1½ teaspoon salt
1/8 teaspoon pepper
½ cup flour
¼ cup yellow cornmeal
1 teaspoon paprika

TROUT IN FOIL, GREEK STYLE

SAUTE SCALLIONS, CELERY, parsley, and mushrooms in butter; season with salt and pepper and a pinch of oregano; add wine and simmer for 10 minutes.

Wash and dry trout. Stuff each trout with the mixture; secure with a skewer and place on individual double sheets of foil.

Sprinkle each trout with salt, pepper, and oregano; squeeze the juice of ½ lemon on each trout and sprinkle with olive oil.

Seal and bake 15 minutes at 400°. Serve the trout in the foil with mixed greens and garlic sauce, accompanied by white wine.

T. W. Poulette, Waupaca

4 trout, cleaned
4 scallions, finely chopped
1 celery stalk, finely chopped
1 teaspoon chopped parsley
6 medium mushrooms, finely chopped
Oregano
1/3 cup white wine
Salt and pepper
Lemons, butter, olive oil

BREADED TROUT

DIP FISH IN SALT milk then egg, then roll in seasoned bread crumbs. Drop in hot fat and cook until golden brown.

Ken Tomaszewski, Janesville

4 fresh trout fillets
½ cup salt milk (½ teaspoon salt)
1 egg well beaten
4 tablespoons bread crumbs
¼ teaspoon garlic salt or powder
½ teaspoon dried parsley flakes
Salt and pepper to taste

BAKED FISH

REMOVE HEAD AND FINS and wash fish thoroughly and salt inside and out. Lay in shallow greased pan lined with foil.

Soak bread cubes in milk to a damp consistency, crumble in bowl, add rest of ingredients.

Mix with fingers and stuff in fish. Score the skin with a knife and brush top with bacon fat. Sprinkle with paprika and bake for 1 hour at 375°, basting occasionally with the fat in pan.

Garnish with lemon slices and parsley, lemon juice, and butter.

Anley Christianson, Ladysmith

Trout 3-4 lbs.
3 cups bread cubes
Milk
1 egg
Dash of pepper
1 teaspoon salt
1 finely chopped onion
½ teaspoon sage
Lemon slices, parsley

CHARCOAL GRILLED NORTHERN LAKE TROUT

BRUSH FISH WITH OIL. Combine ingredients and mix well.

Cook over coals until golden brown, brushing with lemon mixture. Turn fish gently to cook both sides. Pour remaining mixture over fish.

Helen Tschida, Danbury

Trout (2½-3 lbs.)
¼ cup oil
½ cup fresh lemon juice
¾ teaspoon salt
½ teaspoon pepper
1 tablespoon oregano
½ teaspoon Accent

TURTLE SOUP

1½ POUNDS SQUARED TURTLE meat (soak overnight in vinegar water).
Simmer two hours, in four quarts of water with two diced onions.
Put into broth: 2 diced carrots; 1 cup diced celery; salt and pepper to taste. Cover.
Let simmer until vegetables are tender. Add ½ cup barley or one cup narrow egg noodles about ½ hour before serving. Serve with crackers and small cheese wedges. The soup is rich and flavorful.

Jean Harris, Merrill

1½ pounds turtle meat, squared
vinegar
2 onions, diced
2 carrots, diced
Salt & pepper
½ cup barley or 1 cup narrow egg noodles

BOILED TURTLE

SNAPPING TURTLE SHOULD be alive. Sever the head off with an ax. Cover with cold water or hang neck down to drain until blood stops dripping. Wash carefully, drop into boiling salt water and cook 10 minutes.

Drain and cover with cold water; drain again, pull out toenails and rub black skin from legs.

Cover again with boiling water and simmer, covered ½ to ¾ hour or until shell separates easily and legs can be dented.

Cool in water. Place turtle on its back and working from the tail end, loosen and remove under shell. Remove carefully and discard the gall bladder, a sac near the head, and the intestines. The eggs, if any, heart, and the liver should be dropped in water and used in stews, creamed dishes, or croquettes.

Turtle meat can be used in different ways such as soup, stews, ala king, or in mushroom white sauce.

Gib Dutton, Rochester, MN

TURTLE SOUP

IN LARGE POT, PLACE turtle and cover with water, simmer for 1 hour (medium heat).

Add remaining ingredients and cook until carrots and potatoes are tender.

Ken Tomaszewski, Janesville

1 medium turtle (dressed)
cut into pieces
1 bunch carrots (sliced)
1½ lbs. potatoes peeled and cubed
2 large onions chopped
4½ cups beef broth
1 tablespoon flaked parsley
Season to taste

TURTLE SOUP

BOIL TURTLE ON LOW HEAT for 1 hour in 3 qts. water. Drain with colander saving liquid. Let cool and debone and degristle meat, chopping into bite-sized pieces. Take care of vegetables, chopping into bite-sized pieces.

Add all the ingredients to the liquid except salt. Simmer with cover until vegetables are tender. Salt to taste.

Mr. & Mrs. T. Danowski, Milwaukee

5-6 lbs. turtle meat
16 oz. tomatoes, chopped
1 medium onion, chopped
1 cup celery, chopped
1 cup carrots, chopped
2 cups potatoes, chopped
1 tablespoon basil
Salt to taste

SNAPPER SURPRISE

REMOVE FROM SHELL, DRESS, and wash thoroughly. Cut into serving pieces. Roll in flour and brown in cooking fat. When browned, add enough water to cover bottom of pan, season.

Cover and cook till tender. Add water as needed to keep from burning.

Dan Hirchert, Platteville

Snapper
Flour
Season to taste

TURTLE SOUP

COOK TURTLE MEAT in water with salt, onion, and potatoes until meat can be picked off bones. Strain broth to remove onions and potatoes.

Separate meat from bones. Add carrots to broth and cook until almost done. Add tomatoes, uncooked rice, okra, small onion, turtle meat, and chicken gumbo soup (optional).

Simmer until done. Add water for desired consistency.

Michael Hinz, Sheboygan

Turtle meat from large snapper
14 oz. can okra
1 qt. tomatoes
½ cup rice
1 lb. carrots
2 onions, chopped
1 can chicken gumbo soup
Potatoes

BAKED WALLEYE WITH ALMOND DRESSING

WASH THOROUGHLY WITH ICE water and pat dry with paper towels. Gently rub cavity with half of lemon.

Stuff with Almond Dressing. Dissolve broth in boiling water; add margarine. Remove crust from bread, tear into small pieces. Add bread and almonds to broth mixture. Mix lightly.

Place stuffed fish in a buttered baking dish. Melt 8 tablespoons of margarine and mix with 1 teaspoon of chopped parsley and ½ teaspoon pepper. Pour over fish. Bake at 325° for 40 minutes or until fish flakes.

Salt should not be added because of the delicate flavor of walleye and almond dressing.

Serve on warm platter. Garnish with fresh parsley and lemon or lime slices.

Marie Jorgensen, Glenview, IL

3 lbs. dressed walleye

Almond Dressing

4 envelopes (5.3 grams each) instant seasoned chicken broth
2 cups boiling water
½ cup margarine
1 loaf (1 pound) white bread
½ cup finely ground almonds

WINNEBAGO WALLEYE SANDWICH

DRY FILLETS WITH paper towels. In a cast iron frying pan, fry bacon until crisp. Drain off half of bacon grease and add equal amount of Crisco oil.

Blend eggs and milk together. Dip fillets in egg and milk mixture and coat with cornflake crumbs. Fry until golden brown.

Take 2 pieces of rye bread and spread Cheez Whiz on one. Add slices of bacon and fillet. Cover with second piece of rye. Serves 4.

Fantastic over an open fire while camping. Can be used with any other fish from perch to northern.

Thomas Goddard, Brillion

4 walleye fillets
2 eggs
1 lb. bacon
Cornflake crumbs
Rye bread
Cheez Whiz
Crisco oil
1 can Carnation milk

WALLEYE FILLETS AU NOBLE

DIP FILLETS IN MELTED BUTTER, season with salt & pepper and place in shallow baking pan. Mix condensed celery soup with the cream and sherry. Cover fillets with this liquid and sprinkle with grated parmasean cheese. Bake for 30 minutes at 350°.

Karle E. Tonn, Fredonia

Walleye fillets
1 cup condensed celery soup
¼ cup cream
¼ cup sherry
Grated Parmasean cheese
Salt & pepper

BAKED FISH FILLETS ALA WARREN

TAKE A LARGE PIECE OF aluminum foil and place it in a large, flat baking dish. Salt both sides of the fillets, place skin down in the dish. Cut a pattie of butter in half and place each half on two different areas of each fillet. Add two thin slices lemon to each fillet. Sprinkle with paprika. Add enough sweet milk to just cover the bottom of the baking dish. Fold the excess foil over the fish for a cover.

Bake at 325° for 45 minutes. Serve with drawn butter. (The milk we be absorbed by the fish and remove any strong taste they have.) Walleyes, northerns or muskie are excellent served this way.

C.W. Gray, Waukesha

Walleye fillets
1 pat butter per fillet
2 thin slices lemon per fillet
Dash paprika
1/3 cup sweet milk

WALLEYE AND WILD RICE WITH MUSHROOM-WALNUT SAUCE

CUT FILLETS INTO serving-size pieces. Season with 1 teaspoon salt and pepper. Brown bacon, add mushrooms, celery, and onion. Cook until tender, 3-5 minutes. Stir in cooked rice and remaining ½ teaspoon salt.

Arrange fillets in well-greased baking dish large enough to hold fish in single layer. Place ½ cup rice mixture on each fillet. Drizzle melted butter over rice. Cover and bake at 375° for 20 minutes.

Prepare sauce: In pan melt butter, add onion and mushrooms, and saute for 3-5 minutes. Stir in flour, mustard, salt and thyme. Cook 2 minutes. With wire whisk, gradually stir in cream. Cook, stirring constantly until thick (about 3-5 minutes). Stir in nuts. Makes 2½ cups of sauce.

Karen Schmidt, Racine

2 lbs. walleye fillets or other fish fillets
1½ teaspoon salt (divided)
¼ teaspoon pepper
3 slices bacon, diced
1 cup chopped fresh mushrooms
¼ cup minced onion
¼ cup minced celery
2 cups cooked wild rice
2 tablespoons melted butter

Mushroom-Walnut Sauce

3 tablespoons butter
1 tablespoon minced onion
1 cup sliced fresh mushrooms
3 tablespoons flour
½ teaspoon dry mustard
½ teaspoon salt
¼ teaspoon thyme
2 cups cream
¼ cup toasted walnuts, halves or pieces

CRANBERRIED WALLEYE

FRY WALLEYE FILLETS in butter with light seasonings of your choice.

Prepare sauce — melt 5 tablespoons butter in frying pan over low heat and add 4 tablepsoons flour that has been mixed with 1 cup of cranberry juice until all lumps were removed. Stir over low heat until the sauce is like a thin gravy. Add ½ cup medium sharp cheddar cheese and stir until melted.

Pour sauce over the fillets.

Brenda and Paul Ross, Fremont

Walleye fillets
5 tablespoons butter
4 tablespoons flour
Cranberry juice
½ cup medium-sharp cheddar cheese, melted

STEWED WALLEYE

LAYER FISH IN GREASED cast iron skillet, add celery, milk, and garlic powder. Cover with oil and cook at 350° for 15 minutes, add stewed tomatoes and onions. DO NOT STIR. Cover and cook until onions are tender. Serve immediately. Serves 4.

Ken Tomaszewski, Janesville

3-3½ lbs. fresh walleye fillets, skinned
2 large onions, sliced
1 can stewed tomatoes (juice and all)
1 stalk celery chopped
1½ cups milk
¼ teaspoon garlic powder
Salt and pepper to taste

PIKE ROLLS WITH CUCUMBER STUFFING

PREHEAT OVEN TO 450°. Grease 12 muffin cups. Season fillets with salt and pepper. Cut in strips 3x6 in. Coil strips in muffin cups.

Cook onions and celery in fat until tender, about 5 minutes. Add seasonings and toss with bread crumbs and cucumbers. Spoon stuffing in pike rolls and top with a teaspoon of sour cream and sprinkle with paprika. Bake 15-20 minutes or until done. Serve 2 rolls per person.

Mrs. Charles Booth, Waupaca

2 lbs. pike fillets
Salt and pepper

Dressing
¼ cup chopped onion
¼ cup chopped celery
¼ cup butter
½ teaspoon salt
¼ teaspoon thyme
2 cups soft bread crumbs
½ cup chopped cucumber
¼ cup dairy sour cream

PESHTIGO RIVER WALLEYE

LEAVE WALLEYE DRESSED and scaled, but whole (do not fillet). Mix stuffing ingredients and put some inside the fish, and the rest on top and around the fish.

Bake at 325° for 1 hour and 20 minutes or until meat flakes with a fork.

For a microwave, set at full power for 14 minutes. Let sit out for 5 minutes before serving.

Salt and pepper to taste, and add melted butter or lemon juice if desired. Serves 2.

Gary Kraszewski, Pulaski

1 1½-2½ lb. walleye
1 sliced onion
½ cup cut celery
¼ cup butter or margarine
½ teaspoon seasoned salt
1 teaspoon lemon juice

BAKED WALLEYE

HEAT OVEN TO 350°. Season fillets with salt and pepper. Mix juice, onion, and butter. Dip fish in mixture. Place in greased 9x12 pan. Pour remaining mixture over fish. Bake 25-30 minutes or until fish flakes. Sprinkle with paprika.

Michael A. Hinz, Sheboygan

2 lbs. walleye fillets
2 tablespoons lemon juice
¼ teaspoon grated or minced onion
¼ cup butter
Salt and pepper

PIKE BURGERS

GRIND PIKE IN FOOD grinder. Mix ingredients and form into patties. Broil or fry.

David Hraychuck, Sayner

2 lbs. northern pike
2 eggs
1 small minced onion
1 tablespoon lemon juice
Bread crumbs — substitute cornbread for a change

BAKED WHITEFISH

SEASON WHITEFISH BY soaking in mild salt brine for 4 hours.

Stuff fish with mixture and season with seasoning salt such as Lawry's. Place in baking casserole dish and bake at 375° for 40 minutes.

Pour white sauce over fish and serve.

Jerry Ringwelski, Wausau

2 lbs. whitefish
Salt brine

Stuffing

Onion, celery, sprig of parsley
Seasoning salt

White sauce

1 tablespoon butter
2 tablespoons flour
Salt and pepper
¾ cup milk or half & half
Add liquid from fish (about ½ cup)

WHITEFISH-CHEESE APPETIZERS

CUT OUT ROUNDS OF bread with cookie cutter and spread mixture thickly on rounds. Place on cookie sheet and heat in 400° oven for 5 minutes, or until cheese melts and bread is brown. Broiler can be used, but watch carefully.

Marie P. Jorgensen, Glenview, IL

4½ oz. boiled whitefish, flaked
3 oz. shredded cheddar cheese (about ¾ cup)
1 teaspoon minced onion
1½ tablespoons mayonnaise (or enough to hold mixture together)

FISH ALA CRAIG

PLACE FILLETS IN SHALLOW baking dish. Sprinkle crumbs over all. Dot with butter. Salt and pepper and generously cover with paprika. Sprinkle with parsley flakes. Cover each fillet with grated cheese. Bake uncovered for 20 minutes at 375°. Serves 6.

Pollie Rickelman, Naples, FL

8 whitefish fillets
½ cup Italian bread crumbs
3 tablespoons butter
Parsley flakes
Paprika, salt, pepper
1 cup grated cheddar cheese

A.J.'S CARP CAKES

CARP EGGS MUST BE FAIRLY MATURE. Onions to a person's taste (lots of them). Mix all ingredients into pancake batter consistency. Form into patties and fry like pancakes. The taste is much like salmon loaf.
A.J. Bahls, Juneau

Carp eggs
2 or 3 chicken eggs
2 diced onions
Chopped cracker crumbs
Salt & pepper

CARP CAKES

SKIN AND REMOVE BONES FROM FISH. Run carp meat through grinder to crush any remaining bones. Mix fish with ingredients listed (omitting garlic salt if you don't care for the flavor).

Let stand for 10 minutes. Form cakes or patties, roll in flour if you like for easier handling, and fry in bacon fat or shortening.

Karle E. Tonn, Fredonia

2 lbs. raw carp meat
1 medium onion, chopped fine
½ teaspoon salt
1/8 teaspoon pepper
1/8 teaspoon sage
¼ teaspoon garlic salt
¼ teaspoon celery salt
1 tablespoon lemon juice
20 salted crackers, rolled fine

VENISON
Chapter Two

I suppose G. B. Shaw was right when he said: "Do not do unto others as you would have them do unto you. Tastes may be different." There are a lot of people wandering around the countryside claiming they don't like venison, and perhaps some of them are telling the truth.

Most of them, I suspect, don't really know what venison tastes like and have established their bias on an experience with meat improperly treated between field and kitchen, or meat improperly prepared, or both.

No recipe known to man can salvage bad deer meat, but a good piece of venison appropriately trimmed of fat, suet, and membrane is hard to beat. From frying in an iron skillet (cook it hot, cook it fast, and eat it quick) to a fancy rouladen, from pickled heart to broiled liver, the meat of the deer is top-shelf quality.

There are a zillion ways to prepare it, and thanks to excellent game management practices, deer herds are large and vigorous. With such a good supply of the meat easily available and the average I.Q. being in excess of 74, it's hard to explain why more people aren't learning to cook it.

If you are at all hesitant to experiment with these recipes, remember: The second most unpopular person in town is one who *can* cook venison, but won't; the most unpopular person is one who *can't*, but *does;* and, to complete the corollary, the most popular is the one who *can* and *does.*

CARAWAY VENISON MEATBALL CASSEROLE

IN LARGE BOWL, COMBINE ground venison, onions, salt, 1 teaspoon caraway seeds, and pepper; shape into about 20 meatballs.

In large skillet over medium-high heat, in hot oil, brown meatballs well.

In a 3 qt. casserole, spread a layer of sauerkraut with 1 teaspoon caraway seeds. Next put a layer of apples, sprinkle with brown sugar; top with meatballs. Pour apple juice over meatballs; cover; bake 1 hour or until meat is cooked. Makes 8 servings.

Mary Lynn Schroeder, Green Bay

2 lbs. ground venison
½ cup minced onions
2 teaspoons salt
2 teaspoons caraway seeds
¼ teaspoon pepper
2 tablespoons salad oil
2-3 cups well-drained sauerkraut
3 large apples, cut in wedges
2 tablespoons brown sugar
1 cup apple juice

VENISON SPANISH RICE

BROWN VENISON IN OIL. Lower heat, add onion and cook until tender. Drain tomatoes, saving liquid, and chop. Add water to liquid to equal 2 cups. Add all the remaining ingredients to venison and onion, and bring to boil.

Lower heat, cover, and simmer until rice is cooked and absorbs all of liquid. (Approximately 15-20 minutes.)

Remove from heat and let sit with cover on for an additional 10 minutes. Serves 6.

Mrs. Anne Danowski, Milwaukee

1½ lbs. venison with fat cut away and chopped into ½ in. cubes
28 oz. can of tomatoes
¼ cup green pepper chopped
1 small yellow onion chopped
½ teaspoon each of crushed rosemary and thyme
1 teaspoon salt
3 tablespoons sunflower oil, margarine, or butter
1 cup rice

VENISON BURGUNDY

COMBINE ALL INGREDIENTS AND mix well. Place in a small covered roaster and bake at 325° for 2½-3 hours. Stir occasionally.

Serve over cooked noodles. Very good with a green leafy salad and wine. Serves 4-5 people.

Velma Bray, Fennimore

3 lbs. venison cubes (all fat removed)
2 cans consomme soup
2 onions, cubed
1 cup burgundy wine
½ cup flour
½ cup bread crumbs
2½ teaspoons salt
¼ teaspoon pepper

HUNTER'S CABIN ONE DISH MEAL

BROWN VENISON, ONION, AND CELERY in oleo. Mix together and add rice, soups, mushrooms, soy sauce, and seasonings. Place in casserole. Add peas and water. Bake at 325° until meat and rice are tender.

Velma Bray, Fennimore

1½ lb. cubed venison
1 medium to large onion chopped
1 cup celery, diced
Oleo for browning
½ cup uncooked rice
1 can cream of mushroom soup
1 can cream of chicken soup
1 can mushrooms stems and pieces
4 teaspoons soy sauce
Salt and pepper to taste
1 cup peas
1 cup water

AUNT JOYCE'S VENISON CASSEROLE

BROWN VENISON WITH ONIONS and add celery. Combine tomato sauce, tomato paste (½ can of water if too thick), cheese, carrots, and potatoes. Bake at 350° for 1½ hours or until done.

Heidi Scheinert, Shawano

1½ lb. ground venison
2 medium onions chopped
4 stalks celery chopped
1 large can tomato sauce
½ can tomato paste
2 tablespoons parmesan cheese
1 lb. sliced carrots
8-10 potatoes sliced

SATURDAY NOODLE BAKE

BROWN VENISON AND ONION AND cook until tender. Drain.

Combine cream cheese, soup, worcestershire sauce, sugar, and salt and pepper, and add to venison.

Prepare egg noodles as directed. Layer venison mixture and noodles in casserole dish with the venison mixture the last layer.

Add French fried onion rings or buttered corn flakes to the top. Bake at 350° for 20 minutes.

Mrs. Mabel Schroeder, Manitowoc

2 lbs. ground venison, browned and drained
1 medium onion
6 oz. cream cheese
2 cans tomato soup
3 tablespoons worcestershire sauce
½ cup sugar
Salt and pepper
6 oz. egg noodles

SOUR CREAM DEER CHOPS

BROWN CHOPS IN HOT FAT, season with salt and pepper. Drain off excess fat, add next 4 ingredients. Simmer covered until meat is done, about 30 minutes. Put chops to side of pan.

Thicken liquid in pan, add mushrooms and parsley flakes. Top chops with sour cream, cover and heat 5 minutes.

Mary Lynn Schroeder, Green Bay

6 deer chops 1 in. thick
1 can beef bouillon
½ teaspoon thyme
½ cup chopped celery
½ cup sliced green onions
½ cup sliced mushrooms
3 tablespoons flour
1 tablespoon parsley flakes
1 cup sour cream

VENISON MEAT LOAF

IN LARGE BOWL MIX (BY HAND) all ingredients together. Turn into greased loaf pan and bake at 350° for 1 hour and 15 minutes or until done, but not dry.

Ken Tomaszewski, Janesville

1½ lbs. ground venison
½ lb. bulk sausage
½ lb. hamburger
2 medium onions chopped
2 medium eggs well beaten
½ tube saltines (crushed)
¼ teaspoon thyme
¼ teaspoon pepper
½ teaspoon salt
¼ teaspoon parsley flakes
2 tablespoons A-1 Steak Sauce
2 stalks celery chopped fine

VENISON CHOPS WITH RICE

BUTTER A 9x13 IN. PAN. Sprinkle in regular rice. Place chops on rice.

Combine mixture and pour over chops. Cover pan with foil. Bake at 350° for 1¼ hours.

Mrs. Lyle Kothbauer, Mondovi

Venison chops
1 cup regular rice
1 envelope dry onion soup mix
1 can cream of mushroom soup
1½ cans water

MARINATED BARBECUED CHOPS

COMBINE SOY SAUCE, HONEY, and vinegar. Blend in garlic powder and ginger. Add oil and onion. Place meat in plastic food bag; pour marinade over the top, close. Refrigerate 4 hours or longer, turning every hour.

Drain meat. Grill to desired taste, basting occasionally with marinade. Serves 4.

(This marinade can be used with a roast also.)

Nancy Huennekens, Racine

¼ cup soy sauce
3 tablespoons honey
2 tablespoons vinegar
1½ teaspoons garlic powder
1½ teaspoons ginger
¾ cup oil
1 green onion, sliced
1½ - 2 lbs. venison chops or steaks

SAVORY VENISON CHOPS (MICROWAVE)

PLACE CHOPS, CELERY, AND green pepper in a 2 qt. glass baking dish. Cover. Microwave on high for 10 minutes. Drain.

Combine remaining ingredients in small bowl; mix well and pour over chops. Re-cover and continue cooking for 30-35 minutes on simmer, or until fork tender. Let stand 5 minutes before serving. Makes 3-4 servings.

Judy Dixon, Eagle River

6 venison chops 1½ - 2 lbs.
1 medium onion chopped
¼ cup chopped celery
¼ cup green pepper chopped
¼ cup chili sauce
¼ cup dry sherry or water
Salt and pepper to taste

GOOD BURGERS

COMBINE ALL INGREDIENTS. Make into patties, then brown. Put patties in a casserole dish and top with onions, salt and pepper, soup and mushrooms. Place in oven and bake at 300° for ½ hour. Serve with potatoes or delicious on a bun.

Mary Scott, Manawa

1 large onion, chopped
Salt and pepper to taste
2 8-12 oz. cans cream of mushroom soup
1 6 oz. can mushrooms
1-1½ lbs. ground venison

DEER CHOP SPECIAL

SIMMER CHOPS AND ONION, covered with ¼ in. of tarragon vinegar, in a cast iron skillet until tender. Add remaining ingredients and stir until the mixture is thick. Cook at low heat, stirring when necessary, and add more vinegar or chili sauce if needed.

When sauce is thick enough, spread both sides of chops, place them in a shallow pan, and pour bourbon over them. Bake uncovered at 350° for 1½ hours, basting occasionally.

Mary Scott, Manawa

6 venison chops
1 onion chopped
¼ in. tarragon vinegar
Dash tabasco
1 teaspoon hot mustard
Dash worcestershire sauce
Chili sauce
½ cup bourbon (whiskey)

POYHA (CHEROKEE INDIAN MEAT LOAF)

PLACE CORNMEAL IN BOWL, add water, mix, set aside.

In pan, brown venison in the ½ cup bacon fat. Drain off excess fat. Reduce heat. Cook until meat is cooked through.

Add corn and onion. Cook 10 minutes. Add salt and eggs and cornmeal mixture. Stir well. Cook 15 minutes longer. Place in 9x5 in. loaf pan. Bake at 350° for 30-40 minutes.

Karen Schmidt, Racine

1 lb. ground venison
½ cup cornmeal
½ cup water
½ cup bacon fat
1 can (17 oz.) whole kernel corn, drained
1 small onion, chopped
1 teaspoon salt
2 eggs

COCKTAIL MEATBALLS

HEAT CHILI SAUCE, WATER, cranberries, sauerkraut, and brown sugar.

Beat eggs, add to meat with bread crumbs and onion soup mix. Form into bite-size balls. Put in 2 qt. casserole, bake at 350° for 2 hours, uncovered.

Gerald Fahner, Eau Claire

2 lbs. venison, ground
1 jar water
1 16 oz. can whole cranberry sauce
1 jar chili sauce
1 medium-size can sauerkraut
1 pkg. dry onion soup mix
¾ cup brown sugar
3 eggs
¼ cup bread crumbs

QUICKIE VENISON MEATBALLS

MIX MEAT, SEASONINGS, bread crumbs, water, and onion. Form into about 24 small meatballs. Roll in flour and brown in hot fat. Drain.

Mix soup and worcestershire sauce. Pour over meat balls, cover, and simmer about 30 minutes.

Serve hot.

Mrs. Jan Teachout, Waupun

1 lb. ground venison
1 teaspoon salt
1/8 teaspoon celery salt
1/8 teaspoon garlic salt
½ cup dry bread crumbs
½ cup water
2 tablespoons grated onion
1 can cream of celery or cream of mushroom soup
1 tablespoon worcestershire sauce

BURGERS ITALIANO

COMBINE TOMATO PASTE, ONION, and spices. Add ground venison. Top each bun half with mixture. Brown under grill. Top with cheese. Toast again until cheese melts. Serves 8.

Darla Arndt, Fremont

1 lb. ground venison
1 can (16 oz.) tomato paste
1 teaspoon salt
½ teaspoon garlic salt
½ teaspoon oregano
¼ teaspoon pepper
¼ teaspoon anise seed
¼ cup chopped onion
1 cup grated mozarella cheese
4 hamburger buns split

VENISON MEATBALLS WITH ONION GRAVY

SAUTE ONIONS AND CELERY in butter for 5 minutes. Mix remaining ingredients with celery and onions. Shape into 1 in. balls. Brown on all sides in butter, lower heat and cook 10 minutes. Pour onion gravy over meatballs and simmer gently for 15 minutes.

To make gravy, blend butter and flour in skillet. Stir until golden brown. Add water and stir until mixture is smooth and thickened. Add onions and lettuce.

Mrs. Charles Booth, Waupaca

1½ lbs. ground venison
1½ cup bread crumbs
1½ cup finely chopped onions
½ cup chopped celery
1 egg (beaten)
½ cup water
1½ teaspoons salt
½ teaspoon poultry seasoning
2 tablespoons catsup

Onion gravy

2 tablespoons butter
1½ tablespoons flour
1 cup water
1 cup onions thinly sliced
1 cup finely shredded lettuce

HARVEST TIME MEATBALLS

MIX FIRST 8 INGREDIENTS. Shape into 1½ inch balls.

To cook in skillet, heat 1 tablespoon oil and cook meatballs over medium heat for 20 minutes.

To cook in oven, bake uncovered at 400° for 20 minutes.

To cook in microwave, cover with sauce and cook for 9 minutes.

After meatballs are cooked, set aside. (Meatballs may be substituted with 1 lb. cubed venison that has been marinated overnight in dry, red wine and then fried in 2 tablespoons oil.)

Melt butter in large skillet. Add garlic, thyme leaves, mushrooms, and zucchini; cook over medium-high heat for 5 minutes, stirring occasionally.

Add cooked meatballs or cubed venison; cover and simmer, stirring occasionally until vegetables are tender, about 10 minutes. Sprinkle with salt and cheese. Add tomatoes; cover and heat 2-3 minutes.

Marilyn Benish, Yuba

1 lb. ground venison
1 egg
1 small onion, chopped
1/3 cup dry bread crumbs
¼ cup milk
¾ teaspoon salt
1/8 teaspoon pepper
1 teaspoon worcestershire sauce
2 tablespoons butter
1/8 teaspoon garlic powder
½ teaspoon thyme leaves
½ lb. mushrooms, sliced
3 medium zucchini, thinly sliced
(about 4 cups)
½ teaspoon salt
1/3 cup grated parmesan cheese
2 tomatoes cut into 8ths

VENISON STROGANOFF

ROLL MEAT IN FLOUR and seasonings. Brown lightly in fat with onion. Add tomatoes and sugar. Simmer until tender. Ten minutes before serving, add mushrooms, sour cream. Serve with noodles.

Yield: 4 servings.

Robert Weiss, Stoughton

1 pound venison steak cut in strips
3 tablespoons flour
1 onion
2 cups stewed tomatoes
1 teaspoon sugar
1 can mushrooms
½ cup sour cream
Salt & pepper

VENISON STROGANOFF

REMOVE ALL TRACES OF animal fat from venison. Shake pieces of meat in seasoned flour in a paper or plastic bag. Brown quickly in hot cooking oil. Add onions, garlic and mushrooms. Combine remaining ingredients except sour cream and noodles; pour over meat. Simmer till tender about 1 hour, adding more wine if necessary. Stir in sour cream and serve hot over cooked noodles. Sprinkle with Parmesan cheese, if desired.

Howard Kohlhepp, Chippewa Falls

1 lb. venison round steak cut in ½" strips 1½" long
3 tablespoons cooking oil
½ cup onions, chopped
1 clove garlic, minced
1 4oz. can mushrooms
1 10½ oz. can condensed tomato soup
1 tablespoon worcestershire sauce
5 drops tabasco sauce
½ teaspoon salt
1/8 teaspoon pepper
½ cup red wine
1 cup sour cream
1 8 oz. package wide noodles, cooked

TURTLES

COMBINE MIXTURE. FORM INTO 6 patties. Make topping for patties. Set aside.

Mix biscuit dough according to directions on package and roll out 1/8 inch thick. Cut into 4 in. circles and place meat patties between 2 circles. (Spread topping on patties). Seal edges, prick tops, and bake on a baking sheet at 350° for 30 minutes.

After baking, place a dampened towel over sandwiches for a few minutes. (If you don't do this, you will find out why my family named these sandwiches "turtles." As I was experimenting with this recipe and perfecting it, I couldn't get the buns soft until one day a dampened towel accidentally got laid over the buns and like magic they were soft, but the family still continues to call them turtles.)

Marilyn Benish, Yuba

1 lb. ground venison
1/3 cup chopped onion
½ cup dry bread crumbs
2 tablespoons worcestershire sauce
¼ cup evaporated milk
2 tablespoons horseradish
1 teaspoon mustard
1 teaspoon salt
¼ teaspoon pepper
½ teaspoon monosodium glutamate

Topping

Cottage cheese (spread to ½ in. of edge)
2 teaspoons parmesan cheese
1 slice Swiss or Mozarella cheese

VENISON STEW

CUBE TWO POUNDS OF VENISON from the shank, breast, neck, or shoulder and dredge the pieces in flour (about two tablespoons full). Brown the meat in a skillet with two tablespoons of fat. Then season with salt and pepper, place in a stewing pot, cover it with hot water, and simmer for one to one and one half hours.

Peel and quarter six potatoes, six carrots, three onions, four white turnips, and add with one cup of fresh or frozen peas to the stew pot. Simmer the whole for thirty minutes. Quarter three tomatoes and add to the stew and simmer the whole for fifteen minutes longer.

Mix a little flour with water to form a smooth paste and add enough to the stew to thicken the gravy.

Cliff Rauscher, Green Bay

2 lbs. venison
Flour
2 tablespoons fat
Salt & pepper
6 potatoes
6 carrots
3 onions
4 white turnips
1 cup fresh or frozen peas
3 tomatoes

CABBAGE MARINARA

SAUTE MEAT UNTIL NO LONGER pink. Add chopped onion and cook another 5 minutes. Stir in seasoning and rice. Spread half of the shredded cabbage in a 2 qt. baking dish; cover with meat and top with remaining cabbage. Pour undiluted tomato soup over top.

Cover and bake at 350° until cabbage is tender (about 1 hour).

Mrs. Char Schroll, New Richmond

2 lbs. ground venison
1 large onion
1 cup cooked rice
¼ teaspoon thyme
¼ teaspoon oregano
¼ teaspoon garlic powder
¼ teaspoon pepper
1 teaspoon salt
3-4 cups coarsely shredded cabbage
(1 small head)
1 can tomato soup

BARBECUED VENISON BURGER KRISPIES

COMBINE GROUND VENISON, pork sausage, egg, ¾ cup of Krispies, salt, and pepper. Mix well.

Mix together brown sugar, onion, catsup, nutmeg, and mustard. Add ½ of this mixture to the ground meat mixture. Mix well. Shape meat into round balls and place in a baking dish. Top with remaining sauce and sprinkle with the ¼ cup Krispies. Bake at 400° for 30 minutes.

Velma Bray, Fennimore

1 lb. ground venison
¼ lb. pork sausage
1 egg
1 cup Rice Krispies
1 teaspoon salt
¼ teaspoon pepper
1 tablespoon chopped onion
3 tablespoons brown sugar
¼ cup catsup
1/8 teaspoon nutmeg
1 teaspoon dry mustard

ROAST HAUNCH OF VENISON

TO PREPARE A HAUNCH OF VENISON for roasting, wash it in cool water, and pat dry with a soft cloth. Lay over the haunch a thickly buttered piece of brown paper. Then cover the paper with a paste of flour and water, making the paste layer about three quarters of an inch thick. Cover the layer of paste with a couple of sheets of stout paper and secure the paper with twine. Put the meat in a large roasting pan with a little water in the bottom.

Roast the venison in a moderate oven, basting the paper often with butter. Roast the meat for about twenty-five minutes to the pound. When roasting doe venison twenty minutes per pound will be sufficient.

About one half hour before the meat is done, remove the paper and paste from the meat, baste the roast thoroughly, and dredge it very lightly with flour. Return it to the oven and roast until the outside of the roast takes on a pale brown color. Serve the roast hot with unflavored gravy thickened with a little flour. Currant jelly goes quite well with this meat.

Cliff Rauscher, Green Bay

Haunch of venison
Flour
Butter
Currant jelly (optional)

VENISON HASH PUFFS

GRIND UP ONE POUND OF VENISON. Take two eggs and separate them and beat the yolks until, they are thick and very light in color. Add the beaten yolks, one half teaspoon of salt, and eight sprigs of finely chopped parsley to the ground meat. Mix thoroughly. Now beat the egg whites until they stand in peaks, and fold into the meat mixture.

Make eight mounds of mixture and place them on a greased baking sheet. Put the baking sheet under the broiler about four inches from the heat and broil for fifteen minutes.

While the puffs are broiling, mix together two thirds of a cup of catsup, one half cup of water, and one quarter cup of chopped sweet pickles. Serve the sauce over the hot venison hash puffs.

Cliff Rauscher, Green Bay

1 lb. venison
2 eggs, separated
½ teaspoon salt
8 sprigs of parsley
2/3 cup catsup
½ cup water
¼ cup sweet pickles, chopped

STIR FRY VENISON TENDERLOIN

WHEN CUTTING UP YOUR VENISON, save the tenderloin back. Slice in thin, ½ inch slices and stir fry or brown in butter. Eat immediately!
Deer camp delicacy. Can't be beat.
Mrs. Loren Lane, Mt. Hope

BIG GAME HEART

COVER WITH WATER. ADD SALT, bay leaves, and cook until tender. (2½ hours)
Slice thin for sandwiches.

Kevin Voigt, Onalaska

1 cleaned, big game heart
Salt
Bay leaves

VENISON KABOBS

MIX BROWN SUGAR, MUSTARD, soy sauce, water, sherry, tabasco, onion, and garlic in a bowl. Add meat. If using chops or steaks, marinate overnight. If using liver, marinate for 1 hour at room temperature. Remove meat and reserve marinade.

Alternate cubes of meat or liver wrapped in bacon with zucchini, tomatoes, mushrooms, and onions on skewers. Place kabobs on grill about 5 inches from hot coals. Brush generously with marinade. Grill 7 minutes, turn and grill 7 minutes on other side, or until meat is done as desired.

Hint: Most any recipe calling for lamb can be used for the cooking of venison.

Marilyn Benish, Yuba

2 lbs. venison liver, or chops or round steak, cubed
3 tablespoons brown sugar
¼ teaspoon dry mustard
1 cup soy sauce
½ cup water
3 tablespoons dry sherry
¼ teaspoon tabasco
1 tablespoon grated onion
1 clove garlic, minced
½ lb. sliced bacon
Cherry tomatoes
Medium-sized mushrooms
Pearl onions or early garden type
Zucchini, cut in 1 in. slices

VENISON POT PIE

BROWN GROUND VENISON AND onion in margarine.
Add worcestershire sauce and garlic powder. Drain.
Place in bottom of cake pan. Add next 3 ingredients in
order. Mix soup with milk and pour over top. Let soup
settle a bit, then cover with crust.

Make crust by sifting dry ingredients. Add shortening,
and mix as for pie crust. Add milk and place on floured
table. Roll to approximately ½ inch thick.

Pinch crust around the edges. Brush with melted
butter. Bake at 350° for 1 hour.

Deb Schroeder, Lyndon Station

1-1½ lbs. ground venison
1 large onion, chopped
1 tablespoon margarine or
fat for frying
1½ teaspoons worcestershire sauce
Dash of garlic powder
1 cup peas and carrots
1 cup cooked broccoli
¾ cup cooked potatoes, cubed
1 can cream of onion soup
1/3 cup milk

Crust

2 cups flour
4 teaspoons baking powder
¾ teaspoons salt
2 tablespoons shortening
¾ cup milk

VENISON MEAT LOAF FOR A CROWD

MIX ALL INGREDIENTS. Bake in large loaf in angel
food pan at 350° for 1½ hours. Drain off fat. Add 1 can
cream of mushroom soup over top. Put back in oven
until done.

Mrs. Loren Lane, Mt. Hope

8 lbs. ground venison
4 lbs. ground sausage
2 eggs
1 — 2 cups onion
SPICES:
According to taste — sweet marjoram,
thyme and rosemary.

ROAST VENISON

MAKE A MARINADE BY bringing to a boil in a
sauce pan one quart of water, one and one half cups
of vinegar, two chopped onions, one diced carrot,
two cloves of garlic, one teaspoon of diced thyme,
four sprigs of parsley, twelve peppercorns, and one
tablespoon of salt. Simmer the mixture for one hour
and then let it cool. Cover a five to seven pound leg
roast of venison with this mixture and let set in the
refrigerator for at least twenty-four hours before roasting.

The next day, preheat a shallow oven pan in a
450°F. oven. Remove the venison from the marinade,
sprinkle the meat with salt, and cover it with one
quarter pound of sliced fat salt pork. Place the meat
in the preheated pan, adding enough salad oil to
cover the bottom of the pan. Allow fifteen minutes
per pound for medium rare, and twenty to twenty-
five minutes per pound for well done.

Cliff Rauscher, Green Bay

1½ cups vinegar
2 onions, chopped
1 carrot, diced
2 cloves of garlic
1 teaspoon dried thyme
4 sprigs of parsley
12 peppercorns
1 tablespoon salt
5 - 7 lb. leg roast of venison
¼ lb. fat salt pork, sliced
Salad oil

DEER HEART IN SKILLET

ADD SALT TO FLOUR AND PLACE in bag. Shake deer heart pieces until well coated. Melt butter and brown pieces. Add mushrooms and juice, broth, onion, and parsley. Cover and simmer for 1 hour. Serve over hot rice.

Karen Schmidt, Racine

1 deer heart, diced into small pieces
½ teaspoon salt
¼ cup flour
3 tablespoons butter
1 can (8 oz.) mushrooms
1 can (10¾ oz.) chicken broth
1 teaspoon instant minced onion
1 teaspoon minced parsley

VENISON WITH SOUR CREAM

CUT VENISON IN PIECES and melt fat in heavy frying pan. Add meat and garlic. Brown on all sides and arrange in dish. Put vegetables in remaining fat and cook for 2 minutes. Add salt, pepper and water. Pour over meat. Bake in slow oven until meat is tender. Melt butter in frying pan and stir in flour. Add water that the meat was cooked in and boil until thick. Add sour cream and more salt if necessary. Pour over meat and vegetables. Serve with buttered noodles and currant jelly.

Alma E. Morton, Madison

2 lbs. venison
¼ cup fat
1 cup diced celery
½ cup minced onion
1 bay leaf
4 tablespoons butter
1 clove garlic
1 cup diced carrots
2 cups water
1 teaspoon salt
4 tablespoons flour
1 cup sour cream

VENISON RAGOUT

SAUTE THE VENISON in the hot, melted butter, turning until brown. Remove meat from the frying pan and add the sherry and onions turning often so as not to burn. Add tomato paste, flour, blending until smooth, then add beef broth and stir until mixture simmers. Add the venison pieces, bay leaves, mushrooms and ½ cup of wine. Salt and pepper to taste. Stir well and simmer slowly for 1½ to 2 hours or until venison is tender, adding remainder of wine slowly. Serve over rice or buttered noodles.

   Yield: 6 servings.
Eugene N. Russell, Oshkosh

3 lbs. top round of venison, cut into small bite-sized squares
4 tablespoons butter
2 cups onions, diced
4 tablespoons dry sherry
1 tablespoon tomato paste
4 tablespoons flour
1½ cups canned beef broth
2 cups burgundy wine
3 bay leaves
14 whole mushrooms
Salt & pepper, to taste

PICKLED DEER HEART

CUT AND CLEAN HEART. Soak for 1 hour in salt water. Cover with fresh water and boil until tender. Drain.

   Combine vinegar, sugar, sliced onion and pickle spices. Heat just to boiling and pour mixture over heart which has been cooked and cut into bite sized pieces. Ready to serve after 4 - 5 days.

Mrs. Len Johnson, Portage

Deer heart
3 cups vinegar
2 cups sugar
2 tablespoons pickle spices
1 sliced onion

SCHULTZ'S DEER HEART GRAVY

SLICE BOTTOM 2/3 OF HEART thin, and dice. Season with garlic, seasoned salt, and pepper to taste. Brown slightly in oil or margarine.

Add soup and mushrooms and simmer for 1 hour. Thicken with 2-3 tablespoons cornstarch dissolved in 1/3 cup water.

Delicious over mashed potatoes or buttered noodles. Serves 4. (You'll never throw away another venison heart!)

John Schultz, Shell Lake

1 medium deer heart
Garlic, seasoned salt, pepper to taste
1 can cream of mushroom soup
1 small can mushrooms, drained
2-3 tablespoons cornstarch
(dissolved in 1/3 cup water)

VENISON SAUERBRATEN

PUT VENISON ROAST in salt water and 2 cups vinegar. Make sure there is enough liquid to cover the meat.

Let stand overnight.

Wash meat well, place in kettle and cook with 1 cup vinegar, 2 large onions, spices, bay leaves. Add brown sugar when meat is tender, then cook until done.

Take meat out and strain the broth so you can save it for gravy. Add 1 dozen ginger snaps to the broth and a little flour to thicken. Salt and pepper to taste.

Robert Blair, Beaver Dam

Venison roast
3 cups vinegar
2 large onions
2 tablespoons mixed spices
2 bay leaves
1 cup brown sugar
1 dozen ginger snaps
Flour
Salt & pepper

VENISON ROAST IN WINE BARBECUE SAUCE

REMOVE ALL TRACES OF FAT from venison. Sear roast in a heavy frying pan. Mix other ingredients in a sauce pan and bring contents to boiling point. Cover venison with barbecue sauce and bake tightly covered at 350° for 2 or more hours, or until done, turning occasionally, adding more wine if sauce gets too thick. Watch carefully so it does not burn. Serve hot.

Howard Kohlhepp, Chippewa Falls

3 pounds venison roast
¼ cup molasses
¼ cup prepared mustard
¼ cup catsup
Salt and pepper
3 tablespoons shortening
½ cup red wine
¼ cup vinegar

STUFFED VENISON BURGERS

PREPARE STUFFING according to package directions. Combine milk and meat; divide into 5 patties. On wax paper, pat each to a 6 inch circle. Put ¼ cup stuffing in center of each pattie. Draw meat over stuffing and seal.

Place in shallow 1½ quart casserole. Combine remaining ingredients. Pour over meat. Bake, uncovered at 350° for 45 minutes.

Mrs. Loren Lane, Mt. Hope

1 cup herb-seasoned stuffing mix
1/3 cup evaporated milk
1 lb. ground venison
1 - 10½ oz. can cream of mushroom soup
2 teaspoons Worcestershire sauce
1 tablespoon catsup

VENISON LASAGNA

BROWN ONION AND GARLIC LIGHTLY in oil in saucepan. Increase temperature, add meat and cook quickly until brown. Add remaining ingredients and simmer uncovered for 1½ hours. Remove bay leaf before serving.

Cook lasagna noodles according to package directions. After noodles have drained, arrange in baking dish. Make 3 layers each of cooked noodles, ricotta, mozzarella, marinara sauce, and grated cheese. Bake at 325° for about 45 minutes, or until bubbly. Serves 4-6.

Janine Zeutschel, Menomonie

8 oz. Lasagna noodles
1 lb. Ricotta cheese
16 oz. Mozzarella cheese
Marinara sauce
1 cup grated parmesan cheese

Marinara sauce

1 medium onion, minced
2-3 medium garlic cloves, minced
2 tablespoons olive oil
1½ lbs. ground venison
3½ cups (1 lb. 12 oz. can) whole tomatoes
1 can tomato paste
2 cups water
1 teaspoon salt
1/8 teaspoon cayenne
1 teaspoon sugar
¼ teaspoon ground basil leaves
¼ teaspoon oregano
¼ teaspoon parsley
1 bay leaf

VENISON BARBEQUE

COOK MEAT IN WATER in oven until meat falls off bone. Tear up into shreds. Brown onions, green peppers and celery in bacon grease with lots of garlic salt added. Add remaining ingredients to meat and begin simmering for at least 1½ hours without lid (don't let meat become watery). Keep testing and add those ingredients which are needed to make this the delicious recipe which it is.

Eugene N. Russell, Oshkosh

5 - 6 lbs venison
1 cup onions
1 cup green peppers
1 cup celery
garlic
2 - 16oz. canned tomatoes
1 cup vinegar
1 cup sugar
Worcestershire sauce - 4oz.
Catsup - 12oz.
2 tablespoons chili powder

VENISON STEAKS

IT REQUIRES BUT A SHORT TIME to broil venison steaks, and they should be served rare and very hot. Heat the platter on which the steaks are to be served. Put in it two tablespoons of butter, a little salt and pepper, and two tablespoons of melted currant jelly. If the steaks are about one inch thick, ten minutes should be long enough to broil them.

Put the broiled steaks in the heated platter and turn them once or twice in the mixture and serve very hot.

Cliff Rauscher, Green Bay

Venison steaks
2 tablespoons butter
Salt & pepper
2 tablespoons currant jelly, melted

VENISON LIVERS ON TOAST

ROLL LIVER PIECES IN FLOUR and fry in butter until browned. Add all other ingredients and simmer until tender. Serve hot on toast wedges.

Mrs. Jan Teachout, Waupun

½ lb. venison liver (cut in small strips or pieces)
1 can mushrooms
Salt and pepper
1 small can whole tomatoes
½ green pepper

HOME-MADE JERKY

START WITH A GOOD SIZED venison steak, venison roast, commercial chuck roast, round steak, etc. Cut meat into thin strips (cutting with grain of meat).

Boil 2 quarts of water, ½ pint of vinegar, 2 cups of salt, 2 tablespoons pepper. This quantity of brine is adequate for up to 10 pounds of meat.

Soak meat for 5 minutes.

Next, with a rolling pin, flatten out the strips of meat. The jerky should be somewhat rubbery and grey. Now place the strips on the oven rack allowing air to circulate. Set oven at 200° and keep door ajar to allow moisture to escape. Remove meat when almost dry (this is usually about 1 - 1½ hours in the oven).

Now comes the seasoning. Paint both sides with A-1 sauce. Add some Worcestershire sauce or tobasco for a hotter taste. A mixture of ketchup and vinegar is good, too. Dry the sauce on the jerky for about 30 minutes inthe oven.

Store in jars. Kept dry, it will last for years (if you can keep from eating it that long).

Richard Kuhman, Colfax

Venison roast, steak or commercial roast, steak, etc.

FIVE MINUTE BRINE SOAK:

2 quarts water
½ pint vinegar
2 cups salt
2 tablespoons pepper

SEASONING:

A-1 Sauce
Worcestershire Sauce (optional)
Tobasco sauce (optional)

EMIL'S VENISON

REMOVE FAT AND MEMBRANE from venison. Cut meat across grain into slivers 1 — 2" long and about ½" wide. Let meat stand in 1/3 cup soy sauce for one hour. Heat salad oil in a skillet. Add ginger and garlic. After a few minutes remove garlic and add celery. Cook 5 minutes, stirring occasionally. Add venison and soy sauce and cook 5 minutes until all pieces are browned. Add tomatoes and continue cooking a little longer until meat pieces are tender. Mix cornstarch with 2 tablespoons soy sauce and stir into entire mixture and cook until thickened.

Serve with fluffy rice.

Serves 6.

Mrs. Emil Pagel, Algoma

1½ pounds venison round steak
1/3 cup soy sauce
1/3 cup salad oil
1 clove garlic, sliced (optional)
3/4 teaspoon ginger
2 cups celery cut in 1" strips
2 cups drained tomatoes
1 tablespoon cornstarch
2 tablespoons soy sauce

SUPER VENISON LIVER

COMBINE ALL DRY INGREDIENTS in shallow bowl. Brush liver with dressing and dip in crumb mixture. Place on greased cookie sheet and bake in a 400° oven for 12-15 minutes.

Mary De Long, Chippewa Falls

1 venison liver, sliced
1 cup fine bread crumbs
2 teaspoons paprika
1 teaspoon minced parsley
½ cup Thousand Island Dressing
Salt and pepper to taste

THE JUMP MEAT SPECIAL

TAKE A WHOLE front leg of venison, insert a knife between meat and bone about three inches deep. Into these slits on each end of roast insert 1/8 of a clove of garlic, then salt and pepper the entire roast to suit your taste. Place into a large roasting pan, lay 3 thickly sliced strips of good side bacon on the top. Roast in a covered pan, about 30 minutes per pound. At three different intervals during roasting time, baste with 1/3 cup of Port wine (no more). Then add one can cream of mushroom soup to the drippings to form a gravy. Thicken or thin to please your taste, then enjoy.

C.W. Gray, Waukesha

Leg of venison
Fresh garlic
3 strips bacon
1/3 cup Port wine
1 can cream of mushroom soup

VENISON STRIPS IN WINE

REMOVE ALL TRACES OF FAT from venison. Cut meat across grain the width of a pencil and about 1½ inches long. Shake strips of venison in seasoned flour in a paper or plastic bag.

Using a heavy pan, quickly brown in hot oil until meat is no longer rare. Add wine and carrots and simmer for 15 minutes tightly covered. Add potatoes, onions and peppers and stir gently to coat all pieces. Adjust seasoning and add more wine if necessary. Simmer 15 more minutes or until vegetables and meat are tender. Watch carefully and serve piping hot.

Howard Kohlhepp, Chippewa Falls

1½ pounds venison
¼ cup flour
¼ cup cooking oil
4 small carrots, cut in half & quartered
1 medium onion, peeled & quartered
1½ green peppers, cut in strips
½ cup red wine
2 medium red potatoes, peeled & quartere
Salt and pepper

VENISON LIVER

SLICE THE DEER LIVER into serving sized pieces and let it fry in butter in a shallow frying skillet. When it is done, place it on a warm dish and sprinkle with salt and pepper, chopped parsley and pour over the pieces the butter from the pan.

Cliff Rauscher, Green Bay

Deer liver
Butter
Salt & pepper
Parsley, chopped

POOR MAN'S GOOSE

BROWN SLICES OF LIVER lightly on both sides in hot fat, about ½ minute each side. Sprinkle with salt and pepper. Put liver and drippings into bottom of 10-cup casserole. Add onions and potatoes, and sprinkle with more salt and pepper. Top with bacon slices.

Cover casserole and bake at 350° for 1 hour. Remove cover and bake 15 minutes longer to crisp bacon.

Marilyn Benish, Yuba

1¼ lbs. venison liver, sliced
2 tablespoons bacon fat
Salt and pepper
5 medium onions, sliced
5 medium potatoes, sliced
5 slices bacon

DEER HEART STEW

BOIL WHOLE HEART for 15 minutes with quartered carrots and celery. Remove and dice heart, discarding carrots and celery.

Brown pieces of meat in a frying pan with butter. Place in a roaster with 1 can V-8 juice; 1 small can drained green peas; 1 medium chopped onion; 2 sliced carrots; 2 stalks chopped celery; 4 ozs. drained mushrooms. Salt and pepper to taste.

Cover and place in oven at 350° for 45 minutes.

Ray Lardinois, Algoma

Carrots & celery, quartered (to boil with heart)
Deer heart
1 can V-8 juice
1 small can green peas
2 carrots, sliced
2 stalks celery, chopped
4 ozs. mushrooms
1 medium onion, chopped
Salt & pepper to taste

VENISON BAKED IN FOIL

PLACE EACH STEAK ON a 2 foot piece of aluminum foil with two pats of butter on each side of meat. Slice 1 potato over each steak. Season with salt & pepper. On top of potato slice 1 small onion, then slice 2 carrots quartered lengthwise over onion. Over all sprinkle teaspoon Worcestershire sauce. Close foil up tightly. Place on cookie sheet and bake at 350° for 1 hour.

Mrs. John Allen, Chippewa Falls

For each venison steak:
4 pats butter
1 medium potato
1 small onion
2 small carrots
1 teaspoon Worcestershire sauce
Salt & pepper

FRY PAN VENISON STEAK & VEGETABLES

BROWN VENISON STEAK in electric fry pan. Turn temperature down and layer potatoes, carrots, onions and celery on top of the meat. Pour one can of mushroom soup over the top. Add a dash of steak sauce and simmer until done.

Mrs. Loren Lane, Mt. Hope

1 venison steak
Sliced potatoes, carrots, onions, celery.
1 can condensed cream of mushroom soup
Dash steak sauce

LIVER A'LA GOURMET

HEAT OIL IN SKILLET, add sliced garlic and onions and cook slowly until soft and yellow. Add cleaned sliced mushrooms, cover tightly and simmer 3-4 minutes. Put the tomatoes through a sieve to remove seeds and add to skillet; continue simmering gently. Coat liver thoroughly in flour which has been mixed with salt and pepper.

Brown in butter in another skillet until just browned on both sides. Pour sauce over liver, cover and simmer 5 minutes longer.

Marilyn Benish, Yuba

2 tablespoons olive or salad oil
2 cloves garlic
2 medium onions
½ lb. mushrooms
1 can tomatoes or 2¼ cups tomato juice
1¼ lbs. venison liver
3 tablespoons flour
1 teaspoon salt
Dash black pepper
2 tablespoons butter

BIG GAME LIVER PATE

COOK UNTIL TENDER AND PLACE in blender with salad dressing, egg, onion, garlic; blend. Can be frozen.

Kevin Voigt, Onalaska

½ lb. of liver cut into small pieces
¼ lb. oleo
¼ cup onion
2 tablespoons salad dressing
1 hard boiled egg
¼ cup onion minced
1 clove garlic

TERIYAKI VENISON

SLICE VENISON ¼ - 1/8 INCH thick. Mix ingredients. Layer meat and mixture. Cover tightly and refrigerate for 6-12 hours, stirring occasionally. Drain. Dry in food dehydrator for 6-8 hours at 150°.

Sue Hartzell, Cornell

1 lb. venison
½ teaspoon salt
1/8 teaspoon pepper
½ teaspoon ground ginger
2 tablespoons brown sugar
1 crushed clove garlic
¼ cup soy sauce

WOK STIR-FRY VENISON

USE TENDER PART OF VENISON (chops work well). Slice thin strips from them. This is easy when they are partially frozen.

Stir together the cornstarch, salt, sugar, soy sauce, and the water, set aside.

Place wok over high heat. When wok is hot, add oil. When oil is hot, stir-fry the venison, small amounts at a time, and remove from Wok as they are browned.

Next, stir-fry the celery and remove. Then stir-fry the pea pods, remove, and stir-fry the mushrooms.

Add more oil if needed.

Pour the cornstarch mixture into the wok, turn heat down, add all ingredients and stir until the mixture thickens and boils. Cook the instant rice.

Put rice on plates and add the hot stir-fry mixture. Add more soy sauce on top as you like it.

Margie Kmetz, Drummond

2 lbs. thin sliced venison
2 tablespoons cornstarch
½ teaspoon salt
2 teaspoons sugar
2 tablespoons soy sauce
¾ cup water
2-4 tablespoons salad oil or peanut oil
1 large stalk of celery cut in ¼-½ in. slanting slices
4 pkgs. frozen edible pea pods (thawed) (6 oz. each)
Fresh mushrooms sliced
Instant rice

VENISON SUKIYAKI

CUT VENISON ACROSS GRAIN into 1/8 in. strips. Mix soy sauce, ginger, and garlic and toss with beef. Cover and refrigerate at least 1 hour, stirring once.

Cook and stir beef in oil in dutch oven over medium-high heat until brown. Stir in 1 cup broth. Heat to boiling, reduce heat. Cover and simmer until beef is tender, about 20 minutes. Remove beef and broth from dutch oven.

Cook and stir onion, mushrooms, green pepper, and Chinese vegetables in 2 tablespoons vegetable oil over high heat for 2 minutes. Stir in beef and broth. Cover, cook over medium heat for 2 minutes.

Shake remaining broth, the cornstarch, soy sauce, salt and sugar in tightly-covered container. Gradually add into mixture in dutch oven. Heat to boiling, stirring constantly. Boil and stir 1 minute.

Serve over noodles and rice. Serves 5.

Jeanne Urban, Clintonville

1 lb. venison round steak ½ in. thick
1 tablespoon soy sauce
1 teaspoon ground ginger
1 teaspoon garlic powder
2 tablespoons vegetable oil
1 2/3 cups chicken broth (1 2/3 cups boiling water with 2 chicken bouillon cubes dissolved in it)
1 4 oz. can sliced mushrooms
1 medium onion, sliced
1 15½ oz. can mixed Chinese vegetables
1 medium green pepper
2 tablespoons vegetable oil
3 tablespoons cornstarch
2 tablespoons soy sauce
½ teaspoon salt
¼ teaspoon sugar
1/3 cup Chow Mein Noodles
1¾ cups hot rice

VENISON SUKIYAKI

COOK VENISON STEAK QUICKLY in oil in wok or large skillet. Combine bouillon, soy sauce, sugar, and sherry. Add half of this to browned meat. Push meat to side of pan. Cook celery and onion for 3 minutes. Add rest of bouillon mix, bamboo shoots, mushrooms, and spinach. Cook 3 minutes. Add green onions and cook 1 minute. Serve with vermicelli as spaghetti is served.

Note: Cook vermicelli while cooking sukiyaki. Thaw spinach in collander under running hot water to separate.

Gerald Lahner, Eau Claire

1½ lbs. venison steak (cut in 1 in. strips)
¼ cup oil
3 onions
4 green onions
1 cup celery
½ cup beef bouillon
1 tablespoon sugar
½ cup soy sauce
1 cup bamboo shoots
1 small can mushrooms
1 tablespoon cooking sherry
1 pkg. frozen spinach
1 lb. vermicelli

VENISON STIR FRY

CUT MEAT IN LONG THIN PIECES and soak in soy sauce for 5 minutes. (This helps tenderize the meat.)

Heat wok or fry pan on high heat, add oil and meat and stir until brown. Pour juice from meat into bowl and save. Remember, fry the meat, do not boil in juices for this will make it tough.

Remove meat from pan, add celery and juice from meat, mushrooms and onions and cook 2 minutes. Add meat to mixture and cover and heat for 3 minutes or until meat is hot. Uncover and stir in butter or margarine and serve with rice or Chow Mein Noodles.

Cathy Fehrenbach, Milwaukee

1 lb. venison (steak or roast)
2 cups mushrooms sliced (use fresh mushrooms)
½ cup celery sliced thin
1 medium onion sliced for round rings
¼ cup soy sauce
1 tablespoon oil
2 tablepoons butter or margarine

CHINESE VENISON STIR-FRY

IN WOK STIR-FRY MEAT IN OIL till cooked. Remove meat and set aside. Heat remaining oil (add more if necessary) to hot. Add carrots and celery and stir-fry till crisp and tender. Add remaining vegetables and meat. Add sauce mixture and continue to stir-fry until sauce thickens. Serve immediately with rice. Serves 4-5.

Jan Jacobson, Madison

1 lb. venison cut in 1/8x2 in. slices
2 tablespoons oil
2-3 carrots cut in sticks
2-3 green onions cut in ¼ in. pieces
(including tops)
2 stalks celery cut diagonally in
¼ in. pieces
1 can bamboo shoots
1 can water chestnuts sliced
1 can 4 oz. sliced mushrooms

Sauce
¾ cup water
2½ tablespoons soy sauce
2 teaspoons worcestershire sauce
3 tablespoons cornstarch
1 teaspoon sugar
¼ teaspoon pepper
¼ teaspoon garlic powder
½ teaspoon salt
¼ teaspoon ground ginger

ROAST LEG OF VENISON

WITH A SHARPLY POINTED KNIFE, make 1 inch incisions all over the leg of venison and insert small pieces of salt pork. Prepare the marinating sauce.

Marinate the venison in this sauce from 5 to 6 days. Turn the leg over occasionally and baste with the sauce, so that the flavor will permeate the whole leg. Roast in 350° oven, allowing 18 minutes per pound. Venison should be underdone. Serve with piquant sauce.

Eugene N. Russell, Oshkosh

Leg of venison
MARINATING SAUCE:
¼ pint red wine
¼ pint wine vinegar
1 tablespoon salt
½ teaspoon black pepper
Bouquet garnish (3 - 4 sprigs of parsley.
sprig of thyme, small bay leaf)
2 onions, sliced
2 carrots, sliced
4 tablespoons oil

ORIENTAL SUPREME

COOK AND STIR MEAT, ONION, and garlic in large skillet until meat is brown. Drain off fat. Mix soy sauce, cornstarch, and molasses. Stir into meat mixture. Stir in bouillon, water, pea pods, water chestnuts, bamboo shoots, and reserved Mandarin orange syrup; heat to boiling.

Reduce heat, cover and simmer 10 minutes, stirring occasionally. Stir in orange segments; cover and heat 2 minutes.

Nice served with hot cooked rice and additional soy sauce.

Marilyn Benish, Yuba

1½ lbs. ground venison
1 medium onion, sliced
1 clove garlic, minced
¼ cup soy sauce
2 tablespoons cornstarch
1 tablespoon molasses
1 teaspoon instant beef bouillon
¾ cup water
1 pkg. (6 oz.) frozen Chinese pea pods
1 can (5 oz.) water chestnuts, drained
and sliced
1 can (5 oz.) bamboo shoots, drained
1 can (11 oz.) Mandarin orange
segments (reserve syrup)

VENISON CHOP SUEY

MELT ½ STICK OF BUTTER in frying pan. Brown stew meat. Add ½ cup water, cover and simmer until meat is tender (30 min.). Stir in vegetables and juice and chop suey mix, bring to full boil. Simmer 10 min. uncovered. Serve over rice or noodles.

Jim Bruckner, Chilton

2 lbs. venison stew meat (1-2 in. cubes)
1 pkg. chop suey mix
1 1 lb. can chop suey vegetables with juice
1 tablespoon soy sauce

VENISON STROGANOFF

CUT MEAT INTO VERY thin strips or cubes; trim off excess fat. Brown meat in butter; add onions. Combine soup, tomato paste, seasonings and mushrooms then add to meat mixture. Cover and simmer for 1 hour. Stir in sour cream just before serving. Thicken if desired. Serve in ring of fluffy rice; garnish with parsley.

Curtis Heise, Muscoda

1½ - 2 lbs. venison
1 cup butter or margarine
2 lbs. onions, finely chopped
1 can tomato soup
1 6oz. can tomato paste
1 teaspoon salt
1/8 teaspoon pepper
1 can mushroom steak sauce or 1 lb. mushrooms
1 cup sour cream

VENISON PIZZA LOAF

USE YOUR FAVORITE meat loaf recipe. When you put it in the pan make a well down the center of the loaf and pour 1 can pizza sauce into it. Pour sauce 15 minutes before meat loaf is done. Add pizza cheese and put back in oven til cheese is melted.

Mrs. Loren Lane, Mt. Hope

VENISON PARMIGIANA

POUND VENISON AND CUT into 8-10 pieces. Dip into beaten egg. Roll in coating and brown in hot oil in skillet. Arrange in shallow baking dish. Cook onion in skillet drippings then stir in remaining sauce ingredients. Simmer 15 minutes. Stir often. Pour sauce over meat, cover, and bake at 350° for 45 minutes. Top with Mozarella slices and bake uncovered for 15 minutes more.

Sue Hartzell, Cornell

2 lb. venison steaks (½ in. thick, boned)
2 eggs beaten with 2 tablespoons milk
¼ cup olive oil
½ lb. Mozarella cheese, sliced

Coating mixture

2/3 cup bread crumbs
¼ cup grated parmesan cheese

Sauce mixture

1 medium onion, chopped
2 cups tomato juice
1 teaspoon salt
¼ teaspoon garlic powder
6 oz. can tomato paste
½ teaspoon sweet basil
¼ teaspoon pepper

VENISON-YAKI

CUT ROUND STEAKS IN STRIPS 1/8 in. thick and 3-4 in. long. Brown strips in fat in large frying pan. Pour off drippings, measure, and add water to make 1 cup. Combine with soy sauce, sugar, pepper, and garlic and add to meat. Cover tightly and cook slowly 45 minutes.

Cut carrots lengthwise into thin strips and cut strips in half. Add rest of vegetables to the meat, cover, and continue cooking 15 minutes. Combine cornstarch and water and use to thicken cooking liquid. Serve with cooked rice. Serves 6-8.

Steve Windett, Platteville

2 lbs. venison round steak
2 tablespoons cooking fat
Water
1/3 cup soy sauce
2 teaspoons sugar
¼ teaspoon pepper
1 clove garlic, minced
2 green peppers, cut in 1 in. squares
8 green onions, cut in 1½ in. pieces
½ lb. mushrooms, halved
1 can (8 oz.) water chestnuts
2 tablespoons cornstarch
¼ cup water cooked rice
3 carrots

WISCONSIN VENISON CHILI

CUT VENISON IN SMALL CUBES and brown in heated oil in heavy pan. Add onions, garlic, and green peppers. Cook about 5 minutes, stirring constantly. Add chili powder, sugar, tomatoes, tomato sauce, water, and salt, then let mixture simmer about 1½ hours.

Just before serving, add kidney beans. Allow enough time to warm them.

Sue Hartzell, Cornell

2 lbs. venison
¼ cup vegetable oil
1 cup chopped onions
2 cloves garlic minced
1 large green pepper cut in strips
3 tablespoons chili powder
2 teaspoons sugar
3½ cups whole tomatoes
1 cup tomato sauce
1 cup water
½ teaspoon salt
2 cups cooked kidney beans

PEGGY'S LEMON PEPPER VENISON JERKY

SOAK MEAT IN SAUCE OVERNIGHT. Dry in food dryer at 160° for about 6 hours. (Drain meat well first.)

Sue Hartzell, Cornell

2 lbs. venison cut in 1/8 in. strips
2/3 cup soy sauce
1 teaspoon garlic salt
1½ tablespoons lemon pepper

DEEP DISH VENISON PIZZA

PREHEAT OVEN TO 350°. BROWN ground venison with onions. Drain off grease. Stir in tomato paste, mushrooms, oregano, salt, and pepper. Simmer.

Press biscuits into 9 in. pie pan to form crust. Spoon meat mixture into crust. Arrange sliced tomato on top. Add Mozarella cheese. Bake at 350° for 20-25 minutes until cheese begins to brown.

Michael A. Hinz, Sheboygan

1½ lbs. of ground venison
½ cup chopped onions
6 oz. tomato paste
4 oz. can mushrooms
1½ teaspoon oregano
1 teaspoon salt
½ teaspoon pepper
1 refrigerated buttermilk biscuits tube
1 cup shredded Mozarella cheese
1 sliced tomato

VENISON PASTIES

TO MAKE PASTRY, MIX FLOUR and salt in large bowl, cut in butter and lard until mixture resembles coarse crumbs. Stir in ice water until dough gathers into ball. Add remaining water if needed. Cover and refrigerate for 1 hour.

Make filling. Mix all ingredients except butter and egg in large bowl.

Roll pastry on lightly-floured surface until 1/8 in. thick. Cut into 6 in. rounds (use bowl as a guide). Put heaping ¼ cup of filling onto center of each pastry round, dot top with approximately ½ teaspoon butter. Brush edges of pastry with water (warm).

Fold pastry over filling to form half-moon shape. Press seams to seal; use tines of fork for decorative effect. Cut small slit in top of each pastry. Brush tops with beaten egg. Bake on ungreased baking sheet at 400° for 10 minutes. Reduce temperature to 350° and bake for another 20-30 minutes until golden brown. Cool for 5 minutes on wire rack. Makes approximately 12 servings.

Ellen Rosborough, Stoddard

Pastry

3 cups flour
1 teaspoon salt
¾ cup cold unsalted butter, cut into small pieces
¼ cup cold lard, cut into small pieces
6-8 tablespoons ice water

Filling

2 cups finely diced venison steak
2 cups red potatoes, peeled and finely diced
1 cup coarsely chopped white or yellow turnips
1 cup onions chopped
2 medium sized carrots chopped
1½ teaspoon salt
½ teaspoon ground pepper
1 teaspoon ground marjoram
1 teaspoon thyme
1 cup minced, fresh parsley
2 tablespoons butter
1 egg lightly beaten

GROUND VENISON QUICHE

LET PIE SHELL STAND AT room temperature for 10 minutes. Prick bottom and sides with fork. Bake 5 minutes at 425°. Cool.

Melt oil in skillet. Add the meat and brown. Add onion and seasonings and spoon into pie shell. Sprinkle cheese and mushrooms over top.

Beat eggs and milk. Pour over pie. Bake until set, about 20 minutes at 425°. Reduce temperature to 350° and continue baking for 25 minutes. Let stand 10 minutes before cutting into wedges. Serves 4-5.

Karen Schmidt, Racine

1 9 in. deep dish frozen pie shell
1 lb. ground venison
2 teaspoons instant minced onion
½ teaspoon salt
1/8 teaspoon pepper
1/8 teaspoon garlic powder
½ cup sliced fresh mushrooms
1 cup grated cheddar cheese
2 eggs
1 can evaporated milk

BARBECUE VENISON RIBS

CUT RIBS INTO 4x6 IN. PIECES. Place ribs fat side toward sides of pot and place onion around ribs. Cook on low (use crock pot or slow cooker) for 6 hours, then drain all grease, but leaving onions in. Place good portion of Kraft Sauce on ribs so they are covered well. Cook on low ½ - 1 hour.

Mary Scott, Manawa

1-2 lbs. venison ribs
cut into 4x6 in. pieces
1 large onion, sliced
Kraft Barbecue Sauce

VENISON RIBS WITH J-9'S BARBECUE SAUCE

PUT 4 LARGE SERVINGS of venison ribs in roasting pan so all pieces lay flat in pan and do not overlap. Place in oven at 450° for 45 minutes or until nice and brown. Be sure to turn ribs over after 20 minutes to brown both sides.

Remove from oven and pour J-9's Barbecue Sauce over ribs and cover with foil. Lower oven to 275° and cook for 4-5 hours or until very tender.

Take off foil and increase oven temperature if you need to thicken the sauce. If sauce thickens too quickly, just add a small amount of water. Serves 4.

To make sauce, combine all ingredients and cook slowly on top of stove for 45 minutes. Do not cover while cooking.

Janine Zeutschel, Menomonie

4 large servings of venison ribs

J-9's Barbecue Sauce

1 large garlic, minced
1 medium onion, minced
¾ teaspoon prepared mustard
1 tablespoon grated fresh horseradish
1 tablespoon mixed minced herbs, thyme, marjoram, parsley
3 cups water
2 tablespoons wine vinegar
1 tablespoon worcestershire sauce
½ cup catsup
Dash of tabasco sauce
2/3 cup butter or margarine
2 teaspoons sugar
½ teaspoon chili powder
¼ teaspoon black pepper
½ teaspoon salt

BRENDA'S VENISON RIB BARBECUE SAUCE

FOR ABOUT 5 LBS. OF RIBS, combine all ingredients and heat to boiling. Simmer for 45 minutes or more.

Marinate ribs in sauce for 1 day before grilling.

Grill to side of medium coals over drip pan for 1 to 1½ hours. Baste and turn every 20 minutes. Add hickory chips last 15 minutes of cooking.

Brenda and Paul Ross, Fremont

5 lbs. venison ribs
1 cup catsup (use the thickest you can find)
1 tablespoon worcestershire sauce
3 dashes bottled hot pepper sauce
1 cup water
¼ cup cider vinegar
1 tablespoon brown sugar
1 teaspoon seasoning salt
1 teaspoon celery seed

BBQ VENISON SPARE RIBS

ROLL RIBS IN FLOUR then brown in shortening. Mix rest of ingredients together and pour over ribs.

Cover and bake for 3 hours at 350°.

Larry Hitchcock, Sauk City

3-5 lbs. venison ribs
1 medium onion chopped
2 tablespoons vinegar
4 tablespoons brown sugar
¼ teaspoon pepper
1 cup catsup
1 cup water
3 tablespoons worcestershire sauce
½ teaspoon ground mustard
½ cup celery or
1 tablespoon celery salt
Flour
Shortening

VENISON RIBS WITH CARAWAY KRAUT

SEASON RIBS WITH SALT and pepper. Place in dutch oven. Combine all ingredients and pour over ribs. Bake uncovered at 350° for 3 hours. Baste when needed.

Gib Dutton, Rochester, MN

3 lbs. venison ribs,
cut in serving pieces
2 teaspoons salt
¼ teaspoon pepper
1 large can (3½ cups) sauerkraut, undrained
2 medium shredded carrots
1 tart chopped unpeeled apple
1½ cups tomato juice
2 tablespoons brown sugar
2 teaspoons caraway seed

BARBECUED VENISON RIBS ROYALE

COMBINE INGREDIENTS IN SMALL saucepan. Cover, simmer 10 minutes. Brush ribs often with sauce while grilling or broiling. To assure your ribs are going to be tender, marinate them overnight in 1 cup red wine, ¼ cup soy sauce, 1 bay leaf, and 1/8 teaspoon each of garlic and onion powder.

Marilyn Benish, Yuba

3 lbs. venison cut as beef short ribs are cut
¼ cup soy sauce
3 tablespoons lemon juice
¾ teaspoon dry mustard
1 clove garlic, crushed
½ teaspoon salt
¾ cup catsup
2 tablespoons brown sugar
½ teaspoon hot pepper sauce
1 teaspoon onion powder

BARBECUED VENISON RIBS

TRIM FAT FROM RIBS, CUT into serving size. Put ribs in roaster and brown. Cover ribs with sauce.

To make sauce, mix all ingredients and pour over ribs. Bake until done.

Gib Dutton, Rochester, MN

Venison ribs, cut into serving size

Sauce

4 tablespoons minced onions
1 cup tomato puree
¾ cup water
3 tablespoons vinegar
2 tablespoons worcestershire sauce
½ cup brown sugar
1 teaspoon salt
1 teaspoon paprika
1 teaspoon chili powder
½ teaspoon pepper
¼ teaspoon cinnamon
Dash of ground cloves

VENISON ROAST

PUT *FROZEN* ROAST IN ROASTER, add 1 in. water. Sprinkle 1 pkg. of onion soup mix over roast, add onion and beef cube. Cover and put in oven for 2½-3 hours. Baste periodically. Season to taste.

Jim Bruckner, Chilton

3-4 lbs. venison roast (trimmed)
1 onion, chopped
1 pkg. onion soup mix
1 beef bouillon cube

SMOTHERED VENISON

SEASON THE VENISON WITH SALT and pepper, roll in flour. Place in heavy covered pan and brown on all sides in melted fat. Add celery seeds, prepared mustard or horseradish, strained tomatoes. Cover and simmer about 3 hours.

Mary Scott, Manawa

3 lbs. venison, round or rump
1 cup strained tomatoes
Flour
Melted fat
2 tablepoons prepared mustard or horseradish
1 teaspoon celery seed
Salt and pepper

FORGOTTEN VENISON ROAST

LINE BAKING PAN WITH sufficient foil to completely cover roast to retain moisture. Place roast in lined pan. Add a small amount of water. Cover roast with cream of mushroom soup. Sprinkle on onion soup mix. Cover with foil so as to form airtight tent over roast. Bake at 325° for 3 hours. Makes its own gravy.

Michael Hinz, Sheboygan

1 venison roast
1 can cream of mushroom soup
1 package dry onion soup mix

VENISON OVER RICED POTATOES

PLACE VENISON ROAST IN ROASTER. Sprinkle with salt and pepper, place onions on top, add a little water, and roast for 1 hour, then pour cooking wine over roast.

   Roast about 3 more hours until meat is easy to remove from bones. Take meat off bones and cut into small pieces. Put back into broth and thicken to make a gravy. Serve hot over riced potatoes.

Donna Gibert, Medford

5 lbs. venison neck roast
2 large onions, sliced thin
1 cup cooking wine
Salt and pepper

VENISON ALA WEBER

USE THE INDIRECT METHOD for cooking. Coals are placed to the sides of the Weber kettle with a drip pan in the middle. Salt and pepper the roast. Insert meat thermometer and cover with strips of bacon. Roast until thermometer reads medium-rare beef.

Michael Hinz, Sheboygan

1 venison (round) roast
Strips of bacon
Salt and pepper

VENISON KABOBS

USE WOOD OR METAL skewers. Alternate ingredients on skewers, baste with butter. Best over open flame, but can also be done on grill. Cook until desired tenderness of meat.

Ken Tomaszewski, Janesville

2 lbs. venison roast
cut into 1½ in. cubes
2 large green peppers chopped
2 pints cherry tomatoes
1 lb. fresh whole mushrooms
4 small onions quartered

BRAISED VENISON

RUB VENISON WITH DAMP CLOTH and lard and salt pork. Rub with seasoned flour. Saute in ½ cup fat until well browned. Turn frequently. It will take about 1 hour.

Add hot water, vinegar, and cook, covered, for 2½ hours or until done. Add water if needed.

One-half hour before done, cover meat with celery, onion, carrots, and apple. Add lemon juice.

Serve with grape jelly or wine jelly or Tireau sauce.

To make Tireau sauce, combine all ingredients except jelly, simmer for 15 minutes, then add currant jelly and bring to a boiling point, stirring constantly.

Gib Dutton, Rochester, MN

6 lb. cut of venison
Lard
Fat salt pork
Seasoned flour
½ cup hot water
1 tablespoon vinegar
½ cup chopped celery
1 onion chopped
2 carrots sliced
1 tart chopped apple
1 tablespoon lemon juice

Tireau sauce

1 cup port or Bordeaux wine
1 stick cinnamon
6 almonds, blanched and pounded into paste
6 whole cloves
¼ cup brown sugar
Rind of 1 lemon pared very thin
1 cup currant jelly

MUSHROOM VENISON ROAST

TRIM FAT, DREDGE MEAT IN FLOUR, brown slowly in hot fat, season with salt and pepper. Add onions and remaining ingredients. Cover and cook slowly for 2½ hours. Add mushrooms and make gravy.

Mrs. Lyle Kothbauer, Mondovi

3-4 lbs. venison roast
2 onions
½ cup water
¼ cup catsup
1/3 cup cooking sherry
¼ teaspoon each of dry mustard, marjoram, rosemary, and thyme
1 bay leaf
1 6 oz. can mushrooms, sliced

LUAU VENISON

DREDGE MEAT IN FLOUR. Brown in hot oil. Return all meat to skillet; cover and simmer until tender, about 45 minutes. (Time will vary depending on age of deer.)

Remove meat, thicken gravy if desired by combining 1 tablespoon flour with ¼ cup water. Stir into pan juices until thick. Add pineapple, onions, celery, and pepper. Mix sugar, ginger, and soy sauce into gravy. Pour over vegetables and meat and cover.

Bake at 350° for 30 minutes until vegetables are tender but not soft. Lightly mix ingredients. Serve over cooked rice. Makes 8-10 servings.

Karen Schmidt, Racine

5 lbs. boneless cubed venison
¾ cup flour
¾ cup cooking oil
1 cup water
1 can (1 lb. 4 oz.) pineapple chunks drained
3 large white onions sliced
1 cup celery chunks
3 green peppers cubed
¼ cup dark brown sugar packed
2 tablespoons sliced fresh gingeroot or
¾ teaspoon ground ginger
¼ cup soy sauce
4-5 cups cooked rice

VARIETY VENISON

POUR WATER INTO PRESSURE COOKER, add sherry. Remove excess fat from meat, brown on each side, about 5 minutes; salt and pepper. Remove meat from pan and put into pressure cooker. Add onions.

Cook for 35-45 minutes (depending on cut of roast), after the pressure cooker has reached cooking pressure (10 lbs.). Remove from heat, release pressure.

Remove roast and set on a plate to cool (about ½-1 hour). After roast is cooled, slice into thin slices approximately 1/8 to ¼ in.

Mix au jus according to directions. Place sliced meat into crock pot if available. Pour au jus over meat, cover and simmer slowly for 1-2 hours until tender.

Stir frequently, add water when needed. Salt and pepper to taste. Can be served on buns, over mashed potatoes, or over noodles as Stroganoff.

Henry & Mary VanKerkvoorde, Silver Lake

1-3 lb. venison roast
4 cups water
¼ cup sherry cooking wine
2 medium onions, sliced
1 pkg. of Au Jus gravy mix
Salt and pepper

BAR-B-CUE VENISON RIBS

IN A HEAVY 2 QT. FRY PAN, put all ingredients together and simmer at low heat for 1½ hours. Broil ribs on both sides until really brown. Put in a roaster and layer them with barbecue sauce. Bake until tender.

Helen Tschida, Danbury

Venison ribs
1 large onion chopped fine
½ cup butter
1 small can tomato paste
1 cup water
½ cup worcestershire sauce
1/3 cup lemon juice
¼ cup honey
¼ cup brown sugar
1 clove garlic chopped fine
1 tablespoon salt
3-4 dashes tabasco sauce

VENISON SAUERBRATEN

POUR VINEGAR, WATER, BROWN SUGAR, seasonings, and vegetables over meat in glass bowl. Cover and store in refrigerator overnight. Transfer to kettle and cook 2-3 hours. Take meat out and place in warm oven. Strain juice into kettle, remove grease off top and bring to boil. Add crushed cookies, stirring continuously until gravy thickens. Serves 6.

Shane Clarke, Palmyra

5-6 lbs. venison
2 cups wine vinegar
2 cups water
¼ cup brown sugar
1 tablespoon salt
½ teaspoon pepper
½ teaspoon cloves
1 bay leaf
3 medium sized onions chopped
2 large carrots diced
1 cup celery diced
2 tablespoons bacon drippings
8-10 gingersnap cookies, crumbled

VENISON ROAST

SPREAD BUTTER ON VENISON and season to taste. Put onion, carrots, celery, thyme, bay leaves and cloves in roasting pan around meat. Roast at 325°, basting often. When done, take meat out of pan and drain off fat. Put sherry in with the cooking juices and let simmer until nearly dry. Add beef stock, salt and pepper, and heat to boiling. Pour over venison and serve immediately.

Helen Tschida, Danbury

Venison, about 4 lbs.
1 onion diced
1 carrot
1 sprig thyme
2 bay leaves
2 cloves
1 small celery stalk
½ cup sherry wine
1 cup beef stock (1 bouillon cube)
2 tablespoons butter

VENISON ROAST

SOAK ROAST OVERNIGHT WITH ½ cup vinegar. Wash and dry meat well. Brush with ½ cup red wine. Sprinkle with meat tenderizer, salt and pepper and garlic powder. Place slices of lime on top of roast. Add salt pork on top of lime. (Use toothpicks to keep the salt pork and lime in place.) Bake about 5 hours, covered, at 275°. Make a basting sauce with the remaining wine, and add rest of ingredients. Baste often with sauce to prevent drying.

Terry Baumgartner, Kansasville

Venison roast
½ cup vinegar
½ cup red wine
1 teaspoon meat tenderizer
Salt, pepper, garlic powder
4 thin slices lime
5-6 slices salt pork

Basting sauce

Remaining wine
Rosemary (pinch)
½ cup frozen orange juice concentrate
¼ cup honey
¼ cup butter

ROAST VENISON

CUT A POCKET ALONG THE LEG bone from the large end almost to small end. Season the roast well inside pocket and rub well outside. Fill pocket with all the chopped vegetables except onion tops, parsley and mushrooms. Pour wine over roast and add 4 strips of bacon on top.

Place in covered roasting pan and cook at 300° for 3-4 hours until tender. Remove from pan, add flour to juice from mushrooms, and mix well. Add onion tops and parsley to pan juices. Place over high heat and cook 5 minutes until gravy thickens. Put roast back into gravy and cook, uncovered, for 5 minutes to brown. Slice and serve.

Mrs. Lucille Fenski, Iron River

10 lb. roast (hind quarter)
1 chopped green pepper
1 chopped onion
2 sticks celery chopped
4 cloves garlic minced
2 sticks margarine
4 strips bacon
8 oz. can mushrooms
Salt and pepper
1 cup Burgundy wine
1 tablespoon minced green onions (scallions)
1 tablespoon parsley, minced

GUNTHER VENISON ROAST

SALT AND PEPPER VENISON. Place in roaster. Put onion and water on meat and roast 1 hour at 350°. Add more water if necessary.

Take roast out and add 2 more cups of water. Place carrots and potatoes around roast. Mix ½ packet onion soup mix around roast. Place bacon across meat and roast another 2 hours.

Bruce Gunther, Omro

3-4 lbs. venison (can be any cut)
1 large onion
6 carrots
8 medium potatoes
½ package onion soup mix
2 slices bacon

VENISON SCALLOPINE

CUT MEAT IN SERVING PIECES; coat with flour mixture. Fry both sides in hot fat until browned. Add onions, cook 5 minutes. Place in 1½ qt. greased casserole. Add remaining ingredients. Bake at 350° for 2 hours or until tender.

Gail Rigbor, Poy Sippi

2-2½ lbs. venison seasoned with flour, salt, pepper, and paprika
2 medium onions
1 teaspoon sugar
1¼ cup tomato puree
1¼ cup hot water
1 4 oz. can mushrooms
Fat for frying

PAUL'S "MAKE THE JUMPIN' MEAN JUMP HIGH" VENISON CHILI

CUT 4-5 LBS. OF LEAN SHANK, brisket, or bottom round venison into cubes about the size of a dime. Heat this meat in ¼ cup olive oil in a large dutch oven over heat, stirring occasionally until meat is grey and not browned. While the meat is slowly heating and the moisture is disappearing, add the garlic and onions and simmer 10-15 minutes. Then toss in tomatoes, tomato sauce, and malt liquor. Cover and simmer ½ hour. While this is simmering, mix all the remaining ingredients together except the corn flour.

Add this mixture to the meat and cook for 3-4 hours on low heat.

Mix the corn flour with water to make a thin paste, and add to chili just before serving. Top each bowl with 1 heaping tablespoon of chopped sweet Bermuda onion.

Brenda and Paul Ross, Fremont

4-5 lbs. lean venison cubed
1 12 oz. can malt liquor
6 tablespoons chili powder
1 tablespoon ground cumin
1 teaspoon curry powder
2 teaspoons oregano
1 teaspoon seasoning or chef's salt
½ teaspoon cracked or
fresh ground pepper
½ teaspoon cayenne pepper
1 teaspoon paprika (Hungarian Hot is good)
½ teaspoon brown sugar
2 tablespoons corn flour
(or 1 tablespoon flour mixed with 1 tablespoon white corn meal)
1 medium strong onion, minced
4 big cloves garlic finely minced
1 8 oz. can tomato sauce
1 qt. home canned tomatoes
¼ cup home grown dried pulverized hot peppers

HUNTER'S CHILIMAC

BROWN AND DRAIN DEERBURGER. In a large pot, add all ingredients and simmer for 1 hour or until celery is tender. Stir occasionally.

If to be frozen, omit pepper and add later. (It becomes bitter.)

Spencer Anderson, Baraboo

1 lb. deerburger
1 qt. canned tomatoes
2 cans kidney beans
2 stalks celery sliced
1 medium onion, sliced and quartered
2 cups elbow macaroni
2 teaspoons chili powder
1¼ teaspoon salt
¼ teaspoon pepper
1 cup water

WISCONSIN VENISON CHILI

IN A 3 QT. SAUCEPAN OVER medium heat, brown ground venison, onion, and garlic clove; drain off juices. Add remaining ingredients and bring to a boil. Reduce heat to simmer, cover for 1½ hours, stirring occasionally.

Will easily serve 4-6.

Ted Urban, Clintonville

2 lbs. venison (ground)
1 clove garlic chopped
1 medium onion chopped
10-12 fresh mushrooms sliced
1 medium green pepper sliced
1 qt. homemade tomato soup (can substitute 1 16 oz. can of whole tomatoes)
1 8 oz. can tomato paste
1 15 oz. can kidney beans in chili sauce
2 teaspoons salt
1 teaspoon worcestershire sauce
Dash of pepper
Dash of red pepper
2-3 tablespoons chili powder

TEXAS VENISON CHILI

BROWN VENISON IN ¼ CUP vegetable oil. Add onions, garlic, and green pepper cut into strips. Cook 5 minutes, stirring constantly.

Add remaining ingredients and simmer 1½ hours. If a thicker chili is desired, stir in 1 tablespoon flour mixed 2 tablespoons water.

Just before serving, add 2 cups cooked kidney beans. Makes 6-8 servings.

Lori Kramer, Wisconsin Rapids

2 lbs. coarsely ground venison
¼ cup vegetable oil
1 cup chopped onions
2 cloves minced garlic
1 large green pepper cut into strips
3 tablespoons chili powder
2 teaspoons sugar
3½ cups whole tomatoes
1 cup tomato sauce
1 cup water
½ teaspoon salt
2 cups cooked kidney beans

VENISON CHILI

PLACE MEAT, ONIONS, PEPPERS in frying pan and brown. Put rest of ingredients in kettle and simmer all day. Add beans last, just heat until beans are hot and serve.

Gib Dutton, Rochester, MN

3 lbs. of ¼ in. venison cubed or ground
½ onion chopped
1 green pepper cut into cubes
½ bottle chili sauce
2 cans whole tomatoes, drained
¾ stalk chopped celery
1 tablespoon sugar
4 cans kidney beans (or chili beans)
Salt and pepper to taste
Chili powder to taste
1 8 oz. can chopped mushrooms drained

SWAMI'S FAMOUS CHILI

MIX MEAT, GARLIC, ONION in cast iron frying pan and sear until lightly browned. Drain off grease.

In large kettle, put other ingredients and bring to boil. (Leave beans out until heat is lowered.) Add meat. Turn heat down to simmer. Let simmer for 1 hour. Serves 10.

Ed "Swami" Schlumpf, Menomonee Falls

3-4 lbs. ground venison
½ medium onion, chopped
2 cloves garlic, chopped
1 29 oz. can tomato paste
2 15½ oz. cans kidney beans
3 crushed red peppers
1 tablespoon worcestershire sauce
1 teaspoon oregano
1 teaspoon ground cumin
6 teaspoons chili powder
½ cup Open Pit Barbecue Sauce
1 16 oz. can sliced tomatoes
4 cups water

BUSHWACKERS VENISON SOUP

BROWN VENISON IN THE BUTTER. Combine all ingredients in large kettle and add enough water to cover. Over medium-high heat, bring to a light boil. Lower heat and simmer until vegetables are tender, stirring often.

Remove from heat and cool. May be eaten right away, but it will be best when refrigerated overnight and reheated the next day.

Larry Bolchen, Mazomanie

2 lbs. venison cut in 1 in. cubes
1 lb. frozen corn
1 lb. carrots sliced
3 stalks celery sliced
1 lb. potatoes cubed
3 medium onions chopped
1 medium head of cabbage sliced into bite size pieces
5 cans beef bouillon
4 beef bouillon cubes
3 tablespoons butter
1 teaspoon salt
1 teaspoon pepper
1 tablespoon oregano
1 tablespoon basil
4 bay leaves
1½ teaspoons garlic powder
1½ tablespoons sugar

VENISON SOUP

IN DUTCH OVEN OR LARGE KETTLE, brown meat. Pour in 2½ cups water and add vegetables. Cook until all is tender. Add spaghetti. (Tomato juice may be added.)

Gail Nigbor, Poy Sippi

1 lb. ground venison
¾ teaspoons salt and pepper
1 large diced potato
1 cup peas (preferable fresh or frozen, no canned)
1 cup celery chopped
1/3 cup margarine
1/3 cup chopped onion
¼ cup parsley
2-3 medium carrots sliced
1 cup cooked spaghetti

BIG GAME VEGETABLE SOUP

COVER SHANKS WITH WATER and cook until tender at 375°. Remove meat and place in kettle with all vegetables and seasoning. Cook until well done, about 2½ hours.

Kevin Voigt, Onalaska

2 large shanks
1 lb. carrots diced
1 cup onions diced
4 potatoes diced
1 small head cabbage, sliced thin
Salt and pepper
1 large can tomatoes

HUNTER'S SOUP

BOIL THE VENISON FOR 20 minutes, skimming off the foam as it appears. Add the remaining ingredients and simmer for 2 hours.

Ray Baranczyk, Manitowoc

1 venison neck cut into 2-3 in. pieces
2 qts. water
3 tablespoons salt
½ teaspoon pepper
½ teaspoon chili powder
½ head of cabbage
½ lb. carrots
4 average rutabagas or potatoes
4 stalks celery chopped
3 beef bouillon cubes

VENISON DELIGHT

BREAK UP NOODLES IN THE unopened package of Lipton Onion Soup Mix. Keep working until the package feels soft. Trim away all fat and tallow and place remaining meat on a sheet of wax paper and sprinkle flour on both sides. Lightly brown in an oiled frying pan.

Layer in roaster, the meat, onion, and soups. Pour wine over top. Bake at 325° for 3 hours.

There is no need to stir unless the meat is sticking out of the liquid while baking. This recipe makes its own gravy. Serves 6-8.

Kenneth J. Mallak, Wausau

4 lbs. venison steak
1 package Lipton Onion Soup Mix
2 cans mushroom soup
3 medium onions
2½ soup cans Lambrusco wine

TENDER VENISON STEAK

BROWN VENISON IN OIL. Then add soup with ½ can of water. Add basil, onions, and pepper.
  Cover and simmer 1½-2 hours.

Dave Johnson, Neshkoro

2-3 venison steaks
1 can cream soup condensed
(cream of mushroom or celery)
2 teaspoons basil
2 onions chopped
Pepper
Oil

HEARTY VENISON SWISS STEAK

COAT VENISON WITH FLOUR. Brown pieces in shortening in hot skillet. Add remaining ingredients. Stir to mix. Cover and cook over low heat 1-1½ hours stirring occasionally, and adding water if it becomes too thick. Serve with rice.

Carol Bach, Salem

2 lbs. venison cut in serving size pieces
3 tablespoons flour
2 tablespoons shortening
1 large can condensed tomato soup
1/3 cup chopped onion
Garlic to taste
2 tablespoons brown sugar
2 tablespoons worcestershire sauce
2 talbespoons lemon juice or vinegar
2 teaspoons prepared mustard

VENISON SWISS STEAK

TAKE ABOUT 5 ft. OF FOIL 1 in. thick and fold double. Spread mixture of catsup and flour on foil, and put steak on top and season with salt, pepper, and onion and rest of the catsup mixture and squirt lemon juice over it. Fold foil over and crimp tight.
  Grill on a Weber with fire on the sides only, or in the oven (set foil in a roasting pan) bake 1½ hours at 400°.

L.F. Krueger, Fond du Lac

2 lbs. venison round 1 in. thick
1 cup catsup
¼ cup flour
1 large onion sliced
2 tablespoons lemon juice

VENISON SWISS STEAK

DREDGE MEAT WITH FLOUR and season with salt and pepper. Brown in bacon grease or shortening. Add other ingredients. Cover tightly and simmer over low heat for about 1½ hours. Add water if necessary.

Debbie Hoppe, Mukwonago

1½ lbs. venison steak
1 small onion sliced
1 medium stalk celery sliced
1 lb. can tomatoes
2 tablespoons worcestershire sauce
Salt, pepper

STIR-FRIED VENISON STEAK

CUT VENISON STEAK INTO SMALL pieces (as for tenderloin tips). Heat frying pan, add butter, and stir-fry steak to desired doneness.
  Drain small can of sliced mushrooms, and add to steak, season to taste. Add onion rings if you prefer.

Mrs. D.G. Kutcher, Beaver Dam

Venison steak cut in small pieces
Butter
1 small can sliced mushrooms

VENISON STEAK

CUT STEAKS ½ IN. thick, salt and pepper to taste. Sprinkle steaks with flour, Chop steak with french fry cutter and repeat on other side.

Dice onions and green pepper, add mushrooms, and saute in butter.

Fry steaks and garnish with onions, pepper, and mushrooms. Serve with french fries and coleslaw.

Paul Codette, Bayfield

Venison steaks ½ in. thick
Salt, pepper
1 onion diced
1 8 oz. can mushrooms
½ stick butter

VENISON ROULADE

TENDERIZE VENISON ROUND steak by pounding.

Spread horseradish mustard over serving pieces. Over this put slice of bacon, dill pickle, and few slices of onion, garlic salt, salt and pepper. Roll and secure with toothpicks. Brown in hot oil. Remove to platter.

To liquid juice remaining, add wine, water, and mushrooms. Place meat back in frying pan and simmer with cover on until tender. When done, thicken and add ¼ cup sour cram to gravy.

Peter Konopacky, Stevens Point

Venison round steak
Horseradish mustard
Bacon
Dill pickles
Onion slices
Garlic salt
Salt and pepper
Wine
Water
Mushrooms
¼ cup sour cream

VENISON UNIQUE

POUND OUT STEAK AND SEASON with garlic, salt, and pepper. Lay strips of bacon across the steak; place fresh vegetables in center of the steak with tomatoes and cheese. Roll steak up and tie. Cover with juice from tomatoes. Cover and roast at 350° for 2 hours. Makes 6-8 servings. Serve with potatoes or rice.

Judy Debruin, Appleton

3 lbs. venison steak sliced thin and pounded
8 oz. each of onions, celery, carrots, and mushrooms, all diced
4 oz. mozzarella cheese (grated)
1 large can of whole tomatoes (crushed)
6 slices bacon
Garlic
Seasoning

STUFFED VENISON SUPREME

MIX BURGER, ONION, GREEN PEPPER, and bread crumbs to form a stuffing. Spread on steak, covering with another piece of steak around all the edges to seal. Brown under broiler on both sides. Place in roaster with 1 8 oz. can mushrooms, drained, green beans, and carrots. Cover and bake at 350° for 45 minutes.

Mary De Long, Chippewa Falls

2 large venison steaks
½ lb. venison burger
1 onion, diced
1 green pepper, diced
½ cup dried bread crumbs
Salt and pepper
1 8 oz. can mushrooms, drained
1 can green beans
1 can sliced carrots

STUFFED VENISON ROLLS

POUND STEAKS FLAT IN CIRCLES or lengths. Melt butter in small fry pan. Add onions, mushrooms, and celery and saute until tender. Sprinkle sage over bread cubes in medium size bowl. Add onion mixture to bread crumbs and toss. Spread stuffing over steaks. Roll up or fold over. Secure with toothpicks. Brown rolls in butter in large fry pan. Mix gravy mixes with amounts of water specified on pkg. Pour over rolls in fry pan. Cook rolls in gravy until tender. Serve with mashed potatoes. Serves 4.

Jan Jacobson, Madison

3-4 large venison steaks, boneless
2 tablespoons butter

Stuffing

1½ cups day old bread, cubed
1/8 teaspoon pepper
6 tablespoons butter
1 medium onion, chopped
½ cup mushrooms, chopped
1 stalk finely-chopped celery
½ teaspoon sage
2 pkgs. brown gravy mix
Water

VENISON SWISS STEAK

BROWN THE SLICES OF STEAK in bacon grease. Lightly brown the onions and celery, then add the tomato juice, oregano, and spices. Simmer for 1 to 1½ hours until the meat is tender.

Mix the milk, flour, and sugar into a thin paste and pour into the venison to make a thick, rich gravy. Simmer 5 more minutes and serve with mashed potatoes.

Ray Baranczyk, Manitowoc

1 lb. sliced venison round steak
Bacon grease
1 onion, diced
1 celery stalk, diced
1 pint tomato juice
½ teaspoon oregano
1 bay leaf
Salt and pepper to taste
1 cup water
1 cup milk
1 tablespoon flour
½ teaspoon sugar

VENISON ROULADE

CUT VENISON STEAK INTO ¾ in. rectangles and season with salt and pepper. Cut bacon slices in half and place a half slice of onion and bacon on top of meat. Tie with heavy thread or string. Brown in hot oil or margarine.

Add water to the drippings and simmer for at least 2 hours.

The roulades may also be placed in crock pot on low for several hours. Thinly sliced dill pickle may be added to the bacon and onion.

When cooked, removed string and place rolls on a serving plate and thicken juices with corn starch for the gravy.

Mrs. Don Koch, Oshkosh

Venison steak cut into ¾ in. rectangles
Salt and pepper
Bacon slices
Onion slices

VENISON WILD RICE

FRY VENISON IN BUTTER until brown. Add 1 cup water and cook until tender. Add soup, peppers, mushroom soup, water, soy sauce, and wild rice. Cook 30 minutes. Serves 6. Can be served with salad and garlic bread.

Judy Debruin, Appleton

2 lbs. venison steak cut in strips
2 pkgs. onion cup of soup mix
1 can mushroom soup
½ cup chopped green peppers
3 cups water
1 tablespoon soy sauce
1 pkg. Uncle Ben's Grain and Wild Rice Mix

LABELLE'S VENISON SAUTE

SPREAD VENISON STEAKS out in the bottom of a frying pan and warm.

Pour the catsup, steak sauce, tabasco and garlic into a bowl and stir them together. Then pour the mixture into the frying pan, flipping steaks over as the sauce covers the bottom of the pan.

Spread the pepper out evenly over all of the steaks.

Cut onion into rings and spread over the steaks.

Turn the heat to medium but don't fry the steaks; simmer them in the sauce until they're done the way you prefer. You should simmer them until the sauce cooks down to the point where it clings to the meat like a good barbecue sauce.

If you like, mushrooms or peppers can be added to the sauce. Serves 2-4 civilians or 1 mildly-hungry deer hunter.

Wauk Talkradio, Waukesha

2-3 lbs. venison steaks
1 48 oz. bottle catsup
1 small bottle A-1 steak sauce
1 tablespoon black pepper
4 shakes of tabasco
1 medium onion
½ teaspoon garlic

GROUND VENISON GOULASH

BROWN VENISON, ONION, garlic, and celery together and drain. Mix with potatoes and add 1 large can of tomatoes. Bake at 350° for 1 hour.

Heidi Scheinert, Shawano

2 lbs. ground venison
1 medium onion, chopped
1 clove garlic, chopped
2 celery stalks, chopped
1 teaspoon salt
¼ teaspoon pepper
7 potatoes, sliced
1 large can tomatoes

VENISON STROGANOFF

BROWN STEAK CUT INTO strips in shortening. Salt and pepper to taste.

Add rest of ingredients and simmer until done, 30 minutes approximately. Add more wine or water if too thick. Serve over noodles.

Mrs. Ken Radke, Beaver Dam

4 venison steaks cut into strips
1 tablespoon shortening
1 onion
Salt and pepper to taste
1 cup sour cream
1 cup any kind of wine
½ cup water

VENISON STEW

MARINATE 3-4 LBS. OF VENISON roast overnight in mixture of gin and beer. Drain meat, keep marinade. Cut meat into pieces like stew meat. Brown meat in drippings from ½ lb. diced browned salt pork.

Add marinade and vegetables. Add 1 can tomatoes and spices. Simmer several hours until the meat is tender. If desired, diced potatoes and fresh mushrooms may be added.

Serve with rice casserole.

Mary Louise Olson, River Falls

3-4 lbs. venison roast
4 oz. gin
2 bottles beer
1 cup chopped onion
1 cup chopped celery
1 cup chopped carrots
1 clove garlic, diced
½ lb. salt pork drippings
1 can tomatoes
1 teaspoon salt
½ teaspoon pepper
¼ teaspoon oregano
2 bay leaves

SLOW COOKER VENISON STEW

CUT VENISON INTO 1 in. chunks. Roll in flour until coated all around. Cube potatoes, carrots, celery and onions.

Brown venison in oil until half brown. Add 8 pkgs. of Washington Rich Brown Seasoning and brown on all sides until moisture disappears. Add hot water to skillet and simmer for 2 minutes.

Scrape meat and gravy from skillet and add to slow cooker.

Add all vegetables and stir together with meat. Cook on high for 6 hours. Add corn starch to thicken as desired.

Ted Janot, Racine

3 lbs. venison
6 medium potatoes
6 carrots
2 large stalks of celery
1 medium onion
8 pkgs. Washington Rich Brown Seasoning (bouillon)
Cooking oil

CLAY POT VENISON STEW

SOAK CLAY POT and lid in cold water for 10 minutes. In bottom of damp pot, combine venison, onion, celery, garlic, potatoes, and carrots.

In small bowl combine broth, cornstarch, salt, and pepper. Stir until smooth. Add to clay pot with meat. Cover with water soaked lid. Put in microwave on high setting for 15 minutes. Stir and re-cover. Microwave at ½ power (medium) for 45 minutes. Stir and add peas. Re-cover and microwave on ½ power (medium) for 12 minutes or until meat is tender. Let stand covered for 10 minutes before serving. Serves 4-6.

Karen Schmidt, Racine

2 lbs. venison stew meat cut into 1 in. cubes
1 cup chopped onion
½ cup chopped celery
¼ teaspoon garlic powder
2 medium potatoes, cubed
2 carrots, sliced
1 can (10½ oz.) beef broth
2 tablespoons cornstarch
1 teaspoon salt
1/8 teaspoon black pepper
1 can peas

3 GAL VENISON STEW

BROWN MEAT AND bacon in oleo, then add seasonings and onions and water to cover. Simmer until meat is tender. Add more water and celery and cook ½ hour. Add carrots and cook ½ hour. Then add potatoes and canned vegetables and simmer ½ hour.

Serve in bowls with oyster crackers. (Note: always wait until water boils before adding next vegetable.)

John Renard, Green Bay

12 lbs. venison, boneless
½ lb. bacon, diced
1 lb. oleo
2 lbs. onions, diced
2 lbs. potatoes, diced
1 lb. carrots, diced
1 bunch celery, diced
2 cans peas (17 oz.)
1 can whole kernel corn (17 oz.)
1 large can tomato juice (46 oz.)
4½ teaspoons salt
1 tablespoon ground oregano
1 tablespoon pepper
2 bay leaves
2 jars Wyler's Beef Granules

DELUXE VENISON STROGANOFF

IN SKILLET BROWN MEAT AND COOK onion in margarine until tender. Stir in soup, sour cream, and water. Cover and simmer 1 hour or until tender.

Stir often. Serve over noodles. Serves 5.

Mrs. Don Koch, Oshkosh

1 lb. venison steak cut into thin strips
½ cup sliced onion
2 tablespoons margarine or butter
1 can Campbell's Golden Mushroom soup
½ cup sour cream
¼ cup water

BUSY MAN'S VENISON STEW

PLACE THE MEAT IN A crock pot and set on low heat. Add vegetables to meat. Pour the soup over the mixture and add ½ cup water. Cover and allow to cook for 8 hours.

Before serving, prepare rice. Serve stew over rice. Bread or biscuits may be substituted for rice.

Craig Parks, Crivitz

1½ lb. venison stew meat
1 can beefy mushroom soup
3 medium-sized potatoes chopped into thirds
2 carrots, chopped
½ cup water
Precooked rice

VENISON STEW

PUT MEAT IN POT and place on high. Sprinkle flour, salt, and pepper, over meat and mix well.

Add layer of onions, celery, carrots, potatoes. Pour hot water over top and simmer covered for 8-10 hours or until meat and vegetables are tender. Keep warm for serving on low heat.

Mrs. Phyllis Harder, Ripon

1 lb. venison cut in 1 in. cubes
2 tablespoons flour
2 teaspoons salt
½ teaspoon pepper
¼ cup sliced onion
½ cup diced celery
1 cup sliced carrots
1 cup potatoes, cubed
2 cups hot water

VENISON GOULASH

ROLL MEAT IN FLOUR, pressing flour into the cubes. Melt bacon fat in skillet and add onion and garlic. Cook until browned. Add meat and brown well.

Add remaining ingredients except the sour cream. Stir well, cover, and simmer until meat is tender (2-3 hours), adding more stock or water or wine if necessary.

Just before serving, stir in sour cream. Serve with red cabbage cooked with apples, and buttered noodles, or boiled potatoes covered with sour cream.

Shelley Hraychuck, Sayner

2 lbs. venison cut into 1½ in. cubes
3 tablespoons flour
3 tablespoons bacon fat
1 large onion, chopped
2 cloves garlic, minced
1 tablespoon paprika
½ cup red wine
1 qt. boiling water or stock
Salt to taste
1 small can tomato paste
1 cup sour cream

NO PEEK VENISON STEW

MIX TOGETHER WATER, tomato juice or V-8 juice, tapioca, sugar, salt, and pepper. Pour over meat and vegetables in a tightly-covered casserole. Bake at 250° for 4 hours. Do not peek or raise lid!

Mrs. Charles Booth, Waupaca

2 lbs. venison stew meat (cut up)
2 onions, chopped
8 carrots, chopped
2 potatoes, chopped
2 celery stems, chopped
1 4 oz. can drained mushrooms
½ cup water
½ cup tomato juice or V-8
4 tablespoons tapioca
2 teaspoons sugar
Salt and pepper

VENISON LENTIL STEW

COOK AND STIR MEAT, onion and garlic in dutch oven until meat is brown. Drain off fat. Stir in mushrooms (with liquid) and remaining ingredients; heat to boiling. Reduce heat; cover, and simmer, stirring occasionally, until lentils and meat are tender, about 40 minutes. Remove bay leaf before serving.

Marilyn Benish, Yuba

1 lb. cubed or ground venison
1 medium onion, chopped
1 clove garlic, minced
1 can (4 oz.) mushroom
stems and pieces
1 can (16 oz.) stewed tomatoes
1 stalk celery, sliced
1 large carrot, sliced
1 cup uncooked lentils
3 cups water
¼ cup red wine
1 bay leaf
2 tablespoons snipped parsley
2 teaspoons salt
1 teaspoon instant beef bouillon
¼ teaspoon pepper

FIRE-HOUSE STEW

MELT BUTTER IN PAN. Flour venison and brown. Put meat in roaster and pour drippings over meat. Sprinkle lightly with worcestershire sauce. Spread pack of onion soup mix over meat. Add vegetables over meat. Add water to the top of vegetables and add 1 beef bouillon cube, cover and roast in oven at 275° for 3 hours. To thicken gravy, use cornstarch and water. Serves 4-6.

Jim Bruckner, Appleton (Appleton Fire Dept.)

2-2½ lbs. venison stew meat trimmed in 1-2 in. cubes
5-6 potatoes, chopped
5-6 carrots, chopped
5-6 stalks celery, chopped
2 medium onions, chopped
1 pkg. onion soup mix
Flour
Butter (1 stick)
Worcestershire sauce (optional)
1 beef bouillon cube

THE BEST EVER VENISON STEW

BROWN VENISON IN HOT bacon grease. Sprinkle with flour. Combine and heat separately the garlic, onion, bouillon, tomato sauce, pepper, cloves, parsley, bay leaf, and wine. Add meat, potatoes, carrots, and celery. Simmer covered 2-3 hours.

Gretchen Larson, West Salem

¼ cup bacon grease
1½ - 2 lbs. venison cut into stewing size pieces
2 cloves garlic, chopped
1 onion chopped
1 cup beef bouillon
1 cup canned tomato sauce
12 peppercorns
3 whole cloves
¼ cup chopped parsley
1/3 bay leaf
½ cup dry white wine or cooking sherry
6 medium-sized pared, quartered potatoes
6 pared quartered carrots
1 stalk celery, chopped

SPECIAL VENISON DISH

SHAKE VENISON IN FLOUR to coat and brown in oil and margarine. Brown onions with the venison. Transfer to roaster, crock pot, or stew kettle.

Mix according to directions: Swiss Steak seasoning, and hamburger seasoning (brown gravy). Do not use salt as the seasonings are salty.

Pour rest of ingredients over the browned meat and onions and simmer covered 1½-2 hours. Stir often. Serve over cooked rice.

Velma Bray, Fennimore

3 lbs. venison roast cut into cubes
Flour
Oil and margarine
2 medium onions, cubed
1 pkg. Swiss Steak seasoning
Hamburger seasoning (brown gravy)
Red, black or lemon pepper
Garlic powder
Basil
(a dash or two of the spices)
¼ cup cooking wine
1 tablespoon soy sauce
Kitchen Bouquet (a little)
La Choy gravy sauce (a little)
1 can drained mushrooms

HUNTER'S DELIGHT

BROWN MEAT. ADD SOUP, then remaining ingredients. Cook macaroni and add to meat mixture. Cook about ½ hour over low heat to flavor.

Gail Nigbor, Poy Sippi

1½-2 lbs. ground venison
Salt and pepper to taste
1 can tomato soup
1 can whole corn (6 oz. frozen)
1 can green peas (4 oz. frozen)
¼-½ teaspoon sweet basil
¼ teaspoon oregano
1 onion, chopped
1 stalk celery, chopped
1 cup macaroni

CANNED VENISON AND VEGETABLES OVER NOODLES

DISSOLVE BOUILLON CUBE in boiling water, add to venison in medium-sized sauce pan. Heat to boiling, thicken, add mixed vegetables, mushrooms, and seasonings. Heat. Serve over cooked egg noodles.

C. Bison, Appleton

1 cup boiling water
1 beef bouillon cube
1 pint canned venison
Thickening (cornstarch or flour paste)
1 can mixed vegetables, drained
1 can sliced mushrooms (4 oz.), drained
Salt, pepper, parsley, soy sauce, etc. to taste
Wide egg noodles

CANNED VENISON STEW

FOLLOW RECIPE AS ABOVE, except omit mixed vegetables and noodles. Add potatoes, peas, carrots, and onions. Heat, serve with hot rolls or fresh bread.

C. Bison, Appleton

1 lb. canned small whole potatoes, drained
1 8 oz. can small early peas
1 8 oz. can carrots, drained
10-12 small cooked onions

VENISON HAMBURGER TACOS

BROWN VENISON. ADD ONIONS, green pepper to venison.

Put Tacos together as you would hamburger tacos and add all your favorite toppings. Serves 4.

Mrs. Elaine Olson, Racine

1½ lbs. ground venison
1 or more pkgs. flour or corn taco shells
Chopped onion, green pepper, tomatoes
Shredded cheese (any kind)
Shredded lettuce
Black olives
Sour cream
Hot sauce or Salsa sauce

VENISON HAMBURGER BAKE DISH

BROWN VENISON IN BUTTER, add onions.

Cook macaroni in salted water, drain well.

Add macaroni to venison along with the next 5 ingredients. Mix. Simmer at medium heat for 10 minutes.

You may transfer all ingredients to casserole dish and bake at 325° for 30 minutes. Add more milk if it gets dry. Serves 4.

Mrs. Elaine Olson, Racine

1 lb. ground venison
1 medium onion, chopped fine
1 box shell macaroni
1 cup mushrooms, sliced thin
1 can green beans or corn or peas
(any can vegetables you prefer)
2 cans tomato soup (or 1 can tomatoes and 1 can mushroom soup)
1 cup milk
Salt and pepper

VENISON GOULASH

BROWN MEAT IN HOT FAT. Add minced garlic, sliced onions, seasonings, bouillon cubes, and hot water. Cover and simmer until done. More water can be added if necessary.

Thicken as desired with cornstarch or flour dissolved in cold water. Serve over rice or cooked noodles. Canned vegetables may be added just before serving.

Florence Burhans, Horicon

1 lb. venison in 1 in. cubes
1 clove garlic, minced
2 medium onions, sliced
2 teaspoons paprika
1 teaspoon salt
1/8 teaspoon pepper
2 beef bouillon cubes
2 cups boiling water

GAME BIRDS
Chapter Three

Preparation of game birds presents a problem to most cooks. Guests on occasion will gasp, shove their hand(s) in their mouths and come out with all or part of a tooth busted loose from its moorings by the act of chomping down on a #6 chill shot.

All sorts of unpleasantness will develop. Attorneys will serve summonses and complaints. Insurance company claim department executives will turn pale and spend endless nights tossing and turning because of the possibility of having to pay a claim.

But such annoyances can be avoided with the exercise of a modicum of planning. For example, you might take a flat toothpick (a round one won't work), stick it in the BB hole in the duck, twist it around and pull it out. You'll pull out feathers pushed into the duck by the BB and you might retrieve the shot, too. And getting these feathers out of the duck is as important as eliminating the BB.

Ducks have a gland over their tail which exudes an oily substance. When they shake their tails, they are producing a supply of that oil which coats their feathers and makes water run off their backs, almost exactly like water off a duck's back, but not quite.

The oil is not good to eat. (Otherwise folks would eat the feathers and throw the duck away.) But, you may not get all of the shot out of the bird as you are "toothpicking" the feathers.

SMALL BIRD HASH PATTIES

BLEND FLOUR INTO melted butter and add the onion juice, chicken consomme, and cream. Simmer for 1 minute while stirring. Add the meat and wine and bring to a simmer. Serve in either pastry shells or on toast.

Mary Scott, Manawa

2 cups cooked and diced meat from any gamebirds
4 tablespoons flour
4 tablespoons butter
2 teaspoons onion juice
½ cup chicken consomme
½ cup cream
½ cup white wine

SOUR CREAMED WILD FOWL

CLEAN BIRDS, PLACE A slice of fat or bacon over the breast. Bind in place and tie legs tightly to the body.

Brown butter in an iron pan and fry the birds thoroughly, turning constantly so that they are well browned on all sides.

Add water, simmer 15 minutes. Add milk. Allow birds to simmer in the sauce another 3-3½ hours with lid over the pan. Let steam escape. The birds are pot roasted, not boiled.

They should be tender and the meat easily loosened from the bone when ready. During the last half hour, add sour cream. The more the better until sauce is thickened to give it flavor.

Gib Dutton, Rochester, MN

Gamebirds
Bacon or fat
¼ pint boiling water
1 pint boiling milk
Sour cream

GAMEBIRDS

PUT ONION, WINE, WATER and birds (breast down) in cooking bag in a 9x13 in. pan for 3 hours at 250°. Cool, cut bag open, bone meat from body of bird, cut legs and wings off and place in a large ovenware pan. (Slice the breast in serving size pieces.)

Cover with soup and milk, enough to cover meat well. This helps to keep your meat moist.

Refrigerate overnight and return to the oven for 1 or 1½ hours at 250°.

Marjorie Hausen, Wautoma

1 large goose, or 2 small geese, pheasants, ducks, partridge, or woodcock
1 large onion, cut up
1 cup sherry wine
2 cups water
3 cans cream of celery soup
1½ cans milk (½ can milk to every can of soup)

WILD DUCK IN ORANGE JUICE

CLEAN DUCKS AND RUB with salt, paprika, pepper and ground ginger. Place in roasting pan and bake in a 400° oven for one hour.

Remove from rack and drain off fat. Return to oven and pour over mixture made up of orange juice, currant jelly and lemon juice. Baste often and bake until tender.

Robert Blair, Beaver Dam

One duck per person
INGREDIENTS PER DUCK:
2 teaspoons salt
½ teaspoon paprika
1/8 teaspoon pepper
½ teaspoon ground ginger
2 cups orange juice
1 tablespoon currant jelly
1 teaspoon lemon juice

ESCALLOPED DUCK

COVER 3 WILD DUCKS with water and cook until tender, almost 2 hours. Remove meat from bones and cut into ½ in. pieces. Place meat in 3 qt. casserole.

Soak 1 cup wild rice overnight and wash until rinse water is clear. Combine with 4 cups dried bread cubes. Add rest of ingredients and mix. Place on top of duck.

Melt butter and add rest of ingredients. Pour over duck. Bake at 350° for 1 hour. Makes a large batch and freezes well.

Mrs. Don Koch, Oshkosh

3 wild ducks
1 cup wild rice
4 cups dried bread cubes
¾ cup melted butter
1 teaspoon sage
1 teaspoon salt
1 teaspoon pepper
1 small grated onion
1 (8 oz.) can mushrooms

Sauce

¼ cup butter
¼ cup flour
4 cups chicken broth (may use bouillon cubes in water)

EASY DUCK

ADD SALAD OIL to skillet, then brown flour coated duck pieces. Add remaining ingredients and simmer for 1½ to 2 hours or until tender. Serves 4.

Ken Tomaszewski, Janesville

2 large roasting ducks (cut into serving-size pieces)
Flour
½ cup salad oil
1½ cups white wine
1 bay leaf
2 small onions, peeled and stuck with 2 cloves in each
½ teaspoon salt
3 tablespoons fresh chopped parsley
6 peppercorns crushed

CRANBERRY DUCK

MELT MARGARINE. Brown onion and duck. Stir in cranberry sauce. Simmer 1½ hours. Serve with mashed potatoes.

Dave and Shelley Hraychuck, Sayner

2 ducks cut into serving-size pieces
1 can whole cranberry sauce
1 onion
1 stick margarine

ROAST WILD DUCK DELUXE

COVER DUCK WITH WATER, add salt and vinegar. Let soak for 1-2 hours. Combine remaining ingredients, except bacon, with a small amount of milk. Stuff duck with dressing. Place in roaster. Sprinkle with salt and pepper and place bacon on duck's breast. Add ¼ cup water. Bake at 400° for 2 hours. (Baste with liquid or red wine.) Serves 3-4.

Lloyd Recore, Valders

2 tablespoons salt
2 tablespoons vinegar
2½ lb. wild duck
Pepper to taste
1½ cup sage and onion stuffing
¼ cup chopped apple
½ cup pork sausage
1 small onion, chopped
Milk
2 slices bacon

ROAST WILD DUCK

WASH AND PAT DRY ducks. Sprinkle each cavity with salt, pepper, and rosemary leaves, outside, too.

Place half of the onion, apple, and celery in each cavity. Place breast side up in roasting pan.

Pour the orange juice over ducks. Cover and bake 1½ hours at 350° or until done. Uncover and bake 15-20 minutes longer to brown. Split ducks and discard stuffing.

Sue Ziegler, Pewaukee

2 mallards
1 teaspoon salt
½ teaspoon pepper
¼ teaspoon rosemary leaves
1 medium onion cut into 8ths
1 apple cut into 8ths
2 stalks celery, chopped
1½ cups orange juice

DUCK SOUP

BOIL INGREDIENTS for 20-30 minutes until noodles are tender. Salt and pepper to season.

Christina Syverson, Tomah

2 cups duck meat strips cooked
1 cup chopped celery
½ cup onions, diced
1 pkg. egg roll noodles, or homemade noodles

BARBECUED WILD DUCK

MULTIPLY THE INGREDIENT AMOUNTS by the number of ducks to be cooked. Combine all ingredients and warm over low heat. Use whole duck breast with bone, with or without skin. Salt and pepper breasts. Broil for 15 - 20 minutes, basting every few minutes. Save some sauce to use when eating. Serve with wild rice and salad.

Greg Allen, Chippewa Falls

Duck breasts
BARBECUE SAUCE:

2 teaspoons prepared mustard
1 teaspoon tomato catsup
1 teaspoon Worcestershire sauce
1 tablespoon butter

STEWED DUCK

PLUCK, CLEAN, WIPE AND disjoint neatly, a couple of ducks. Cover the bottom of a sauce pan with thin slices of fat salt pork. Add a little pepper and lay in the pieces of duck on top of the pork. Then add another layer of salt pork on top of the duck. Cover the top layer of meat with sliced onions and fit a tight lid over the pan. Cook over a low heat until the meat is tender. This will take two and one half to three hours for young birds and up to four hours for old birds.

Take the meat out of the pot and keep hot. Strain the gravy and add a half teaspoon of powdered sage, a teaspoon of currant jelly, a tablespoon of browned flour, and a pinch of parsley. Boil the whole up sharply and pour it over the duck.

Cliff Rauscher, Green Bay

Fat salt pork
2 ducks
Pepper
½ teaspoon powdered sage
1 teaspoon currant jelly
1 tablespoon browned flour
Pinch of parsley
Onions, sliced

BARBECUE DUCK

CLEAN AND SOAK DUCKS overnight in water (to cover ducks), salt, vinegar, and baking soda. Rinse well and dry off on paper towels. Rub salt and pepper on ducks, brown on both sides with Crisco shortening.

Combine all ingredients for sauce. Pour over ducks. Cook in slow oven 2-2½ hours.

Shirley Peterson, Wausau

Ducks
Salt, vinegar, baking soda

Barbecue Sauce

¼ cup Mazola oil
1 cup chopped onion
1 8 oz. can tomato sauce
½ cup water
¼ cup brown sugar
¼ cup lemon juice
3 tablespoons worcestershire sauce
2 tablespoons prepared mustard
2 tablespoons salt
¼ teaspoon pepper

FRIED DUCK

PLUCK AND CLEAN several ducks. Fill the body cavity of each with one raw carrot and parboil them until the meat comes off the bones freely.

Cut the meat into neat pieces. Make a batter of beaten eggs and fine bread crumbs, seasoned with salt, pepper, nutmeg, add a few sprigs of parsley. Dip the pieces of meat into the batter and fry in a hot fat until the pieces are golden brown.

If gravy is desired, take that from some previous meal, flavor with mushrooms and pour over the meat. This will make a delicious breakfast dish.

Cliff Rauscher, Green Bay

FOR EACH DUCK USE:

1 raw carrot
Eggs
Bread crumbs
Salt & pepper
Nutmeg
Parsley sprigs

QUICK ORANGE GLAZE FOR DUCKS

COMBINE ALL INGREDIENTS in a pot. Cook over high heat stirring constantly until mixture comes to a boil. Reduce heat and simmer until thickened and clear.

Dip meat in glaze in serving dish or just pour sauce over ducks before serving.

Especially good with mallards.

Mrs. Al Zierden, Shawano

3 teaspoons Tang (instant orange drink)
1 cup hot water
1/3 cup brown sugar
1/3 cup white sugar
1 tablespoon corn starch
¼ teaspoon salt

BAKED DUCK

CLEAN, WIPE AND DRY the ducks. Then brown them in butter in a hot skillet. Insert a whole raw onion into the body cavity of each and place them in a roaster. Pour a large cupful of red wine into the pan. Bake the birds for about one hour in a moderate oven (350°F.). Baste the birds often during the baking period to insure that the meat doesn't become too dry.

Cliff Rauscher, Green Bay

Butter
1 onion
1 cup red wine

SUPER ROAST WILD DUCK

CLEAN, WASH, AND dry ducks. Season well with salt and pepper inside and outside. Roll in flour, be sure breast is well coated.

Fry in bacon or pork drippings, slowly until crust is formed. (This rids fat from under skin.)

Make dressing by frying pork and then adding ground-up ingredients. Season well with salt and pepper and G. Washington (Rich Brown). Add to bread that has been soaked and squeezed out. Stuff ducks and bake at 250° for 2 hours. Raise heat to 300° for 1-1½ hours more. (use roaster with cover.)

Mrs. Charles Miller, Menasha

Ducks
Salt, pepper
Flour
Bacon or pork drippings

Dressing

1 lb. ground pork
8 cups dried bread or croutons
2 large onions, ground up
3 stalks celery, ground up
Gizzards and hearts (cooked)
2 packets of G. Washington
(Rich Brown)

POTTED DUCKS

CLEAN, WASH WELL, and truss the ducks without stuffing, tying down the legs and wings with tape.

Fry one half dozen strips of fat salt pork until they are crisp in a broad bottomed pot, adding one half of a sliced onion, and one half a teaspoon of sage. Lay the ducks in the pot and cover with warm, not hot water. Put a tight lid on the pot and cook very slowly and steadily for three hours.

Take the ducks out of the pot and undo the tapes. Lay them on a hot dish. Strain the gravy and thicken with brown flour. Boil up sharply and pour a little over the ducks and the rest can be served separately. Tart jelly will go well with this dish.

Cliff Rauscher, Green Bay

6 strips fat salt pork
½ onion, sliced
½ teaspoon sage
Brown flour

DEVILED DUCK

BOIL OR ROAST A DUCK and let it become cool. Remove the skin and bones and cut the meat into bite size pieces.

Boil the livers of the ducks and mash them up until a smooth paste is formed. Put the paste in a sauce pan with one tablespoon of dry mustard, one teaspoon of salt, a dash of cayenne pepper, and the juice of one lemon. Mix thoroughly, add two tablespoons of melted butter and one quarter cup of water. Mix well. To this mixture, add one and one half pints of cold duck. Place the sauce pan over a moderate heat and stir the mixture until it is smoking hot. Pour the whole out on a hot dish and garnish with sliced lemon and sprigs of parsley.

Cliff Rauscher, Green Bay

1 tablespoon dry mustard
1 teaspoon salt
Dash of cayeene pepper
Juice of one lemon
2 tablespoons melted butter

BROILED WILD DUCK

CLEAN, SPLIT DOWN THE back, and dry ducks. (Teal and small ducks are left whole.) Rub with olive oil. Sprinkle with salt and pepper. Lay skin side down on rack. Broil at 350° for 15-20 minutes or until done.

Turn several times to brown evenly. Serve with lemon butter.

Gib Dutton, Rochester, MN

Ducks
Olive oil
Salt and pepper

Lemon Butter

¼ cup butter
Grating of lemon rind
2 teaspoons lemon juice
Beat butter, grating of lemon rind, and lemon juice. (Lime or orange rind and juice may be substituted.)

CLASSIC HUNTER'S SAUCE FOR WILD DUCK

COMBINE IN SMALL SAUCEPAN ½ cup red currant jelly; ¼ cup each Port wine and catsup; ½ teaspoon Worcestershire sauce and 2 tablespoons butter. Melt over low heat, serve warm.

Makes 1 cup.

Howard Kohlhepp, Chippewa Falls

FRED'S WILD DUCK

PREPARE STOVE TOP DRESSING, adding ½ cup Wild Rice Stuffing mix.

Remove from stove, add apple, onion, and mushrooms, salt and pepper.

Stuff ducks and place in cooking bag. Add Vermouth. Place in roasting pan and roast at 325° for 2½-3 hours or until tender.

Fred Hoekstra, Lake Villa, IL

2 ducks
1 box Stove Top Dressing (chicken flavor)
1 box Uncle Ben's Wild Rice Stuffing Mix
1 diced onion
1 thin sliced apple
1 can mushroom stems and pieces, drained
Salt and pepper
1½ cups sweet Vermouth
Cooking bag

DUCK A LA CREOLE

MELT BUTTER AND MIX in flour. Stir in ham, onion, celery, pepper, and parsley. Season with salt, pepper, and paprika. Stir for 2 minutes. Add consomme. Simmer for 1 hour. Strain, and add the cold roast duck.

Cook just long enough to heat thoroughly. Serve over hominy, mush, rice, or toast.

Karen Schmidt, Racine

2 tablespoons butter
1 tablespoon flour
2 tablespoons finely chopped ham
2 tablespoons finely chopped onion
2 tablespoons finely chopped celery
2 tablespoons finely chopped sweet peppers
2 tablespoons finely chopped parsley
1 cup consomme
2 cups cold roast duck cut into cubes

ROAST WILD DUCK OR GOOSE

CLEAN BIRD AND WIPE dry; rub inside with salt and place medium onion or apple in cavity. Tie and place on rack in roaster, rub surface with oil, lay slices of bacon over breast. Salt and pepper. Bake uncovered in slow oven 350° until done. (15-20 minutes per pound.)

Bake duck ½ to 1 hour (goose 1-2 hours), basting often. Remove bird to hot platter and serve with gravy made from drippings and stock made from giblets.

Gib Dutton, Rochester, MN

Duck or goose
Salt
1 medium onion or apple
Bacon slices

DUCK STEW with DUMPLINGS

CLEAN AND CUT UP THREE DUCKS. Put the pieces in a stewing pot with two cut up onions, a crumbled bay leaf, one whole clove, ten cracked peppercorns, one tablespoon of salt, and two quarts of water. Bring the whole to a boil, reduce the heat, cover the pot, and simmer for one and one half hours. Add six more quartered onions, cook for fifteen minutes more, add six cut up carrots and two cut up stalks of celery. Simmer for another fifteen minutes.

Remove the ducks and vegetables and keep them warm. Strain the broth and return it to the pot. Add enough water so that there is four cups of broth in all. Mix one half cup of flour with one half cup of water and stir it into the broth. Cook, stirring constantly until the gravy is thickened. Add the ducks again to the pot along with the cooked vegetables. To this add one cup of peas, cover and simmer for five minutes. Mix one third of a cup of milk, two tablespoons of butter, and one cup of sifted self-rising cake flour. When the flour is dampened, form into little balls and drop them into the pot. Cover the pot and simmer for fifteen minutes.

Cliff Rauscher, Green Bay

3 ducks
2 onions, diced
bay leaf, crumbled
1 whole clove
10 peppercorns, cracked
1 tablespoon salt
6 onions, quartered
6 carrots, diced
2 stalks celery, diced
½ cup flour
1 cup peas
1/3 cup milk
2 tablespoons butter
1 cup sifted self-rising cake flour

ROASTED WILD DUCK

CLEAN, WIPE AND DRY the ducks. Sprinkle generously with flour, salt and pepper. Place whole peeled onion inside each duck and place them in self-basting roaster. Fasten with toothpicks 2 or 3 strips of bacon across each bird. If desired, ducks may be stuffed with wild rice dressing made by boiling rice (wild) and seasoning with salt, pepper and chopped onion. Cover bottom of roaster with water. Cover tightly and roast in oven at 350°for 1½ to 2 hours, depending on the number for last 15 - 20 minutes, before taking from oven to allow skin to brown.

Alma E. Morton, Madison

Flour
Salt & pepper
Onion (whole - peeled)
Bacon (2 - 3 strips)
Wild Rice dressing (optional)

ROAST WILD DUCK

RUB INSIDE OF BIRD with salt. Place breast up on rack in shallow pan. Brush with salad oil or lay bacon over breast.

Pour boiling water in pan. Add celery and onion. Roast at 350° 20 minutes per pound. Baste frequently with pan drippings. (If duck has had a fish diet, or if bird isn't young, stuff loosely with carrot or peeled potato, simmer in water for 10 minutes, discard stuffing, then roast.)

Jim Tilkens

Duck
Salad oil
Bacon
2 cups boiling water
Celery, chopped
Onion, chopped

TEMPTING, TENDER TEAL IN CREAM SAUCE

CLEAN 4 TEAL AND LEAVE whole. Rub outsides with Wesson Oil. Place in oven and broil briefly.

Take out and salt and pepper and place back in oven for approximately 10 minutes at 450°.

Brown onion in pan on top of stove, add rest of ingredients. Place ducks and mixture and carrots in pan and cover with foil. Cook at 325° for 2-2½ hours or until tender. Serves 4.

Janine S. Zeutschel, Menomonie

4 teal
Salt
Pepper
Wesson Oil
1 medium onion
1 can Cream of Mushroom soup
1 can Cream of Celery soup
¾ can water
¼ to ½ cup Sherry
¼ teaspoon sage
¼ teaspoon rosemary
¼ teaspoon thyme
4 carrots

MALLARD WITH ORANGE/MUSTARD SAUCE

CUT 2 MALLARDS IN HALF through the breast and brown in a dutch oven over medium high heat, in olive oil.

Combine ingredients and cook over medium heat for 15-20 minutes and then pour over the ducks, and bake at 300° for 1-1½ hours. Baste at least every half-hour.

Remove ducks to warming tray. Add blended corn starch and water to meat drippings, and stir for 10 minutes to make sauce. (There should be enough heat retained in dutch oven to lightly cook properly.)

Pour over ducks and garnish with braised oranges.

Brenda and Paul Ross, Fremont

2 mallards — olive oil
1 tablespoon olive oil
¼ cup strong orange juice
1½ tablespoons soy sauce
1 tablespoon Dijon Mustard
1½ teaspoons Orange Blossom Honey (Clover is 2nd choice)
1½ teaspoons finely minced ginger root
1 garlic clove crushed
1/8 teaspoon cracked or freshly ground pepper

FRIED DUCK BREASTS

CUT SKINNED BREASTS into slices about 1/8 in. thick. Add dash of flavor salt and a sprinkling of cornmeal or flour. Cook on flat, solid griddle or in lightly-greased frying pan for about 10 minutes on each side and serve hot. (You may use flour instead of cornmeal.)

Mary Scott, Manawa

Skinned duck breasts
Flavor salt
Butter or bacon fat
Flour or cornmeal

DUCK OR GOOSE

SEASON CAVITY WITH SALT and pepper and Lawry's Seasoned Salt. Put 3-4 prunes per duck, (double for goose), wedges of apple, apricot, and butter in cavity.

Rub breast with salt, pepper, and Lawry's. Use Ginger Ale or 7-Up for moisture. Cook uncovered at 400° for 20-30 minutes. Baste with melted butter.

Cover roaster and reduce heat to 300°. Baste every 20 minutes.

During last ½ hour of roasting pour orange juice concentrate over duck.

Herb Behnkl, Shawano

Duck or goose
Salt, pepper, and Lawry's
Seasoned Salt
3-4 prunes
Apple wedges
Apricot pieces
½ stick butter
Ginger Ale or 7-Up
1 stick melted butter (for basting)
1 can orange juice concentrate

DUCK SUPREME

SEASON DUCKS WITH Nature's Seasons, or salt and pepper. Brown in a little oil in electric fry pan.

Add soups and 1 can water. Cover and simmer 1 hour.

Scrub potatoes and carrots, and chop and add to pan. Cover and simmer 1 hour or until tender. Add more water as needed.

Venison can be used in place of ducks.

Mike Berger, Kewaskum

2 wild ducks, quartered
1 can Campbell's Golden Mushroom soup
1 envelope Lipton Onion soup
Morton Nature's Seasons
Small red potatoes
Carrots

(SCOTER) OR COOT STEW

SKIN (REMOVING ALL ADHERING FAT) two coots and cut out breast and legs and thighs.

Prepare a large pot, preferably of thick iron with a heavy cover, with the following:
6 egg-sized onions, 5 carrots (cut in 1-inch sections), 5 diced tomatoes (peeled), 1 hefty pinch of marjoram, 2 tablespoons chopped parsley, 1 tablespoon of salt, 1 teaspoon of pepper, 2 bay leaves. Add 1 quart of water and 3 tablespoons of wine or cider vinegar. Bring to a simmer. Then salt and pepper the coots, dredge sections thoroughly with flour, and brown in a large skillet with 1/8 pound of butter. Tilt browned coot sections and butter gravy (thinned and simmer very slowly in covered pot for about 2 hours or until coot is tender.) Do not be misled by the popular superstition that "coot will not get tender", it will.
Ron Sarauer, Kewaskum

2 coots
6 onions
5 carrots , cut in 1" sections
5 tomatoes, diced
1 hefty pinch of marjoram
2 tablespoons chopped parsley
1 tablespoon salt
1 teaspoon pepper
2 bay leaves
3 tablespoons wine or cider vinegar
Flour
1/8 lb. butter

ROAST COOT

SOAK COOTS IN SALT WATER overnight. Cut bacon into squares and fry until done. Add onions. Add the birds and pot roast until brown. Add dash of whole spices. When nearly done, add a small bottle of grape juice and cook slowly uncovered until birds are tender.

Louis A. Loboda, New Lisbon

4 coots (mudhens),skinned and cleaned
5 strips bacon
2 chopped onions
Dash whole spices
Small bottle of grape juice

HUNTER'S STYLE GOOSE

MIX FLOUR, SALT, AND PEPPER together; lightly roll the goose in the mixture. Heat the oil in a deep skillet. Saute the onion and goose until well browned.

Add the tomatoes, green pepper, jalepeno peppers, oregano and wine. Cover and cook over low heat 50 minutes or until the goose is tender.

Skim the fat, then taste for seasoning. (This recipe can also be used with pheasant or duck.)

Mrs. Maureen Steele, Fond du Lac

3 tablespoons flour
1½ teaspoon salt
½ teaspoon pepper
½ goose, disjointed, or 1 duck or pheasant (about 4 lbs. of meat)
1 tablespoon olive oil
1 onion, chopped
2 cups canned tomatoes
1 green pepper, chopped
¼ teaspoon dried oregano
¼ cup dry white wine
1-2 jalepeno peppers (optional)

FRIED GOOSE

SKIN 1-3 GOOSE BREASTS and cut meat into ¼ in. strips. Place meat in 1-2 quarts boiling water and add salt and vinegar. Boil 20-30 minutes, rinse, and lightly roll strips in flour and garlic and onion salt to taste.

Dip into batter and fry until golden brown.

Dean Dasher, Neenah

1-3 goose breasts
¼ cup salt
2 tablespoons vinegar
1 cup flour
Garlic and onion salt to taste

Batter

1 cup flour
1 teaspoon baking powder
½ teaspoon salt
1 egg
1 cup milk
¼ cup vegetable oil

ROAST GOOSE

STUFF THE GOOSE WITH THE FOLLOWING: three pints of bread crumbs, one quarter pound of butter, one teaspoon of sage, one teaspoon of black pepper, one teaspoon of salt, and one chopped onion. Do not stuff too full. Stitch the openings together in order to keep the flavor in and the fat out.

Place the stuffed goose in a baking pan with a little water. Roast in a 425°F. oven, basting frequently with salt and water, and turning often so that the sides and back are nicely browned. The goose should be allowed to roast twenty-five minutes for every pound of bird.

After the goose has been roasting for one hour, the oven should be allowed to cool and the rest of the roasting should be done in a 350°F. oven for the remainder of the roasting time.

The goose should be served with giblet gravy and apple sauce. When roasting a young small bird, fifteen minutes per pound of roasting will be sufficient.

Cliff Rauscher, Green Bay

1 goose
3 pints of bread crumbs
¼ lb. butter
1 teaspoon sage
1 teaspoon black pepper
1 teaspoon salt
1 onion, chopped

ORIENTAL GOOSE

MARINADE GOOSE OR DUCK in Teriyaki sauce for 3 hours.

Make sauce for basting. Mix all ingredients in sauce pan and heat to blend.

Roast at 350° until bird is tender, basting often to keep moist.

For sauce to serve with bird, pour drippings off bird, add water, and 1 can of mushrooms, and flour to thicken.

Gerald Lahner, Eau Claire

Sauce for basting

1 cup pineapple juice
½ cup soy sauce
2 teaspoons ginger
½ bottle brown gravy sauce
1 stick margarine
1 teaspoon garlic powder
1/3 cup cooking sherry
4 tablespoons sugar

Sauce for serving

1 can mushrooms
Flour to thicken

WILD GOOSE WITH WILD RICE AND BREAD STUFFING

CLEAN GOOSE, AND SALT inside and outside. If skinned, omit salt on outside and lay bacon strips over breast and leg meat.

Prepare stuffing; wash and drain rice. In medium-size sauce pan, dissolve bouillon cube in boiling water. Add rice, cover tightly and simmer 40-50 minutes. Drain, reserve liquid.

Saute celery and onion in butter until tender, add to rice.

Lightly brown sausage or ground beef in skillet, drain excess fat.

Combine reserved liquid, egg, and ½ cup milk, add with remaining ingredients to rice mixture. Mix well. Add extra milk only if stuffing is too stiff.

Stuff goose, remainder of stuffing can be baked in a covered casserole for 1 hour at 325°.

Place goose in roasting pan that has ½ cup oleo spread on the bottom. Cover and bake at 350° for 4-6 hours, depending on size and age of bird. (If unsure, allow more time, goose can be kept warm in oven.) Baste with oleo during roasting, and add water as needed to keep from cooking dry. Juices from pan can be used for gravy.

C. Beson, Appleton

1 goose

Stuffing

1 chicken bouillon cube
1½ cup water
½ cup raw wild rice
½ cup chopped celery
½ cup chopped onion
¼ cup butter or oleo
¼ lb. pork sausage or ground beef
½ cup chopped apple (if desired)
1 can (5 oz.) sliced mushrooms
½ teaspoon salt and sage
¼ teaspoon pepper
2 tablespoons soy sauce
2½-3 cups sage and onion dressing mix
½ to 1 cup milk
1 egg

WILD GOOSE FILLET

FILLET BREAST AND LEGS. Fry in bacon grease. Cover with sliced onions.

Mix together ingredients and pour over goose. Cover and simmer 1½ hours or until done.

Add about 1 cup sliced fresh mushrooms. Cover and cook until mushrooms are done.

Ralph and Sue Ziegler, Pewaukee

Goose breast and legs
Bacon grease
1 medium onion

Sauce

1 can cream of mushroom soup
1 can cream of celery soup
½ cup white wine
1 cup sliced fresh mushrooms for top

LIVER PATE DE HOOT

SIMMER LIVERS IN SAUCE pan with enough water to cover. Drain and save liquid.

Chop onion and grind liver and onion fine. Blend in all other ingredients and refrigerate, but allow to reach room temperature before serving.

L. F. "Hoot" Holzwarth, Madison

1 lb. duck or goose livers, cleaned
6 large green onions
1 stick butter
6 tablespoons buttermilk
or heavy cream
1½ teaspoons Hoot's Seasoning
½ teaspoon nutmeg
2 teaspoons dry mustard
(Chinese preferred)
¼ teaspoon ground cloves

Hoot's Seasoning

Salt	Onion salt
Pepper	Garlic salt
Accent	Celery salt
Seasoned pepper	(equal parts of all)

HOOT'S GOOSE AND GRAVY

PREHEAT OVEN TO 450°. Put goose in covered pan with butter on top. Do not season goose. Cut temperature to 400° and cook for 3 hours or until done. Baste every 45 minutes.

Put heart, liver, and giblets into small sauce pan with chunks of celery and onion and enough water to cover well, and simmer till done. Chop and put back in pan for stock.

Cut carrots, 'baga, and mushrooms and set aside.

Cut up goose, discarding skin.

Add stock to pan, and water for gravy, using flour and corn starch as gruel and mix very well. Season to taste using poultry and Hoot's Seasoning. Add Kitchen Bouquet to darken.

Add meat and vegetables to pan and set aside for the next day's meal or if you wish to use today, precook the vegetables and use the water for gravy. For use the next day, simmer 3 hours at 275° stirring so that it will not stick. This will amply serve 12 hungry hunters.

L. F. "Hoot" Holzwarth, Madison

1 large wild goose
1 pint wine (cheap port)
¼ lb. butter
Poultry seasoning and
Hoot's Seasoning (see below)
Heart, liver, and giblets
Flour and cornstarch
8 medium carrots
1 medium rutabaga
1 lb. fresh mushrooms
1 cup wild and long grain rice
Kitchen Bouquet

Hoot's Seasoning

Salt, pepper, accent, seasoned pepper, onion salt, garlic salt, celery salt, equal parts of all.

WILD GOOSE WITH PRUNE & APPLE STUFFING

STUFF GOOSE with ingredients.

Now place the goose on rack in roasting pan. Roast in hot oven (400°) for 20 minutes. Pour off fat and then proceed to baste with your own choice of basting. Reduce heat to very moderate and continue to roast allowing 20 minutes per pound.

Robert Blair, Beaver Dam

1 goose
1 quart bread crumbs
2 cups chopped prunes
2 cups peeled and chopped apples
Salt
Generous grating of fresh nutmeg
Apple juice to moisten

GOOSE NOODLE SOUP

PUT ALL INGREDIENTS, except noodles, salt, and pepper, in crock pot. Cook on low for about 8 hours. Add noodles and continue cooking until they are the right texture. Salt and pepper to taste. Serves 6-8.

Joe and Dean Dashner, Neenah

1-2 lbs. boned goose
½ cup chopped onion
1 tablespoon butter or margarine
4 tablespoons chicken bouillon
8 cups hot water
3 cups (6 oz.) uncooked medium egg noodles
Salt and pepper

WILD GOOSE — MARINATED

REMOVE BREAST OF GOOSE from carcass. Trim off all fat and skin, legs may also be used.

Marinate meat in mixture of teriyaki sauce and honey, for a minimum of 24 hours (can go longer), turning at least once.

Grill goose breasts over a hot charcoal fire from 12-15 minutes.

T. W. Poullette, Waupaca

Goose breasts

Sauce
¼ cup honey
1 cup teriyaki sauce
¼ cup sherry (optional)

BRAISED GOOSE 'N APPLE

STUFF A GOOSE WITH CELERY and onion slices. Season with salt and pepper, place in covered roaster.

Peel and core several large cooking apples, cut into thick slices and place around goose.

Roast covered at 425° for 20-25 minutes per pound, basting frequently with cider.

Uncover the goose the last few minutes while baking to allow it to brown. Remove celery and onion before serving.

Heidi Scheinert, Shawano

1 goose
Celery and onion slices
Several large cooking apples
Cider (for basting)

GOOSE CRUNCH CASSEROLE

MIX TOGETHER AND THEN add soup mixed with mayonnaise.

Bake at 350° for 30 minutes in 8x8 in. baking dish.

Mrs. Maureen Steele, Fond du Lac

3 cups diced, cooked goose
2 hard boiled eggs, chopped
½ cup sliced almonds
1 can mushrooms
¾ cup diced celery
1 tablespoon chopped onion
1 can cream of mushroom soup
¾ cup mayonnaise

STUFFED PARTRIDGE

SALT AND PEPPER BIRDS. Stuff with wild game stuffing and place in crock pot or slow cooker. Add 1 cup warm water and any vegetables you prefer and cook on low for 8 hours or on high for 3-4 hours.

Mary Scott, Manawa

2 whole partridges
Wild game stuffing
Salt and pepper

PHEASANT OR GROUSE CASSEROLE

COOK 1 PHEASANT OR 2-3 GROUSE, celery stalks, onion, salt, and pepper in boiling water until tender.

Debone birds into bite-size pieces. In a 9x13 pan, line bottom with a package of herb stuffing cubes made according to package directions. Put bird pieces on top of stuffing mix. Add 1 8 oz. can of mushroom pieces. Pour 2 cans cream of mushroom soup over top. Spread evenly with spatula.

Bake at 325° until hot.

Mrs. Jeff Van Caster, Conover

Pheasant or grouse
Celery stalks, onion, salt and pepper
1 pkg. herb stuffing cubes
1 8 oz. can mushroom pieces
2 cans cream of mushroom soup

ROAST GROUSE

CLEAN THE GROUSE and wash them in water containing a little soda. Then take some narrow strips of fat pork, two inches in length, and with needle and thread, sew them to the breasts of each bird. Tie the legs together and sprinkle all over with salt and pepper. Rub the birds with butter, then dredge them in flour.

Place the birds in a dripping pan with an onion cut into slices and add a little water. Roast the whole in a hot oven, 425° for 45 minutes, basting freqiently with the stock. When done, place the grouse on a hot platter and serve as soon as possible.

Cliff Rauscher, Green Bay

Two grouse
Strips of fat pork, 2" long
Butter
Salt and pepper
Flour
1 sliced onion

DEEP FRIED GROUSE

CLEAN THE BIRDS WELL and joint. Salt and pepper the jointed bird parts, and then dredge them with flour.

Fill a deep frying pan half full of hot fat. Put the grouse in and cook for 10 — 15 minutes over a hot flame. Serve on a hot platter with parsley sprigs.

Cliff Rauscher, Green Bay

ROAST GROUSE WITH WINE

CLEAN AND WASH each bird and then salt and pepper them. Put an onion in the cavity of each bird and place them breast up in a roasting pan. Lay four slices of salt pork over the breasts.

Roast the birds in a 400° oven for 20 — 25 minutes, basting every five minutes with a mixture of one cup melted butter and one cup of dry wine.

Serve with wild rice, fresh green peas and currant jam.

Cliff Rauscher, Green Bay

Two grouse
2 medium onions
8 slices salt pork
1 cup melted butter
1 cup dry white wine

ROAST GROUSE, PARTRIDGE

CLEAN, WASH, AND DRY GROUSE. Rub cavities and outside with salt and pepper. Fill with sage stuffing, place thin slices of fat pork or bacon over openings and fasten with toothpicks.

Place in roast pan and add ½ cup boiling water. Bake at 450° for 15 minutes, then reduce heat to 350° and bake until tender.

Remove fat, brush surface with cooking oil, dredge lightly with flour, and bake until brown.

Garnish with red pickled apple and sprigs of watercress.

Gib Dutton, Rochester, MN

Grouse
Salt and pepper
Sage stuffing
Fat pork or bacon slices
½ cup boiling water

BOHEMIAN GROUSE SOUP

COMBINE ALL INGREDIENTS IN A large kettle. Bring to boil and simmer 2 hours. Remove grouse from broth. Remove meat from bones (meat will come off easily) and place grouse back in broth.

In separate kettle, boil 4 medium potatoes until done. Mash 1 potato in bottom of each bowl first. Ladle broth on top. Season with salt and pepper. Serves 4.

Gary Kraszewski, Pulaski

2 grouse (whole)
2 qts. water
1 bay leaf
3 chicken bouillon cubes
½ teaspoon pepper
3 carrots, chopped
2 stalks celery, chopped
1 medium onion, chopped

PARTRIDGE IN RED WINE

COMBINE FLOUR and 1 teaspoon salt in paper or plastic bag; add two or three pieces of partridge at a time and shake to coat. Brown partridge in butter in heavy pan or Dutch oven. Add onion and beef broth. Cook covered over low heat 50 to 60 minutes. Remove birds to serving dish. Add wine to pan; simmer 5 minutes, stirring and scraping brown bits from bottom of pan. Pour sauce over partridge.

Serves 2 to 3.

Howard Kohlhepp, Chippewa Falls

½ cup flour
2 — 1 pound ready to cook partridge, cut up
¼ butter
2 tablespoons finely chopped onion
1 — 10½ oz. can condensed beef broth
3/4 cup claret or red Burgundy

DEVILED GROUSE

CHOP VERY FINE, left over pieces of grouse (cooked and cold). Melt one tablespoon of butter in frying pan. Add ½ pint of milk, 1 pint of chopped grouse, 1 tablespoon of parsley, ¼ teaspoon grated nutmeg, 2 tablespoons bread crumbs, ¼ teaspoon of salt and a pinch of cayenne to taste.

Stir the mixture over the heat until it boils. Add three chopped hard boiled eggs. Then fill the individual dishes with the mixture, sprinkle lightly with bread crumbs and brown in a quick oven.

Cliff Rauscher, Green Bay

1 pint of chopped, cold, cooked grouse
½ pint milk
1 tablespoon butter
1 tablespoon parsley
¼ teaspoon grated nutmeg
2 tablespoons bread crumbs
¼ teaspoon salt
Pinch of cayenne pepper
3 chopped hard boiled eggs
Bread crumbs

PARTRIDGE PIE

CLEAN BIRDS, SPLIT DOWN back. Cut veal in strips, season with salt and pepper. Saute in drippings in fry pan until lightly brown. Put birds in casserole, cover with veal and lay bacon strips over top.

Stir flour into drippings, add stock, stir and cook until thickened. Add cloves and pour over meat. Cover and bake at 350° until done.

Place mushroom, parsley, and sherry on top. Adjust pastry dough over casserole, and cut gashes in crust to let steam out. Bake at 450° until brown.

To make pastry cover, mix and sift flour and salt, cut in shortening, and blend. Add water until dough is formed.

Gib Dutton, Rochester, MN

3 cleaned partridges
½ lb. veal steak
1 teaspoon salt
1/8 teaspoon pepper
¼ cup bacon drippings
6 slices bacon
3 tablespoons flour
2 cups stock or water
2 whole cloves
1 cup sliced mushrooms
1 tablespoon chopped parsley
½ cup sherry

Pastry cover

1¼ cups sifted flour
2/3 cup shortening
½ teaspoon salt
1/3 cup cold water

TASTY GROUSE

SPLIT 2 GROUSE IN HALVES and sprinkle with salt and pepper. Fry 10-15 minutes in butter. Remove from pan.

Add pear juice from a 16 oz. can of pears, wine, half-and-half, and paprika to the pan drippings. Simmer 10 minutes. Add salt and pepper.

Place pears in pan with grouse. Pour sauce over and broil just until brown.

Terry Baumgartner, Kansasville

2 grouse
Salt and pepper
1 16 oz. can pears
½ cup white wine
1 cup half-and-half
Dash of paprika

FOIL BAKED PARTRIDGE

SALT AND PEPPER WHOLE BIRD inside and outside. Place 1 bay leaf in cavity. Lay bacon on bird, wrap in foil, and bake at 300° for 30 minutes.

For grill, lay wrapped partridge on hot coals, turn once. Takes approximately 30 minutes.

Bob Vosen, Fond du Lac

Whole partridge
Salt and pepper
1 bay leaf
3 strips bacon

GROUSE DEVON

COOK BROCCOLI FOR 7 MINUTES and drain. Place on bottom of buttered casserole dish. Place grouse meat only on top of broccoli.

Combine soup, Miracle Whip, lemon juice, and pour over grouse. Add cheese over all.

Bake at 350° for 40 minutes. Crush Wheaties or cornflakes over top. Serve with wild rice. Serves 4-6.

Chris Dorsey, Stevens Point

4-5 cooked grouse
2 pkgs. frozen or fresh broccoli
2 cans cream of chicken soup
½ cup Miracle Whip
1 teaspoon lemon juice
½ cup shredded cheese
1 cup Wheaties or cornflakes

GROUSE IN WINE SAUCE

CLEAN GROUSE THOROUGHLY. Pat dry.

Brown onion and garlic until translucent. Put flour, salt, and pepper in a small plastic bag and shake meat pieces one at a time. Put floured meat and herbs into pan and brown meat well on all sides. Pour wine and lemon juice over meat.

Cover skillet and reduce heat. Simmer slowly for 1 hour or until meat is well cooked. Turn meat once while simmering. Add more wine if needed. Serve with wild rice. Serves 2-4.

Dr. Karl Johnson, Clear Lake

2 grouse, quartered
½ cup flour
1 teaspoon salt
1 teaspoon pepper
1/3 cup oil
1 small chopped onion
1 large clove garlic, chopped
1 teaspoon marjoram leaves
1 teaspoon basil leaves
1 teaspoon thyme leaves
1 tablespoon parsley, chopped
1 cup white wine
¼ cup lemon juice
(other herbs as desired)

DAVE'S SAUTEED GROUSE

CUT GROUSE FROM BONE into pieces and roll in flour mixture. Brown in oil. After browning, sprinkle any remaining seasoned flour on top. Cover with oinions and celery. Add water mixture and simmer until tender. (2 hours) Serve over noodles. Serves 2.

Dave Post, Sheboygan

2 grouse

Water mixture

3 teaspoons oil
1 medium chopped onion
¼ cup chopped celery
1 cup water
3 teaspoons worcestershire sauce

Flour mixture

Flour
½ tablespoon celery salt
½ tablespoon garlic salt
1 tablespoon onion salt
2 teaspoons seasoned salt
1 tablespoon oregano

BRAISED PARTRIDGE

RINSE BIRDS AND PAT WITH damp paper towel. Sprinkle with salt and pepper. Combine pate with mushrooms and enough mixture (water, whiskey, wine) to make it moist.

Stuff each bird with ½ of the mixture.

Heat oil in electric fry pan or heavy skillet; brown birds on all sides. Reduce heat, add butter, cover and cook over low heat, basting occasionally with pan juices, about ½ hour or until tender.

David Manson, Sister Bay

2 partridge (approximately 1 lb. each)
Salt and pepper
6 oz. pate or liverwurst (skinned and mashed)
½ cup mushrooms
2-3 tablespoons oil
¼ cup butter, melted

CRISPY FRIED GROUSE

BAKE GROUSE BREAST IN covered pan until almost done. Cool and cut breast in ¼ in. slices. Dip into blended egg and milk mixture, roll in cracker crumbs. Fry in cast iron frying pan with butter until golden brown. Works with pheasant, also.

Thomas W. Goddard, Brillion

4 grouse breasts
2 eggs
1 can carnation milk
Saltine cracker crumbs
Butter

LARDED GROUSE

ON EACH BIRD lay thin slices of bacon until bird is completely covered. Wrap with string to keep bacon in place. Put in roasting pan and pour over birds sufficient water to provide basting. Roast 20 - 25 minutes at 400°. Remove strips of bacon, brush birds with melted butter, dredge with flour and place in oven again until the birds turn a rich brown.

Alma E. Morton, Madison

1 grouse per serving
Enough bacon to cover each bird
Butter
Flour

GROUSE QUICHE

PUT GROUSE AND MUSHROOMS in shell, sprinkle with cheese. Combine soup and milk, add eggs, mix well. Pour soup mixture over cheese. Bake at 350° about 45 minutes or until center of pie comes out clean when a knife is inserted.

Season with salt and pepper. Note: For variation, you can also add finely chopped onion, celery, and/or green pepper.

Mrs. Jeff Van Caster, Conover

1 cup diced grouse (or pheasant)
4 oz. mushrooms sliced, drained
1 cup Velveeta Cheese, shredded
1 can 10¾ oz. cream of chicken soup
¼ cup milk
4 eggs, slightly beaten
1   9 in. unbaked pie shell
Salt and pepper

PHEASANT, PARTRIDGE

BROWN 4-6 MEDIUM BREASTS in butter. Combine ingredients and pour over meat. Sprinkle with paprika. Bake at 325° for 1½ hours. Serve with rice.

Jim St. Laurent, Green Bay

Pheasant breasts
1 can cream mushroom soup
1   8 oz. can mushrooms and liquid
1 cup sour cream
½ cup sherry
Paprika

SMOTHERED PHEASANT

ROLL PHEASANT PIECES IN FLOUR, season with salt, pepper, and garlic. Brown slowly in hot oil, turning once. Place in baking dish. Pour on soup. Bake in covered dish at 325° until tender.

Serve with gravy made from drippings.

Lloyd Plank, Augusta

1 pheasant cut in serving pieces
Flour, salt, pepper
1 clove of garlic
Cooking oil
1 can mushroom soup

PHEASANT STEW

MELT BUTTER IN HEAVY, deep pot. Brown pheasant pieces on both sides. Add remaining ingredients, cover, and simmer 1¼ hours until pheasant is tender. Add more cider if necessary.

Mary Scott, Manawa

¼ cup butter
1 pheasant, quartered
3 apples, peeled and sliced
2 teaspoons cinnamon
2 cups apple cider
Salt to taste

ROAST PHEASANT

CLEAN, WASH, AND DRY BIRD, rub inside with salt and pepper. Stuff with desired dressing. Truss.

Place in roaster, breast side up, rub olive oil or butter and salt and pepper on outside. Roast uncovered at 350° until done. Baste at 20 minute intervals. (Allow 25-30 minutes per pound.)

Remove bird, skim off fat, make a gravy from drippings.

Gib Dutton, Rochester, MN

1 pheasant
Salt and pepper
Olive oil or butter

ROAST SWEET POTATO PHEASANT

WIPE THE CAVITY OF EACH BIRD carefully with a damp cloth. Rub them inside and out with oil and dust with salt and pepper. Mix flour cups of freshly mashed sweet potato with one cup of minced walnuts and pack the mixture loosely into the cavities and truss them. Place the birds in a roasting pan and lay three strips of bacon over each breast. Pre-heat the oven to 350° and pour one quarter cup of melted butter and one cup of white wine over the pheasants, and put them in the oven. Roast for 75 minutes, basting frequently so as not to allow them to dry out.

At the end of the cooking time, remove the birds to a platter, stir one cup of chicken consomme and one half cup of cream into the pan juices. Use this for gravy. Boiled onions and a salad go well with this meat.

Cliff Rauscher, Green Bay

Per pheasant:
Vegetable oil
Salt and pepper
Two cups freshly mashed sweet potato
½ cup minced walnuts
3 strips bacon
¼ cup melted butter
½ cup white wine
Chicken consomme
½ cup cream

PHEASANT ALEXANDER

SEASON PHEASANT HALVES with salt and pepper. Brown in butter, turning once.

In bowl, combine tomato, wine, onion, parsley, and thyme. Pour over pheasant in skillet. Cover and simmer 45 minutes to 1 hour, or until tender.

Remove meat from pan. Measure juice, if necessary add water to make ¾ cup. Blend flour and cream. Stir into pan juices. Cook and stir until thickened and bubbly. Serve over pheasant and rice. Sprinkle with paprika. Makes 4 servings.

Karen Schmidt, Racine

2 2-2½ lb. dressed pheasants
halved lengthwise
Salt and pepper
4 tablespoons butter
1 tomato peeled and chopped
½ cup white wine
¼ cup sliced green onions
2 tablespoons snipped parsley
¼ teaspoon dried thyme, crushed
1 tablespoon flour
½ cup cream

PHEASANT DELIGHT

MIX EGG AND MILK. Dip pheasant pieces into mixture. Place flour and cornmeal in plastic bag. Add pheasant and shake. Brown pheasant in fat.

Place in baking dish; add onion and water. Bake at 325° for 1 hour. Serves 2.

Lloyd Recore, Valders

1 pheasant cut into serving pieces
1 egg
½ cup milk
½ cup flour
½ cup cornmeal
Fat
½ cup chopped onion
1 cup water

ROAST STUFFED PHEASANTS

SINGE, CLEAN, WASH, and dry pheasants. Rub inside with salt. Put the stuffing lightly into cavity and inside the neck where the crop was removed. Skewer or sew the openings. Truss. Brush breast, legs, and wings with butter and place pheasants on their backs on a rack in a shallow pan. Roast, uncovered, in a moderate oven (325° to 350° F.). Baste pheasants with melted butter at half hour intervals during the roasting. Cover any parts of the pheasants which become too brown with two thicknesses of cheesecloth which has been wrung out of hot water and then dipped into melted butter. The time of roasting depends on the size and age of the pheasants, degree of fatness, etc.

2 pheasants
Salt
Stuffing
¼ cup butter

STUFFING

MELT BUTTER IN A skillet, add onion and cook until onion is transparent. Add crumbs and seasonings and stir and heat until crumbs are slightly brown.

Beverly Rychter, Gleason

2/3 cup butter
½ cup onion minced
2½ quarts soft bread crumbs
2½ teaspoons salt
2½ teaspoons ground sage
¼ teaspoon pepper

PHEASANT CREOLE

ON EACH BIRD lay several thin strips of bacon until each bird is completely covered. Then bind the birds with string to keep the bacon in place. Place them in a roasting pan and pour enough water over them for basting.

Roast the birds 20 — 25 minutes in a 450° oven. Remove the bacon strips, brush the birds with melted butter, dredge them with flour and return them to the oven until they turn a golden brown. Thicken the pan liquid, season and add a cup of sherry. Use this as gravy.

Place the birds on a platter, garnish them with green pepper rings and the bacon strips.

Cliff Rauscher, Green Bay

Two pheasants
Enough bacon strips to cover birds
Melted butter
Flour
1 cup sherry
Green pepper rings (garnish)

BRAISED PHEASANT

CUT BIRD IN PIECES for serving. Roll in seasoned flour, saute in bacon drippings in heavy pan. Add bacon, carrots, celery, and rest of ingredients.

Add 1 cup shelled and blanched chestnuts 10 minutes before meat is done.

Gib Dutton, Rochester, MN

Pheasant
Seasoned flour
4 slices chopped bacon
4 carrots, chopped
4 stalks celery, chopped
1 large onion, chopped
1 sprig thyme crushed
1 bay leaf, crushed
2 teaspoons chopped parsley
1 cup water
1 cup shelled chestnuts

HERBED PHEASANT ROSE'

SHAKE PHEASANT IN FLOUR mixed with garlic salt and paprika. Brown on both sides in hot shortening. Sprinkle with herbs, add wine, cover and cook slowly until tender. Skim any excess fat from liquid in pan. Thicken liquid in pan with 1 - 1½ teaspoons cornstarch mixed with 1 tablespoon water, if desired. Stir in sour cream.

Howard Kohlhepp, Chippewa Falls

4 pieces pheasant
¼ teaspoon garlic salt
¼ teaspoon paprika
3 tablespoons flour
2 - 3 tablespoons shortening (½ butter)
¼ teaspoon each: rosemary & basil
½ cup California Rose wine
½ cup commercial sour cream

COVERED PHEASANT

PREPARE PHEASANT BY FIRST rolling in seasoned flour. Put it in a baking pan and cover it with 2 cups of sliced onions. Pour 1 cup of milk or cream and 2 tablespoons barbecue sauce over bird and bake at 300° until tender for about 1 hour and 15 minutes. Gravy can be made from the drippings. Quail is also very good this way.

Yield: 3 - 4 servings.
Bill Gloeckler, Milwaukee

1 pheasant
Seasoned flour (season with salt & pepper)
2 cups onions, sliced
1 cup milk or cream
2 tablespoons barbecue sauce

PHEASANT RICE BAKE

SPRINKLE SOUP MIX into buttered 2-quart casserole. Sprinkle rice over soup mix. Add pheasant pieces. Dilute soup with milk and pour over pheasant. Cover and bake in 350° oven for 1 hour and 15 minutes. Uncover, sprinkle with onion rings. Cook 15 minutes more.

Yield: 6 servings.
Robert Weiss, Stoughton

1 pheasant, cut into pieces
1 package dry onion soup mix
1 cup uncooked rice
1 can cream of chicken or mushroom soup
1 soup can of milk
1 can french fried onion rings

GERMAN PHEASANT

PLACE SAUERKRAUT IN DEEP ovenware pot, add broth, wine, and caraway seeds. Cover and simmer for 1 hour at 350°.

In skillet, brown pheasant in ¼ cup butter. Season to taste. Place pheasant in pot with sauerkraut and cook covered until pheasant is tender. Serves 2.

Ken Tomaszewski, Janesville

1 young pheasant
¼ cup butter
1 cup white wine
2 cups chicken broth
2 lbs. sauerkraut, drained
½ teaspoon caraway seeds
Salt and pepper

PHEASANT ALA WEBER

CUT PHEASANT INTO SIX PIECES. (Brown in fry pan). Put can of mushroom soup, 1 can milk, 1 diced onion and 2 cut peppers into small roaster. Place pheasant in mixture and let simmer for 1½ hours. Also have tried goose, duck and venison this way.

Andy Weber, Merton

1 pheasant
1 can cream of mushroom soup
1 can milk
1 diced onion
2 cut peppers

ROAST PHEASANT, GROUSE or PARTRIDGE

COVER EACH BIRD completely with thin slices of bacon and tie with a string to keep bacon in place. Place in a roasting pan and pour in just enough water to cover the bottom of the pan. Bake at 400°F. for 20 to 25 minutes. Remove bacon, brush birds with melted butter. Sprinkle with flour and continue baking at 325°F. until the birds turn a rich brown color.

To make gravy, thicken the liquid in the pan with flour or cornstarch, and add ½ cup dry sherry if you desire. Heat to boiling and cook 3 to 5 minutes.

Robert Weiss, Stoughton

Pheasant, grouse or partridge
Enough bacon slices to cover each bird
Butter
Flour
Sherry (optional)

BAKED PHEASANT

BROWN PHEASANT IN ½ CUP BUTTER. Add rest of ingredients to pheasant and bake at 300° for 2 hours.

Make cream sauce by frying mushrooms and adding the rest of the ingredients. Serve over baked pheasant.

Mrs. Ken Radke, Beaver Dam

1 pheasant, cut into pieces
½ cup butter
1 tablespoon worcestershire sauce
1 onion chopped
1 clove garlic
Cream to cover pheasant

Cream Sauce

1½ cup fresh mushrooms
2 tablespoons butter
1/8 tablespoon crushed rosemary
1 can cream chicken soup
1/3 cup half and half
2 tablespoons dry white wine

SMOTHERED PHEASANT

CUT BIRD IN PIECES for serving. Roll in seasoned flour and saute in butter until browned. Add cream and simmer, covered, ½ to ¾ hours. Add milk if necessary. Turn occasionally. You can also bake in moderate oven 350° until done.

Serve with gravy made from cream in pan.

Gib Dutton, Rochester, MN

Pheasant
Seasoned flour
Butter
1 cup cream

PHEASANT FEASTERS

COMBINE MILK AND EGGS in bowl. Mix well. Dip meat in mixture then in bowl of crumbs and then fry in ½ cup of grease at low temperature.

Christina Syverson, Tomah

3 cups bite sized meat (pheasant, turkey, chicken, grouse)
2/3 cup milk
2 eggs
3 cups finely crushed bread crumbs (whole wheat)

BAVARIAN PHEASANT SOUFFLE

COOK THE PHEASANT BREASTS in the water and bouillon cubes for 20 minutes. Save the broth.

Debone and cube the pheasant. Sprinkle the croutons in a 9x13 in. pan and add onion, sage; salt and pepper to taste. Pour 1 cup of broth over the croutons. Put meat on top of the croutons.

In a separate pan, melt the butter and mix in the flour, 1 cup of broth, and the eggs. Pour the remaining broth into the egg mixture and pour this mixture over the meat.

Bake at 375° for 45 minutes.

Prepare the sauce about 15 minutes before the souffle is finished. Heat the soup, sour cream, and pimentoes on the stove and pour over individual pieces of the souffle. Serves 6.

Ray Baranczyk, Manitowoc

2 pheasant breasts
4 cups water and 2 chicken bouillon cubes
1 8 oz. pkg. of croutons
1 onion, diced
½ teaspoon sage
Salt, pepper
½ cup butter
¼ cup flour
6 eggs, beaten
1 can cream of mushroom soup
1 cup sour cream
1 small jar pimentos

PHEASANT IN WINE

CUT BIRDS INTO serving sized peices and roll in flour seasoned with salt and pepper. Brown in melted butter or margarine. When each piece is browned, place in a Dutch oven or heavy casserole dish. Add one can cream of chicken soup or can of cream of mushroom soup and 2 tablespoons finely chopped onion combined with 3/4 cup of white wine. Sprinkle with paprika. Cover and bake at 350° for 1½ hours or until tender. Serve with wild rice.

Robert Weiss, Stoughton

2 pheasants
Flour
Butter or margarine
1 can cream of chicken or mushroom soup
2 tablespoons finely chopped onion
¾ cup white wine
Paprika
Salt & pepper

PHEASANT STEAKS

CUT AND BONE THE ENTIRE breast of pheasant in 2 pieces. Pound real well. Pat flour mixed with seasoned salt into the breasts.

Fry quickly in skillet over moderate heat. This is good with partridge breast, too.

Gerald Lahner, Eau Claire

Pheasant breast
Flour
Seasoned salt

PHEASANT IN CREAM SAUCE

COMBINE SOUP, SOUR CREAM, tarragon, parsley, and sherry. Heat ¼ cup water to boiling; add chicken bouillon and mix till dissolved. Add to soup mixture.

Saute onions in butter until tender. Add to soup mixture. Mix together, add enough of the remaining water to make sauce thin enough to pour.

Pour sauce over pheasant pieces in flat casserole dish. Cover with foil and bake at 350° until almost done. Remove foil and cook uncovered until pheasant is tender and sauce thickens slightly. Serve with noodles. Makes 4 servings.

Jan Jacobson, Madison

1 pheasant, cut in serving size pieces
1 (10½ oz.) can cream of mushroom soup
½ cup sour cream
1 teaspoon instant chicken bouillon
¼ cup water
1 teaspoon tarragon leaves
1 teaspoon parsley flakes
¼ cup chopped onion
2 tablespoons butter
1½ tablespoons sherry
1-2 tablespoons water

PHEASANT

FLOUR BIRD AND FRY IN OIL and onions. Put pheasant in roaster with oil and onions. Add soup and fill ¼ of the roaster with water.

Bake at 350° for 2 hours.

John Milani, Rockford, IL

Pheasant
Flour
Oil
Onions
1-2 cans cream of mushroom soup

QUAIL WITH GRAPES AND HAZELNUTS

SPRINKLE QUAIL INSIDE and out with salt, pepper, and flour. Melt butter in skillet. Add quail and brown on all sides.

Add water, cover, and cook over low heat 15 minutes or until tender.

Add grapes and cook 3 minutes longer. Stir in nuts and lemon juice. Serves 4.

Donna St. Laurent, Green Bay

4 quail
Salt, pepper, flour
¼ cup butter
½ cup water
½ cup seedless grapes
2 tablespoons chopped hazelnuts
1 tablespoon lemon juice
4 buttered toast slices

BROILED QUAIL

CLEAN BIRD, SPLIT DOWN the back. Brush with olive oil or lemon butter. Season with salt and pepper. Broil at 350° for 15 minutes or until done. Baste when turning.

Serve with wild rice and gravy on buttered hot toast with mushroom, cream cheese, and broiled tomatoes.

Gib Dutton, Rochester, MN

Quail
Olive oil or lemon butter
Salt and pepper

STUFFED QUAIL WITH SEASONED RICE

COAT INSIDE OF BIRDS with butter and poultry seasoning. Stuff full of seasoned rice. Close all openings with skewers (or tie). Place in uncovered baking dish. Bake at 375° for 1 hour, basting every 10 minutes.

To make seasoned rice, saute onions and garlic in olive oil until onions are golden. Add remaining ingredients and simmer about 15 minutes, until rice is tender.

To make the baste, mix all ingredients in saucepan. Heat until butter has melted, stirring occasionally.

Terry Collard, Mundelein, IL

Quail
Poultry seasoning

Seasoned rice

2 cups onions, diced
2 teaspoons olive oil
1 cup uncooked rice (not Minute Rice)
1 bay leaf
¼ cup white wine
1½ cup water
Salt and pepper to taste
1 clove garlic, minced
Hot sauce, to taste

Baste

4 tablespoons butter
1 clove garlic, minced
2 tablespoons red wine
Salt and pepper to taste
Hot sauce to taste

ROAST QUAIL

CLEAN BIRD, WIPE DRY. Brush inside and out with butter and rub with salt. Wrap each bird in grape leaves. Set in roasting pan. Roast uncovered at 350° for 20 minutes, then remove leaves, brush with butter, and brown.

Garnish with parsley and serve on hot toast with plum or grape jelly. Allow 1 quail per person.

Gib Dutton, Rochester, MN

Quail
Butter
Grape leaves

QUAIL BREAST WITH SAUERKRAUT

IN LARGE CASSEROLE MELT 3 tablespoons butter. Add breasts and saute until brown, about 3 minutes. Turn and brown other side for 3 minutes. Remove and set aside.

In same casserole, melt the remaining 1 tablespoon butter. Add onion and saute 5 minutes. Add drained sauerkraut, apples, raisins, wine, and caraway seeds. Season with salt and pepper. Place browned bird breast on top of sauerkraut. Push down into kraut to keep moist. Cover and bake at 350° for 45-50 minutes.

To serve breasts, make a nest of sauerkraut mixture and place breast on nest.

Karen Schmidt, Racine

¼ cup butter divided
4-6 quail breasts
¼ cup chopped onion
1 can (27 oz.) sauerkraut, drained
1 cup unpeeled, chopped apple
1/3 cup raisins, soaked in water for 30 minutes and drained
½ cup dry white wine
½ teaspoon caraway seeds
Salt and pepper to taste

BROILED SNIPE

CLEAN BIRD, SPLIT DOWN the back. Brush with olive oil or lemon butter. Season with salt and pepper. Broil at 350° for 15 minutes or until done. Baste when turning. Serve on buttered toast.

Gib Dutton, Rochester, MN

Snipe
Olive oil, lemon butter
Salt and pepper

WILD GAME STUFFING

SHREAD THE BREAD. Mix all ingredients together and put enough water in to moisten, but not soak. Use to stuff the game or bake separately at 350° for 1 hour.

Mary Scott, Manawa

10 slices bread
1 large onion, chopped
1 green pepper, chopped
Poultry seasoning

ORANGE STUFFING

SOFTEN BREAD CUBES in hot water for 15 minutes. Add remaining ingredients and combine lightly.

Carole Tilkens

3 cups dry bread cubes, toasted
½ cup hot water
2 teaspoons grated orange peel
2/3 cup diced orange
2 cups diced celery
¼ cup melted butter
1 beaten egg
½ teaspoon salt
Dash pepper
¼ teaspoon poultry seasoning

ROAST WILD TURKEY AND STUFFING

PARBOIL GIBLETS, CHOP FINE. Add bread crumbs. Blend in seasonings. Add pecans, eggs, and giblets.

Saute mushrooms in ½ the butter. Combine mushrooms, onions, and bread mixture, moisten with enough sherry to stick together.

Stuff the turkey and roast at 325° for 2½ hours. Baste several times. Serves 8-10.

Jill Delforge, Green Bay

1 10 lb. turkey and giblets
10-12 slices dried bread, crumbled
2 teaspoons celery salt
1 teaspoon nutmeg
4 tablespoons chopped parsley
Salt and pepper to taste
¼ teaspoon ground mace
2 teaspoons chopped pecans
4-5 hard-cooked eggs, chopped
1½ cup chopped mushrooms
¼ lb. butter
1 large onion, chopped fine
2/3 to 1 cup sherry wine

ROAST WILD TURKEY

PREPARE WILD TURKEY the same as a domestic one. Stuff with a good oyster dressing or type you prefer. Rub skin with oil and place uncovered at 350° until done. Allow 20-25 minutes per pound.

Remove bird and make gravy from drippings. Use leftovers the same as a domestic turkey.

Gib Dutton, Rochester, MN

Turkey
Oil
Dressing

WOODCOCK WITH WINE AND GRAPES *

IN LARGE SKILLET, FRY BACON until half-cooked. Remove bacon from pan and cut into 10 pieces. In skillet used to fry bacon, saute mushrooms. Remove, set aside.

In bowl, combine flour, salt, and pepper. Dredge each woodcock in seasoned flour. In skillet, brown woodcock.

Arrange woodcock in baking dish and place bacon pieces across each breast. Add broth, wine, celery, and carrots. Cover and bake 20 minutes at 350°. Add grapes and mushrooms. Cover, and bake 15 minutes longer.

Place woodcock on serving platter, garnish with mushrooms and grapes. Makes 6-8 servings.

Karen Schmidt, Racine

10 woodcock (can use doves) cleaned and dressed
3-4 strips of bacon
½ cup sliced mushrooms
¾ to 1 cup flour
Salt and pepper
1 cup chicken broth
1 cup dry sauterne wine
1 stalk celery chopped
3 carrots thinly sliced
2 cups seedless grapes
½ cup orange juice

FRIED WOODCOCK

CUT THE WOODCOCK INTO serving pieces. Flour, salt, and pepper each piece and fry quickly over high heat to brown the outside and retain the moisture of the meat inside.

Lower heat, add marjoram, onion, celery, and water. Simmer 1 hour adding water if necessary to prevent burning.

(Squirrel meat is very compatable in this recipe with the rich dark meat of woodcock.)

Serves 2.

Ray Baranczyk, Manitowoc

3-4 woodcock
Flour
Salt and pepper to taste
½ cup vegetable oil
½ teaspoon marjoram
1 onion, diced
1 stalk celery, diced
½ cup water

WOODCOCK SUPREME

WRAP BACON AROUND EACH ½ breast. Salt and pepper. Bake 12-15 minutes at 450° or until bacon is almost crisp. Take out and keep warm.

Slice apples, saute in butter, do not let them get mushy. Add sugar to glaze them.

Make sauce by using bacon fat (pan drippings), brandy, and chicken bouillon, and flour to thicken.

Put woodcock on apples, and pour sauce over and serve.

T. W. Poulletle, Waupaca

Woodcock breasts, filleted out
Bacon
Salt and pepper
Green-skinned apples
Butter
Sugar

Sauce

Bacon fat
¼ cup brandy
½ cup chicken bouillon
Flour to thicken

BROILED WOODCOCK

CLEAN BIRD AND WRAP IN a blanket of thin slices of salt pork or bacon. Broil at moderate heat 350° about 15 minutes. Turn often. Serve on toast with wild rice, currant, or wild-plum jelly.

Gib Dutton, Rochester, MN

Woodcock
Thin slices of salt pork or bacon

WOODCOCK DELIGHT

PREPARE RICE. WHILE IT IS cooking, bone and dice the woodcock breasts. Melt butter in a small frying skillet and add the bird. Brown the meat over low heat while stirring regularly. When pieces have been browned, but still are moist, pour the red wine over the meat. Allow to cook for 3-5 minutes. Add starch to thicken the sauce which results.

When sauce reaches desired thickness, serve the woodcock over the rice. Serves 2.

Craig Parks, Crivitz

4 breasts of woodcock
2 teaspoons butter
½ cup red wine
1/3 teaspoon cornstarch
2 cups prepared wild rice

CREAMY SAUCE FOR GAME BIRD MEAT

TO 2-3 CUPS REGULAR WHITE SAUCE add all ingredients. Heat mixture to boiling, but do not boil. You may add some milk or cream to desired consistency. Take from heat and stir in beaten egg. Add flakes or cubes and bring to boiling again.

Serve over regular or wild rice.

Margie Homer, Cable

White sauce
1 tablespoon chicken bouillon flakes
or 2 cubes
½ stick butter or margarine
1 teaspoon dill weed
1 teaspoon lemon herb seasoning
1/3 cup grated cheese
1 teaspoon dry sherry wine
Touch of onion

* WOODCOCK FOOTNOTE: One out of fifty upland bird dogs will retrieve a woodcock. Two out of fifty woodcock hunters will put woodcock in their mouths. This shows that upland bird dogs are twice as smart as woodcock hunters.

GAME
Chapter Four

If you are going to be popular, have neighbors that all speak to you, and a wide circle of friends, you must first learn when to keep your mouth shut and then develop the sensitivity to know when to lie.

When the wife of a visiting Boston banker tastes the stew and says something like: "Delicious, my dear. What is it?" It is not only permissable, but damn near essential that you lie. Don't say: "It's a stew Dirty Joe DuQuette used to serve in logging camp. It's made out of skunk and muskrat." This may result in a nervous cat (frightened by the lady's screaming). And, possibly, some spitting up on the rug. You should reply: "It's a meat ragout — which was originally brought into the area by a French chef."

Most of the smaller four-footed animal recipes require the disjointing of the limbs. This is because raccoon, possum, and even squirrel, if cooked whole, may look a lot like a rat, a monkey, or a small child. You're well advised to bake an entire small animal only for close friends who like game and don't have delicate constitutions — or small children.

Of course, the meat is delicious, but your guests will enjoy it more if (particularly the first time around) it is cooked in small pieces and if they don't know it is porcupine or beaver tail.

Some of the smaller animals (squirrel, muskrat, and raccoon, for example) have glands which must be removed before cooking unless it be your purpose to alienate your guests and create a class of people who will never again eat small game.

But if the psychological barrier is broken and the meat is properly prepared for the oven, the small game animal meal can be magnificent.

WILD GAME BARBECUE

BEAVER, RACCOON, WOODCHUCK, Muskrat, can all be roasted like other roasts. Best way to satisfy taste probably is in a barbecue. Be sure all game is cleaned well. Don't forget to remove the kernels from the coon and all the fats you can.

Gib Dutton, Rochester, MN

Beaver, Raccoon, Woodchuck, Muskrat

BARBECUE GAME DISH

IN SAUCE PAN, MIX ALL ingredients well, cook over low heat for 45 minutes, strain through sieve.

Layer meat in pan; just cover with sauce and bake covered for 1 hour at 350°, remove cover and bake for another ½ hour or until lightly brown.

Ken Tomaszewski, Janesville

2 lbs. any fresh game cut into pieces

Barbecue sauce

4 large onions, minced
1 large bay leaf
1 teaspoon salt
1 cup tomato juice
2/3 cup vinegar
½ teaspoon oregano
½ teaspoon marjoram
1 teaspoon celery salt
1 cup catsup
½ cup vegetable oil
3 garlic cloves, minced

ROAST SADDLE OF BEAR

COMBINE INGREDIENTS. Season with salt and pepper. Pour over bear and roast uncovered at 325° for 35-45 minutes per pound. Baste with pan juices.

Heidi Scheiwert, Shawano

Bear meat
1 cup cider
1 tablespoon lemon juice
2 tablespoons honey
1 tablespoon ginger
2 tablespoons soy sauce

BARBECUED BEAR

PLACE BEAR IN ROASTER. Season with salt and pepper. Rub with garlic. Roast at 350° for 1 hour or until well done. Slice thin.

Mix remaining ingredients with 1 teaspoon salt. Simmer in skillet for 15 minutes. Add meat and simmer for 1 hour until meat is tender. Serves 6-8.

Jill Delforge, Green Bay

1 2-3 lb. bear roast
Salt and pepper
1 clove garlic
2 tablespoons brown sugar
1 tablespoon paprika
1 teaspoon dry mustard
¼ teaspoon chili powder
1/8 teaspoon cayenne pepper
2 tablespoons worcestershire sauce
¼ cup vinegar
1 cup tomato juice
¼ cup catsup
½ cup water

ROAST BEAR

REMOVE ALL FAT FROM ROAST. Place in large kettle and cover with water. Add vinegar, bring to boil. Simmer for 20 minutes. Remove roast and discard water. Place in roaster. Add salt and pepper. Place onion slices on roast and add ham skin or bacon and cover and roast at 350° for 3 hours. Add water as needed. Serves 8.

Lloyd Recore, Valders

1 4-5 lb. Bear roast
½ cup vinegar
1½ teaspoons salt and pepper
2 onions, sliced
Ham skin or bacon

BEAR ROAST

PLACE ROAST IN PAN. Fill bottom of pan with ½ in. of water. Sprinkle packet of onion soup mix on top of roast. Cover and bake at 325° for 8-9 hours, until tender, turning once.

About 2 hours before roast is done, add more water and vegetables. Cover and cook until vegetables are tender.

Make sour cream gravy by adding 1 beef bouillon cube to drippings in roasting pan. (Remove vegetables and roast, keep warm.) Thicken gravy with milk and flour. When thick, add sour cream. Heat through but do not boil. Season with salt and pepper.

Mrs. Jeff Van Caster, Conover

Bear roast
1 packet onion soup mix
Carrots, chopped
Potatoes, chopped
Onion, chopped
Fresh mushrooms, chopped

Sour cream gravy

1 beef bouillon cube
1/3 cup milk
2-3 tablespoons flour
½ cup sour cream
Salt and pepper

BEAR ROAST

MARINATE 3-4 LBS. MEAT in Adolf's Meat Marinade for 24 hours. Dredge with flour and sear meat on all sides in dutch oven.

Make a paste of mustard and brown sugar and spread on meat. Add rest of ingredients and simmer 3-4 hours until tender.

Thicken liquid for gravy, and season to taste. Serve with rice or mashed potatoes.

Penny Hickman, Gordon

3-4 lbs. Bear roast
Adolf's Meat Marinade
Flour
Bacon fat
½ cup mustard
½ cup brown sugar
1 cup dry wine
4 cups water
1 pkg. Lipton's Onion Soup Mix

BEAR MEAT TREAT

USE A LARGE HEAVY cast iron skillet. Add 1½ lbs. butter (no margarine).

Place the skillet over campfire or stove and allow butter to get sizzling hot (but do not burn).

Add paper-thin slices of bear meat into the hot butter. Fry about 1 minute, dip them out, and start eating!

Kevin Voigt, Onalaska

Hind quarter bear meat cut in paper-thin slices
1½ lbs. butter

BEAR STEAK

TRIM ALL FAT FROM STEAKS and marinate in dressing for 20 minutes. Cook at medium heat. Rare steaks 4-6 minutes, and medium steaks 7-10 minutes. Don't overcook!

Mary Scott, Manawa

1 lb. bear steak per person
1 cup oily Italian salad dressing

BROILED ELK STEAK

WIPE STEAK. RUB BOTH SIDES with cut surface of garlic and brush with butter. Place on rack in broiler at 500° and cook for 5 minutes; turn steak and brush with melted butter.

Place mushrooms, dipped in butter, on rack for 5 minutes. Place steak and mushrooms on hot platter. Season with salt and pepper. Garnish with parsley, serve with tart jelly, cranberry sauce, relish, or pickled apple. Serve with wild rice.

Gib Dutton, Rochester, MN

Elk steak, 1 in. thick
1 clove garlic
½ cup butter, melted
8 large mushrooms (caps)
Salt and pepper
Parsley

BRAISED ELK

SEAR A THICK ELK ROUND STEAK in drippings, season with ground pepper and salt. Cover with dry red wine. Add vegetables and simmer until tender and liquid is almost evaporated.

Mrs. Joseph Vross, Two Rivers

Elk steak
Ground pepper
Salt
Dry red wine
2 small onions studded with cloves
Celery cut in small strips
Parsnips cut in small strips
Turnips cut in small strips

COUNTRY STYLE GROUNDHOG

SOAK GROUNDHOG OVERNIGHT in salt water to remove wild flavor. Cut meat into serving pieces. Combine flour, salt, pepper, and baking soda; rub into meat. Brown in hot oil; sprinkle with sugar. Reduce heat and add water. Cover and simmer 40 minutes or until tender; remove cover the last 10 minutes to brown.

Jill Delforge, Green Bay

1 groundhog skinned
½ cup flour
¼ teaspoon salt
¼ teaspoon pepper
¼ teaspoon baking soda
4 tablespoons cooking oil
½ teaspoon sugar
½ cup warm water

GROUNDHOG FOOTNOTE: I was surprised to discover the popularity of groundhog. I learned it is commonly used as a breakfast meat in a majority of the households of the republic — all breakfast sausage is composed of ground hog.
(We take no responsibility for Winter's footnotes — the Editor.)

MOOSE CURRY

BROWN GARLIC AND ONIONS in fat. Brown meat dredged in seasoned flour. Add remaining ingredients and simmer until meat is tender. Serve over rice. Serves 6.

Jill Delforge, Green Bay

1 lb. round steak cut in ¾ in. cubes
½ clove garlic, minced
2 cups sliced onions
4 tablespoons fat
1 tablespoon flour
1 1/8 teaspoon salt
1/8 teaspoon pepper
1 cup beef bouillon
1 teaspoon curry powder
½ cup tomato juice
1 cup raw rice, boiled

BRAISED MOOSE

WIPE MEAT WITH DAMP CLOTH. Lay strips of salt pork or bacon, which have been dipped in claret or unsweetened cranberry juice, over meat. Baste with juice. Sprinkle with mixture of salt and pepper, cinnamon and cloves. Marinate in mixture for 1-2 days in refrigerator. Turn meat several times a day. Drain, brown in drippings from salt pork in frying pan, turning often.

When browned, place meat in pan, add water to drippings, bring to boil, and pour over meat. Cover and bake at 350°. Allow 35 minutes per pound. Turn every ½ hour and when half done, add salt and pepper, bay leaf, onion, and juice. When done, place meat on platter. Add 1 cup heavy cream to liquid in pan and bring to boil and beat well; serve in separate bowl. Serve with green olives, a tart jelly, cranberry sauce, or relish.

Gib Dutton, Rochester, MN

6 lbs. moose
Salt pork or bacon
Claret or cranberry juice
Salt and pepper
Cinnamon
Cloves
½ cup water
½ bay leaf
1 onion
1 cup claret or cranberry juice
1 cup heavy cream

MOOSE SWISS STEAK

COMBINE FLOUR, SALT AND pepper and pound into steak with the back of a cleaver. In heavy skillet, brown meat on both sides in drippings with onion. Add rest of ingredients, cover and simmer until tender.

Heidi Scheinert, Shawano

Round steak 1 in. thick
Bay leaf
Flour
Onion, chopped
Canned tomatoes or V-8 juice
Salt and pepper

WISCONSIN MUSKRAT

CUT BACK LEGS OFF 5-6 nice-sized muskrats; trim off all fat. Boil the legs in water seasoned with salt and pepper for 45 minutes. Remove legs from water. Rub nutmeg on legs. Saute onion and butter. Remove onions. Brown muskrat legs in the butter until well browned. Add onions and celery and salt and pepper. Stir together. Serve hot with boiled potatoes.

Dick Baumgartner, Jr., Kansasville

5-6 nice-sized muskrat legs
Salt and pepper
Nutmeg
1 onion
1 cup celery

MUSKRAT IN ONION SAUCE

SOAK WHOLE MUSKRAT IN SALT and water in crock or glass bowl overnight. Drain, cut in serving-size pieces. Mix flour, salt, and pepper together and roll meat in mixture, coating all pieces.

In deep heavy skillet, fry bacon until transparent and light brown. Add meat and brown on all sides. Add soup and sour cream. Stir. Cover tightly and simmer for 1 hour.

David and Shelley Hraychuck, Sayner

1 plump muskrat
2 tablespoons salt
2 qts. water
½ cup flour
1 teaspoon salt
½ teaspoon pepper
6 strips bacon, chopped
1 can undiluted onion soup
1 cup sour cream, warmed

RIVER BOTTOM MUSKRAT

METHOD 1: QUARTER MUSKRAT, parboil with celery and onion for 20 minutes. Drain meat, dredge with flour and fry in bacon fat.
Method 2: Follow Method 1, but brown in Crisco, cover pan, and bake 1 hour at 350°.

Bob Vosen, Fond du Lac

Method 1:

Muskrat
Celery
Onion
Flour
Bacon fat

Method 2:

Muskrat
Celery
Onion
Flour
Crisco

MUSKRAT STEW

CLEAN MUSKRAT, REMOVING all fat and the glands in the forelegs. Soak overnight in water and vinegar (1 gallon to 1 cup).

Drain and cut into pieces. Brown in bacon grease or margarine with 1 onion. Add water to cover, bay leaf, salt and pepper to taste, and flour to thicken the gravy. Bring to boil and simmer until done.

Kathryn Cowdery, Havana, FL

Muskrat
Water
Vinegar
Bacon grease or margarine
1 medium onion
Bay leaf
Salt and pepper
Flour

APPLE ROASTED OPOSSUM

PARBOIL A YOUNG CLEANED opossum until tender in salted water. Stuff with any favorite dressing. Place on rack in roaster, cover with strips of bacon.

Dissolve sugar and lemon juice in water and add to pan and bake at 350° for 2 hours. Drain all but about 1 cup of liquid from pan. Surround opossum with pared, quartered apples. Continue baking for ½ hour until opossum is tender. Serves 3-4.

Joseph Vross, Two Rivers

1 young opossum
Dressing
Bacon strips
3 cups water
1 tablespoon sugar
1 tablespoon lemon juice
Pared, quartered apples

'POSSUM OVER COALS

CUT A YOUNG POSSUM into serving-size pieces and broil over the coals of a campfire, turning frequently until brown. Serve with sweet potatoes which have been roasted in the coals of the fire in their jackets.

Tracy Johnson, Shawano

1 young opossum cut into serving-size pieces
Sweet potatoes

BRAISED OPOSSUM

CLEAN OPOSSUM BY PLUNGING animal into hot water just below boiling. Hold by tail about 1 minute or until hair will strip: Place on table and scrape with with dull knife or pull hair off. Don't cut skin. Make incision from throat to hind legs and remove intrails: Do not cut off head or tail. Remove brains and cut off feet. Wash thoroughly in cold water.

To braise, wipe dry. Rub with salt and pepper and place in dutch oven or roaster; sprinkle with juice of lemon, add water to pan. Cover tightly and bake at 350° about 1½ hours or until done. Turn meat when half done. Serve on hot platter, place red apple in mouth and garnish with watercress. Serve with boiled sweet potatoes, cornbread, and guava jelly.

Gib Dutton, Rochester, MN

1 opossum
Salt and pepper
Juice of 1 lemon
1 pint hot water

SWEET AND SOUR OPOSSUM

CUT OPOSSUM INTO SLICES or cubes. Combine with soy sauce and wine. Let marinate for 1 hour then drain and save marinade. Brown possum. Add drained marinade and chicken broth. Cover and simmer until tender, 35-45 minutes.

Add remaining broth. Add ¼ cup syrup from pineapples, brown sugar, cornstarch, vinegar, salt, rest of soy sauce, green pepper, and onion. Cook until tender. Add tomato, drained pineapple, and sweet pickle pieces. Cook a few minutes to blend and serve with rice or Chinese noodles.

Jean Bradtke, Shawano

1½ lbs. boned opossum (no fat)
¼ cup soy sauce
1 tablespoon sherry
1 cup chicken broth
1 can pineapple chunks
1 cup packed brown sugar
1 tablespoon cornstarch
1/3 cup vinegar
1/8 teaspoon salt
1 small green pepper, cut in strips
1 medium onion, cut in 8ths
1 large tomato, cut in wedges
3 large sweet pickles, chopped

WISCONSIN'S WILD GAME PASTRIES

MIX ALL TOGETHER, cut rolled out pie crust in 4x4 squares, place ¾ cup of mixture on each square. Fold sides together, seal tightly, puncture with fork.

Bake at 350° for 55 minutes.

Kevin Voigt, Onalaska

Pie crust
2 lbs. steak cut into small cubes
½ cup sliced onion
4 potatoes, sliced

RABBIT SOUP

BROWN DISJOINTED RABBIT with herbs and vegetables in melted butter. Add lemon peel and stock and simmer on low heat for several hours until rabbit is tender.

Season to taste with salt and pepper. Strain soup through collander, remove meat from bones and cut up. Puree vegetables and return puree to broth along with meat. Thicken with roux, stir until smooth, add wine and serve.

Heidi Scheinert, Shawano

1 Rabbit
2 cups chopped onions
2 cups chopped celery
2 cups chopped turnips
2 cups chopped carrots
3 sprigs parsley
Pinch of rosemary
1 bay leaf
1 teaspoon grated lemon peel
¼ cup butter
2 qts. stock
1 tablespoon roux
Salt and pepper to taste
Wine (port or sauterne)

RABBIT STEW

BROWN RABBIT IN SHORTENING. Add remaining ingredients. Simmer until meat is done. Add vinegar 5 minutes before serving. Makes 4 servings.

Lloyd Recore, Valders

1 rabbit cut in serving pieces
3 tablespoons shortening
1 medium onion, chopped
¼ cup celery, chopped
2 tablespoons tomato paste
½ cup wine
1 teaspoon mixed spices
1 clove garlic, minced
Salt and pepper to taste
2 teaspoons vinegar

PRESSURE COOKER RABBIT

IN PRESSURE COOKER, SAUTE ONION with 2 tablespoons of shortening until tender. Remove onion and brown serving-size pieces of rabbit.

Blend drippings from bottom of pot with water. Return onions and add 1 bay leaf, salt and pepper. Cover and cook at 15 lbs. pressure for 15 minutes. Cool until pressure is released.

Thicken gravy with mixture of cornstarch and water. Serve over buttered noodles or mashed potatoes. Easy, quick, and delicious!

David & Shelley Hraychuck, Sayner

1 rabbit cut in serving-size pieces
1 onion, sliced
1 bay leaf
Salt and pepper

FRICASSEED RABBIT

CUT RABBIT IN QUARTERS, fasten bacon across pieces of meat with toothpicks. Roll in flour.

Brown onions in fat, then brown pieces of rabbit. Season with salt and pepper. Add sour cream slowly. Cover, and let simmer 20 minutes.

Debbie Hoppe, Mukwonago

1 rabbit, cut in quarters
4 slices bacon
1 medium onion, sliced
1 cup sour cream
2 tablespoons fat
½ teaspoon salt
1/8 teaspoon pepper

CREAMED RABBIT WITH MUSHROOMS

COAT RABBIT WITH FLOUR MIX. Brown in cooking oil. Saute onions and mushrooms in butter. Add onion soup mix and chicken bouillon and heat. Pour mixture over rabbit. Pour sour cream over top of mixture and stir.

Cover and simmer for 1 hour. Serve with hot rice.

Dennis Mayer, Manitowoc

2 rabbits, boned
½ cup flour
½ teaspoon pepper
Cooking oil
¼ cup diced onions
8 large mushrooms, sliced
1 pkg. onion soup mix
2/3 cup chicken bouillon
1½ cup sour cream

HASSENPFEFFER

PLACE PIECES OF RABBIT in a crock or glass dish. Add wine, spices, onion and enough vinegar and water in equal parts to cover. Marinate rabbit for 2 days in refrigerator. Remove the rabbit and dry the pieces well. Sprinkle with salt and pepper and roll lightly in flour and brown in shortening. Add marinade to make a depth of ¼ inch in pan. Cover tightly and simmer until done, adding more marinade if needed. Remove rabbit from pan, thicken drippings and add sour cream to gravy.

Howard Kohlhepp, Chippewa Falls

1 rabbit, cut into serving pieces
Cider vinegar & water
1 onion, sliced
1 cup burgundy-type wine
6 peppercorns
3 whole cloves
1 bay leaf
3 tablespoons shortening
¼ teaspoon pepper
½ teaspoon salt
1 cup sour cream

GRILLED HASENPFEFFER

PLACE RABBIT PIECES in shallow glass container. Combine wine, garlic, parsley and rosemary. Pour over rabbit and let stand at room temperature for an hour, turning rabbit pieces several times.

Meanwhile, light charcoal fire and let coals burn until covered with gray ashes.

Combine and shake oil, brown sugar and pepper in tightly covered jar. Remove rabbit from marinade and place on grill. Lay bacon pieces on top of each rabbit piece. Grill, basting alternately with oil mixture and marinade. Remove bacon pieces and turn rabbit after 30 minutes. Grill another 30 minutes, then remove to platter and serve hot.

Yield: 4 servings.
David Brower, Cloquet, Minn.

1 (2 to 3 lb.) snowshoe rabbit, cut up
1 cup red wine
4 large garlic cloves, pressed
1 tablespoon rosemary
4 bacon slices, cut into 2 inch pieces
½ cup salad oil
1 tablespoon brown sugar
½ teaspoon pepper

QUICK AND EASY RABBIT

CUT RABBIT INTO PIECES. While wet, coat each piece with flour and salt and pepper. Brown in frying pan that can be put into oven. Pour soup over rabbit and add ½ soup can of water. Cover, place in oven at 350° for 1 hour.

Mrs. Paul Marty, Madison

1 rabbit cut into pieces
Flour
Salt, pepper to taste
Cooking oil
1 can golden mushroom soup
½ soup can water

RABBIT AND MUSHROOMS

CUT RABBIT INTO PIECES. Make mushroom sauce by sauteing mushrooms with butter, and adding rest of ingredients. Simmer for 5 minutes. Add water, milk, and parsley, and mix. Pour over rabbit and cook for 1 hour or until done.

Ken Tomaszewski, Janesville

2 lbs. rabbit cut into pieces

Mushroom sauce

1 lb. fresh mushrooms
3 tablespoons butter
4 tablespoons dry sherry
¼ cup tomato juice
½ cup milk
½ cup water
1 tablespoon dried flaked parsley
Salt and butter to taste

RABBIT SOUP

JOINT ONE LARGE RABBIT and put it into a soup kettle with one quarter of a pound of salt pork and one onion which has been sliced and fried. Cover the ingredients with two quarts of water and cook slowly for two hours.

Strain out the meat and bones being sure to squeeze all the juices from the meat. Then put the soup back over the fire and add four tablespoons of rice, some parsley, and some salt and pepper. Simmer the soup until the rice is soft. Some people desire that the meat be minced up very finely and added to the soup at the end.

Cliff Rauscher, Green Bay

1 large rabbit
¼ lb. salt pork
1 onion, sliced & fried
4 tablespoons rice, uncooked
Parsley
Salt & pepper

JUGGED COTTONTAIL

CUT RABBIT IN CUBES. Place a layer of rabbit cubes in bottom of casserole and season with spices. Cover with a layer of bacon. Add another layer of rabbit pieces, season as before, and cover with bacon. Continue until meat is used up. Add water, cover, and bake 2 hours at 350° or until rabbit is tender. Add more water if it becomes dry.

Mary Scott, Manawa

1 rabbit cut in cubes
Salt and pepper
Pinch of thyme
Pinch of savory salt
¼ teaspoon celery seed
¼ teaspoon parsley flakes
Pinch of ground cloves
1 bay leaf
Bacon strips

WILD RABBIT

CUT RABBIT IN QUARTERS, and halve the back. Brown rabbit in bacon grease. Add salt and pepper to taste. Layer rabbit in casserole dish with sliced onions. On top of rabbit, lay bacon strips side by side to cover rabbit. This keeps it moist and adds flavor. Baste with juice often. (Add water if it doesn't make its own juice.) Back at 350° for 1 hour, then at 300° until tender, usually 2-3 hours.

Carol Nushart, Brillion

2 rabbits cut up
1 large onion cut into thin slices
5-6 strips bacon

KRAUT AND RABBIT

QUARTER AND HALVE THE BACK of the rabbit. Brown in bacon grease. Layer sauerkraut and rabbit in baking pan starting with sauerkraut on the bottom. Bake at 350° for 2-3 hours or until tender. Serve with dumplings.

Carol Nushart, Brillion

2 rabbits cut up
2 quarts sauerkraut
Bacon grease

ROAST RABBIT

CLEAN RABBIT, WASH AND DRY. Leave whole or cut into servings. Rub meat with oil, salt and pepper, and place in roaster uncovered.

Bake at 350° for 1½ hours or until done. Baste every 15 minutes with melted fat and turn when half done. Serve hot with pan gravy made from drippings.

To make gravy, add flour to drippings and cook until browned. Gradually stir in 1 cup water or stock and cook and stir until smooth and thick. Season to taste.

Note: Adding milk or sour cream makes gravy a lighter color and gives a delicious flavor.

Gib Dutton, Rochester, MN

1 rabbit
Oil, salt and pepper

Gravy

Flour
1 cup water or stock

FRIED RABBIT

WIPE RABBIT DRY. CUT INTO SERVINGS. Combine egg yolk and milk and stir gradually into flour. Add seasoning and beat until smooth. Dip rabbit into batter and fry about 15 minutes or until done. Brown all sides. Cook at reduced heat and turn often.

Serve on platter with creamed gravy.

To make gravy use the drippings, flour, and milk, and season to taste. Add chopped parsley and 2 teaspoons currant jelly.

You may also serve fried rabbit with orange sauce. To make the sauce, combine all ingredients and mix.

Gib Dutton, Rochester, MN

2 rabbits
2 egg yolks, slightly beaten
3 cups milk
1¼ cup flour
Salt and pepper
½ cup fat
Parsley
Currant jelly

Orange sauce

2 tablespoons flour
¼ cup water
1 cup orange juice
Salt and pepper
1 teaspoon grated orange rind
1 tablespoon brown sugar

COMPANY RABBIT

PLACE RABBIT IN BUTTERED casserole and sprinkle other ingredients on top. Add water. Bake at 350° for 1 hour (covered). Uncover and bake and additional 30 minutes.

Mary DeLong, Chippewa Falls

1 rabbit cut up
½ teaspoon salt
½ teaspoon pepper
½ teaspoon thyme
3 large bay leaves
5 slices bacon, diced
1 large onion, sliced

RABBIT BALLS

PARBOIL RABBIT FOR ½ HOUR in water, salt, onion, and celery tops. Remove meat and cool. Remove meat from bones and put through meat grinder.

After grinding, add pork sausage, eggs, and rest of ingredients, and mix together until well blended. Shape into golf ball-sized balls. (These meatballs can be used in any meatball recipe.)

Penny Hickman, Gordon

Rabbit
Salt
Onion
Celery tops
1 lb. seasoned pork sausage
2 eggs
1 cup bread crumbs
1 teaspoon sage
1 teaspoon marjoram
1 teaspoon salt
1 teaspoon pepper

GRANDPA'S HASSENPFEFFER

PLACE MEAT IN LARGE KETTLE. Cover with water (about 1 in. over meat). Add rest of ingredients and let stand 24 hours.

Boil till meat is nearly done, take out the meat only, and cook the rest until the apples and prunes are well cooked.

Strain through fine sieve, mashing all ingredients to save all juices.

To the juice, add browned flour, enough to make a thin gravy.

Add meat and simmer until meat is fully cooked. Add sugar, vinegar, and salt to taste. More water may be needed depending on toughness of meat. Serve over rice, mashed potatoes, or bread.

Susan Stray, Menomonee Falls

5 lbs. rabbit meat
1 cup vinegar
1 cup brown sugar
½ lemon, sliced
1 large apple
6-8 prunes
¾ cup raisins
2 medium onions, sliced
2-3 tablespoons pickling spice
5-8 dried red peppers
1 stick cinnamon
Salt
Browned flour
Sugar, vinegar, salt to taste

ROAST RABBIT

SKIN AND CAREFULLY CLEAN and wash the rabbits. Fill them with a forcemeat of crumbs and fat salt pork chopped very fine. Some minced onion may also be added. Sew up the rabbits and tie on slices of fat salt pork on the outsides of each of them. Roast the rabbits about two minutes longer per pound than you would fowl of the same weight.

Baste frequently, adding a little vinegar (two tablespoons) to the drippings near the end of the roasting period. When done, cut the strings and remove the crisp pork. Lay the pork around the rabbits on a hot dish. Then thicken the gravy, which should be strained, with browned flour. Bring the gravy to a boil and serve with the meat.

Cliff Rauscher, Green Bay

Fat salt pork, chopped very fine
Onion, minced
2 tablespoons vinegar
Flour

BAKED RABBIT

CUT RABBIT INTO QUARTERS. Mix flour and spices in a shallow bowl; roll rabbit pieces into flour mixture.

Melt butter in frying pan and brown rabbit. Place rabbit in roaster with the water and butter left from the frying pan. Add onions. Bake for 1½ hours at 350°.

Serve with mashed potatoes and vegetables.

Paul Codette, Bayfield

1 rabbit
1 cup flour
1 tablespoon sage
½ teaspoon pepper
½ stick butter
2 cups water
1 onion

BETSY RABBIT

DRAIN PIECES OF RABBIT and dredge in seasoned flour. Brown in hot skillet using butter or bacon drippings. Place browned pieces in casserole.

Brown onions, mushrooms, green pepper, and garlic in skillet and then sprinkle over rabbit. Add water. Bake at 350° until fork tender.

David Post, Sheboygan

2 rabbits cut up and soaked in salt water with 1 tablespoon baking soda
1 cup flour
3 cloves garlic, chopped
2 large onions, chopped
1 cup mushrooms, chopped
1 green pepper, chopped
1 tablespoon fresh parsley, chopped
3 whole tomatoes, chopped

RABBIT OR SQUIRREL CRUNCH

MIX SOUP, MILK AND ONION. Dip meat in mixture and then roll in stuffing. Place in shallow baking dish with small amount of water on the bottom to prevent sticking. Pour butter over the meat. Bake at 400° for 1 hour. Any remaining liquid may be heated and served as a gravy over the meat or accompanying side dish of rice, noodles, or potatoes.

Note: Most any recipe for chicken can be used to cook either rabbit or squirrel.

Marilyn Benish, Yuba

2 lbs. game (rabbit or squirrel — they may be combined if both are young and tender. Older game will have to be boiled until tender.)
1 can creamed soup (mushroom, celery, etc.)
¾ cup milk
1 tablespoon chopped onion
1 cup finely crushed packaged herb-seasoned stuffing

SNOWSHOE DELIGHT

THIS RECIPE IS SIMPLE TO PREPARE. First, use a roaster just a bit bigger than the hare you plan to cook. Large hares may be cut up for a smaller roaster. Pour 1 can of cream of celery, mushroom or onion soup in the roaster. Add ½ can of tap water. Stir the liquid until the soup blends. Add 3 whole potatoes, 2 stalks of celery, 1 onion and 4 carrots to the roaster. Cover the roaster and put it in the oven at 350° for 1 hour. Baste the meat every 20 minutes.

Remove the roaster from the oven and let it cool for a few minutes. Serve the liquid as soup. The meat and vegetables should be served later for the main course.

Yield: 2-3 servings.

Donald Kender, South Milwaukee

1 snowshoe hare
1 can cream of celery, mushroom or onion soup
½ can tap water
3 whole potatoes
2 stalks celery
1 onion
4 carrots
Salt & pepper

FRIED RABBIT

THE RABBIT MUST BE very tender for this method
of cooking. After it has been cleaned, and washed,
put it into boiling water and let it boil for ten minutes.
Then drain it and when it is cold, cut it up at the joints.
Dip it into beaten egg, then dip in cracker crumbs.
After the pieces have been seasoned with salt and pepper,
fry them in butter and sweet lard until they are browned
on all sides.

   Take the pieces of rabbit out of the skillet and thicken
the gravy with a spoonful of flour and add a cup of milk
or cream. Let it all boil up and pour it over the meat.
Serve it hot with onions and garnish the platter with
slices of lemon.

Cliff Rauscher, Green Bay

1 rabbit
1 egg
Cracker crumbs
Salt & pepper
Butter
Sweet Lard
Flour
1 cup milk or cream
Onions, fried
Lemon slices

ROASTED RACCOON

CLEAN AND SKIN RACCOON, soak in salted water
overnight. Remove, rinse, and dry thoroughly.

   Fill cavity with onion, apple, and onion last. Add
pieces of seasoned bread if more stuffing is needed.
Butter meat and sprinkle with seasonings.

   Roast uncovered at 350° for 20 minutes per pound.
Discard filling and replace with rice. Serves 6.

Jill Delforge, Green Bay

1 tender adult raccoon
2 medium onions
3 large apples
3 tablespoons butter
Salt, pepper, and sage to taste
Cooked rice

RACCOON

CUT OFF AS MUCH FAT AS possible. This is easier
when the raccoon is partially frozen.

   Cut into serving pieces and brown in shortening. Salt
and pepper to taste. Add onion, vinegar, bay leaves,
pepper, and water (to cover half the raccoon) and bake
at 400° or cook on top of stove until tender. (2-2½ hours)

Alice Wilker, Two Rivers

Raccoon cut in serving pieces
Shortening
Salt and pepper
1 large onion, diced
½ cup vinegar
2 bay leaves
½ teaspoon whole black pepper

RINGTAIL PIE

CUT PREPARED RACCOON IN serving pieces. Mix
water, seasonings, sugar and spices together. Put raccoon
pieces in this brine about 8 hours or more. Drain and
put in stewing kettle and cover with water. Cook until
meat is tender. Add vegetables and cook until tender.

   When all ingredients are done, remove from broth.
Thicken liquid with browned flour and butter and season
to taste. Place meat and vegetables in a dish and cover
with gravy. Top with baking powder biscuits and bake
at 450° until brown. (12-15 minutes) Serves 8.

Dan Hirchert, Platteville

1 raccoon
1 qt. water
1 pt. vinegar
1 tablespoon salt
1 tablespoon pepper
1 tablespoon brown sugar
¼ oz. pickling spices
1 onion, diced
4 small potatoes
4 small carrots

RACCOON PATTIES
(ALSO FOR OPOSSUM OR WOODCHUCK)

CLEAN RACCOON AND REMOVE meat from bones and grind. Add bread crumbs and rest of ingredients. Form into patties, and dip into beaten egg and then into bread crumbs. Fry until brown in hot fat. Cover with currant jelly sauce and bake at 350° for 1 hour.

Make currant jelly sauce by mixing seasonings with flour and butter. Add stock gradually bringing to a boil for a few minutes. Melt ¼ cup of currant jelly in the sauce and season with sherry wine.

Karen Schmidt, Racine

Raccoon (ground)
½ cup bread crumbs
1 small onion, chopped
1 egg
Salt and pepper
3 slices bacon, cubed

Currant jelly sauce

2 tablespoons bacon fat or butter
3 tablespoons flour
¼ cup currant jelly
1 cup water or stock
¼ teaspoon salt
¼ teaspoon pepper
2 tablespoons sherry wine

BAKED RACCOON

TRIM OFF FAT FROM MEAT and cut into chunks. Roll meat in flour which has salt and pepper added to it; brown in frying pan with bacon strips and onions.

Place meat in roaster (add bay leaves if desired) and bake in moderate oven until done.
Donald Welch, Spencer

Raccoon meat
Flour
Salt & pepper
Bacon strips
1 onion cut into large chunks
2 bay leaves (optional)

ROASTED COON

REMOVE ALL FAT AND DEBONE COON. Remove all glands located in the back of each hind leg and underneath the front legs.

Place coon in roaster and add all ingredients. Cook at 350° for 2½-3 hours, or until done.

You can stuff the raccoon with your favorite stuffing.

Gail Nigbor, Poy Sippi

1 raccoon defatted and deboned
2 bay leaves
6 whole allspice
Salt and pepper to taste
2 medium onions
4 stalks celery, chopped
5-6 carrots chopped in quarters

STUFFED BAKED RACCOON

BOIL RACCOON IN WATER with sliced onion for 3 hours or until tender. Remove raccoon and stuff. Place in roaster with 3 cups water and bake at 350° for 1 hour. (Be sure to always remove all glands on raccoons as they can flaw the taste.)

Make stuffing by mixing all ingredients and enough water to moisten but not soak.

Mary Scott, Manawa

1 5-10 lb. raccoon
1 large onion, sliced

Stuffing

10 slices bread (shredded)
1 large onion, chopped
1 green pepper, chopped
Poultry seasoning

RACCOON STEW

PUT ALL INGREDIENTS IN crock pot or slow cooker. Add additional water if there isn't enough liquid from tomatoes. Cook on low heat for 10 hours. (You can also cook on high for 5-6 hours.)

Mary Scott, Manawa

1 medium raccoon, cubed
1 large onion, chopped
3 carrots, chopped
2 stalks celery, chopped
7 tomatoes, peeled and chopped
4 medium potatoes, cubed
1 can corn
1 teaspoon black peppercorns
1 teaspoon allspice
1 clove garlic, chopped
2 teaspoons chili powder
1 teaspoon thyme
2 bay leaves

OUR FAVORITE RACCOON RECIPE

REMOVE ALL FAT AND BONES from raccoon; cut into ¾ in. cubes. Place meat in frying pan with butter and brown all sides. Put meat into deep cooking pot and place several strips of bacon and sliced onions over meat; add only enough water to cover ingredients. Add vinegar, salt, and pepper to taste.

Place covered in oven at 350° for 1 hour. Remove and place 8-10 prunes into the juices. Reduce heat to 325° and replace pot in oven for 45 minutes.

Remove pot when done. Mix gravy sauce if desired by mixing flour and water. Place on top of stove over medium heat, stirring until gravy thickens. Serve over potatoes with sliced, cooked carrots.

Dick Baumgartner, Kansasville

Raccoon, deboned and cut into cubes
Butter
Bacon
Onion slices
2 tablespoons vinegar
Salt and pepper to taste
8-10 prunes

Gravy sauce

1½ tablespoons flour
1 cup water

ROAST STUFFED COON

PLACE THOROUGHLY DEFATTED and cleaned coon in a roaster or large dutch oven and add enough water to cover. Add vegetables and cover and simmer for ½ to 1 hour depending on size of coon.

Remove and allow to cool for 1 hour, then rub coon inside and out with mixture of 2 parts salt to 1 part pepper plus a strong dash of Hungarian sweet paprika. Save 1 cup of the broth.

Stuff the cooled coon with dressing and then skewer. Make the dressing by mixing all ingredients.

Return to pan, cover tightly and roast at 350° for about 2 hours depending on size (add 1 cup water to roast). When done, brown as you would a turkey, if desired.

Brenda and Paul Ross, Fremont

1 Raccoon, defatted
2-3 large chopped onions
2 chopped carrots
3 stalked chopped celery leaves and all
Salt
Pepper
Dash Hungarian sweet paprika

Dressing

2 or more qts. soft bread crumbs
1 teaspoon salt
¼ teaspoon pepper
1½ teaspoon poultry seasoning
1 egg beaten
1 chopped sweet onion
1 chopped apple
1 cup broth

ROAST SKUNK

DISSOLVE BOUILLON CUBE IN 1 cup hot water. Skin, clean, and remove scent glands from skunk. Parboil in salted water for 15 minutes. Drain off water. Place meat in fresh water and steam until tender. (approximately 1 hour)

Transfer to roasting pan and bake at 375°. Add 1 cup of bouillon soup, carrots, and onion juice and cook uncovered 2 hours.

Dan Hirchert, Platteville
Harold Knudtson, Eau Claire

1 skunk, skinned, cleaned, scent glands removed
Salt
1 bouillon cube
2 sliced carrots
1 teaspoon onion juice

SUPER GOOD SQUIRREL

COOK ONION AND SQUIRRELS in water until meat falls off the bone. Slow cooker works well for this. Debone, being careful to get all small bones.

Mix rest of ingredients and add squirrel to it. Cook over low to medium heat until heated through. Serve over rice or noodles. Serves 4.

Deb Schweder, Lyndon Station

3-4 squirrels
1 medium onion, quartered
1 can cream or chicken or cream of mushroom soup
½ cup milk (add slowly, may not need quite ½ cup)
1 tablespoon worcestershire sauce
¼ teaspoon garlic powder
¼ teaspoon poultry seasoning
Salt and pepper to taste

SQUIRREL STEW

CUT SQUIRREL IN STRIPS and roll in flour and brown slowly in butter. Add spices. When brown, add enough water to cover meat. Add vinegar and worcestershire sauce. Simmer for 1 hour or until meat is tender. Add potatoes and rest of vegetables and cook until tender.

Rick Peterson, Osseo

3 squirrels
¼ cup butter
1 teaspoon salt
½ teaspoon pepper
1 teaspoon thyme
1 teaspoon paprika
1 teaspoon parsley flakes
2 tablespoons vinegar
1 tablespoon worcestershire sauce

SQUIRREL STEW

SKIN, CLEAN, WASH, and cut up three gray squirrels as you would cut up chicken to be fricasseed. To the stew pot add the squirrels, one half pound of lean pork cut into bite size pieces, one sliced onion, some parsley and enough water to just cover the meat. Bring the whole to a boil and let simmer for ten minutes.

Then to the pot add the corn from a can of whole kernel corn with the liquid drained off, and continue to simmer until the meat is tender. Add six large pared and sliced tomatoes and stew for twenty more minutes. Then stir in three tablespoons of butter rolled in flour. Simmer the whole for ten more minutes and pour into a large, deep serving dish.

Cliff Rauscher, Green Bay

3 gray squirrels
½ lb. lean pork
1 onion, sliced
Parsley
1 can whole kernel corn
6 large tomatoes, pared and sliced
3 tablespoons butter rolled in flour

SQUIRREL PIE

PLACE SQUIRREL IN LARGE KETTLE, cut up in any manner. Cover with water. To water add bay leaves, peppercorns, cloves, and onion. Bring to boil, reduce heat to medium-high, and continue to cook and add water as necessary to keep meat covered. Cook until meat falls away from bones.

Let cool until easy to handle. Remove meat from bone. Reserve liquid. Prepare 1 package of herb-seasoned stuffing using reserved, strained cooking liquid to moisten. Some butter may be added if there isn't enough natural fat in the liquid. Place the stuffing mixture in the bottom of a 9x13 in. pan. Place deboned squirrel on top of stuffing. Over the top, pour 2 cups brown gravy. (Add onion, garlic, parsley, chives, chopped celery, etc., to prepared types of gravy for a homemade taste.)

Bake at 350° for 30 minutes.

Marilyn Benish, Yuba

Squirrel, cut up in any manner
2 bay leaves
6 peppercorns
6 cloves
1 sliced onion
1 package herb-seasoned stuffing mix
Brown gravy

SQUIRREL AND NOODLES

MELT TWO TABLESPOONS of butter in a large frying skillet. Skin, clean and cut up into serving pieces two squirrels. Rub the pieces of meat with a clove of garlic and sprinkle with salt and pepper. Saute the pieces in the butter until they are evenly browned. Push the meat to one side of the skillet and add a chopped onion, stirring gently until the onion is transparent.

Pour one and one half cups chicken consomme over the squirrel. Cover and simmer gently until tender. This should take about 1 hour. Then remove the meat and keep it warm. Blend 1 pint of sour cream into the juices in the pan, adding more consomme if necessary, to obtain the desired consistency. Add 1 teaspoon of caraway seeds, blend in 3 tablespoons of paprika, a little at a time.

Return the meat to the pan, simmer for a few more minutes until the whole dish is piping hot. Serve with noodles and green peas.

Cliff Rauscher, Green Bay

Two squirrels, cut up
Clove of garlic, cut up
Salt and pepper
2 tablespoons butter
1 chopped onion
1½ cups chicken consomme
1 pint sour cream
1 teaspoon caraway seeds
3 tablespoons paprika
Noodles

SQUIRREL STEW

WASH AND SOAK BEANS IN 1½ qts. cold water overnight. Drain. Wash squirrel and cut into servings. Place squirrel and beans in large kettle, cover with boiling water. Add salt and pepper and cook covered for 1½ hours until done. Add water if needed, and green pepper and butter the last ½ hour of cooking.

Gib Dutton, Rochester, MN

1 squirrel
1 pint dried lima beans
2 large green peppers
Boiling water
2 teaspoons salt
1/8 teaspoon pepper
2 tablespoons butter

ROAST SQUIRREL

CLEAN SQUIRREL, WASH AND DRY. Leave whole or cut into servings. Rub meat with olive oil, salt, and pepper.

Roast uncovered at 350° until done. Turn and baste every 15 minutes.

Pan gravy — stir flour into fat and cook until browned, gradually stir in 1 cup water or stock and cook for 5 minutes. Stir until smooth and thickened. Season to taste.

Gib Dutton, Rochester, MN

Squirrel
Olive oil
Salt and pepper

COUNTRY SQUIRREL SPECIAL

SALT AND PEPPER SQUIRRELS. Flour meat and brown on both sides in hot vegetable oil and remove. Drain excess oil. Add flour to make gravy. Add meat, onion, salt and pepper. Cover and cook on low heat for 2 hours. Add more water if necessary.

Mary Scott, Manawa

2 squirrels, quartered
1 cup vegetable oil
1¼ cups flour
2 cups water
1 large onion, chopped
Salt and pepper to taste

SMOTHERED SQUIRRELS

PLACE BROWN SQUIRRELS, onions, and mushroom soup in skillet. Cover and simmer 45 minutes or until tender.

Mary Scott, Manawa

2 medium squirrels
1 large onion, chopped
1 can mushroom soup

SAUTEED SQUIRREL & RICE

SIMMER SQUIRRELS IN WATER, salt and onion until meat can be picked off bones. Separate meat from bones.

Saute 2 sliced onions with butter in cast iron frying pan until partially done. Add mushrooms and squirrel meat with additional butter and finish sauteing. Serve over wild rice. Note: Duck may be substituted for squirrel.

Michael Hinz, Sheboygan

Several squirrels
3 onions
Fresh mushrooms
¼ lb. butter
1 pkg. wild rice mix

ITALIAN STYLE SQUIRREL

DIP SQUIRREL IN FLOUR and brown in shortening. Season with salt and pepper. Add remaining ingredients and simmer, covered for about 1 hour. Serve over rice or noodles.

Lorraine Overturs, Nekoosa

1-2 squirrels (depending on size)
Flour
Shortening
Salt and pepper
1 onion, chopped
1 teaspoon oregano
1 teaspoon sweet basil
Dash garlic powder
1 15 oz. can tomato paste
1 4 oz. can mushrooms
2 tomato paste cans water

SQUIRREL BRUNSWICK STEW

PLACE SQUIRREL IN DUTCH OVEN with water and spices. Cook until tender, about 1 hour.

Remove meat from bones, cut up and return to broth. Add rest of ingredients and cover and simmer for 40 minutes. Remove bay leaf. To serve, ladle into soup bowls. Serves 8-10.

Karen Schmidt, Racine

1 fox squirrel 2½-3 lbs. or 2 gray squirrels cut up
6 cups water
1 tablespoon salt (divided)
1 teaspoon dried leaf rosemary
1 bay leaf
2 medium potatoes, diced
1 can (16 oz.) tomatoes (drained)
1 can (16 oz.) cream-style corn (undrained)
1 pkg. (10 oz.) frozen cut okra
1 pkg. (10 oz.) frozen lima beans
1 large onion, chopped
1 tablespoon sugar
½ teaspoon pepper

SUNDAY SQUIRREL DINNER

CLEAN 3-4 SQUIRRELS, CUT INTO serving pieces. Brown pieces in butter, do not cook through. Put squirrels in deep pan.

Saute onions. Put over meat and add water to cover. Add vinegar and spices. Place covered in oven at 350° for 1 hour or until meat is tender. Add prunes and continue baking for 45 minutes longer, with oven down to 325°. Remove from oven. Thicken pan juices and serve squirrel and gravy with brown rice and parsley.

Dick Baumgartner, Jr., Kansasville

3-4 squirrels
Butter
2 onions, sliced
3 tablespoons vinegar
Pinch of thyme
Salt and pepper to taste
Prunes (dozen)
Cornstarch and water to thicken pan juices

CRUNCHY PARMESAN SQUIRREL

COMBINE ONION, CHEESE, CRUMBS, and seasonings. Dip squirrel in combined egg and milk, coat with cheese mixture. Place in shallow baking pan with small amount of water to prevent sticking. Pour melted butter over squirrel. Bake at 350° for 55-60 minutes until tender and golden brown.

Marilyn Benish, Yuba

2½-3 lbs. quartered squirrel
3 oz. can french fried onions, crushed
¾ cups (3 oz.) grated parmesan cheese
¼ cup dry bread crumbs
1 teaspoon paprika
½ teaspoon salt
Dash of pepper
1 egg, beaten
1 tablespoon milk
¼ cup melted butter

SOUPER SQUIRREL

MIX SOUP MIX AND WATER according to package directions in large dutch oven. Add squirrel. Simmer 1 hour or until meat is tender.

Lorraine Overturs, Nekoosa

2-3 squirrels
1 envelop onion soup mix
Water

WILD GAME STEW

ANY VARIETY OF WILD GAME may be used, grouse, pheasant, quail, woodcock, duck, rabbit, squirrel, venison.

Cut breasts into bite-size pieces. Brown in butter and onion. Add mushroom; cover and simmer.

Prepare thickening by mixing water, cornstarch, and bouillon cubes and bring to a boil stirring occasionally. Let simmer.

In crockpot, add thickening, layer potatoes, meat mixture, and carrots until all ingredients are used up. On low, cook approximately 4 hours, stirring occasionally.

(A touch of Lawry's Seasoned Salt adds to the taste.)

Robin Nelson, Hollsboro

Wild game cut into chunks
Butter
Onion slices
Mushrooms, chopped

Thickening

4 cups water
2 tablespoons cornstarch
2 beef bouillon cubes

6 medium potatoes
4 carrots
Lawry's Seasoned Salt (optional)

Chapter Five
SMOKING, CANNING & PRESERVING

Before the days of electrically operated freezers, and even further back when the village's supply of ice didn't last over the summer months, the preservation of game foods was more complicated than in today's electron, atom, and ethoxyquin era. And the food tasted better.

That's why they called them the "good old days." It wasn't because of the typhoid, the child labor, or the open-sewerage systems of the time.

Game meats were salt cured, canned, pickled, made into mincemeat, and smoked. The strips of venison, dried in the sun, became jerky. I suspect the old-fashioned way of making jerky may have fallen out of favor because, nowadays, people would get upset when they saw flies crawling around on the drying meat. If you prefer an antiseptic kind of existence, you can still make jerky by drying the strips of venison in the oven. The trick is to get enough heat to drive the water out, but not enough to cook the meat.

While smoking and pickling are returning to popularity, sausage making has largely been left to the professional. But the canning of wild meats did not disappear with the passenger pigeon, and mincemeat and jerky are still made in the land.

Sure, you can freeze the 1¼'' salmon steaks, venison chops and burgers supplied to you by the meat market to which you deliver your game, but, next year, why not do your own butchering? Then make your own mincemeat, smoke some fish, can, make jerky, and try your hand at sausage making. It'll keep you off the streets.

CANNED CHINOOK SALMON

FILLET FISH AND TAKE OUT dark meat and large bones. Cut fish into 1 in. chunks. Pack into pint jars. Leave ¼ in. air space at top.

Stir in ingredients as jar is filled with fish. Tighten lids. Pressure cook at 1#-12# for 1 hour and 50 minutes. (110 min.) Reduce pressure normally.

This recipe is good for making loaf, patties, for salad sandwiches or just snacking with crackers.

Laverne C. Wubben, Hazel Green

Fish fillets
1 tablespoon catsup
2 tablespoons vinegar
2 tablespoons Wesson Oil
¼ teaspoon canning salt

CANNED SALMON

WASH FRESH SALMON, soak in brine for 1 day, wash, skin, and fillet; cut in pieces easy to pack in jars. (pints or quarts)

Mix ingredients and pack in jars 1 in. from top. Seal. Process 10 pounds pressure for 90 minutes. Hot water bathe for 3 hours. Do not underprocess.

Mrs. Elaine Heiar, Bloomington

Salmon
2 tablespoons catsup or barbecue sauce
1 teaspoon salt for qt. or ½ for pt.
½ teaspoon liquid smoke (scant for 1 qt. raw salmon
2 tablespoons vinegar
1 teaspoon oil

KAROLYN'S CANNED SALMON OR REDHORSE

PACK FISH TO NECK OF pint jars. (Use only pint jars.)

To each jar add salt, vinegar, catsup, and oil. Pressure cook at 15# for 60 minutes.

Great on crackers, in salads, hot dishes, or sandwiches.

Jane Paulsen Grosvold, Holcombe

Salmon
1 teaspoon canning salt
1 tablespoon white vinegar
1 tablespoon catsup
2 teaspoons salad oil
(add these amounts to *each* jar)

CANNED SALMON

FILLET SALMON, CUT IN 2 in. chunks. Add salt and mustard and pack in pint jars. Process 90 minutes at 10#.

Use as you would canned chicken for sandwiches or hot dishes.

Mary DeLong, Chippewa Falls

Salmon
½ teaspoon salt
1 tablespoon yellow mustard

CANNED FISH

CLEAN AND DRY FISH THOROUGHLY. Mix the following for each pint jar.
1 teaspoon salt; 2 teaspoons olive or vegetable oil; 2 teaspoons catsup; 2 teaspoons vinegar. Pack fish fillets into sterilized pint jars, and pour above mixture over. Seal jar and process in pressure cooker for 1 hour and 40 minutes at 15 lbs. of pressure.

The fish can be eaten straight out of the jar, in a sandwich or salad. Any kind of fish can be used.
Mrs. Rhea Sasse, Fremont

Any type of fish
1 teaspoon salt
2 teaspoons olive or vegetable oil
2 teaspoons catsup
2 teaspoons vinegar

CANNED CARP

CUT FISH IN PIECES to fit in a pint jar. Put fish in jars and to each pint jar add the rest of the ingredients.

Cook in pressure cooker for 90 minutes at 15 lbs. Turn heat off. Let cool and take out.

Mrs. Richard Strauman, Prairie du Chien

Fish
2½ teaspoons catsup
2½ teaspoons white vinegar
2 teaspoons Mazola Oil
1 teaspoon salt

SALMON

CLEAN FISH, SKIN IF DESIRED. You need not remove bones, they will dissolve. Cut fish in chunks and put in brine of salt and water for 24 hours.

Remove fish, rinse well, drain and pack chunks snugly in fruit jars adding 2 tablespoons each of catsup, sugar, vinegar, and oil. Place in pressure cooker or canner and cook 10 minutes at 10# pressure or until you think it is cooked through.

Fish will resemble salmon, bones will be soft like salmon. Can be eaten immediately or sealed for future use. You may use any kind of fish.

Esther Heath, La Crosse

Salmon or any kind of fish
1½ cups salt
2 gals. water
2 tablespoons catsup
2 tablespoons sugar
2 tablespoons vinegar
2 tablespoons vegetable oil

CANNED FISH

CLEAN AND WASH FISH, cut in chunks, and pack in jars. Jars should be packed quite tightly with raw fish. Mix sauce together and pour over fish in jars.

Put on lids and process in pressure cooker at 10# pressure for 100 minutes. Note: If backbone is not removed at time of canning, it should be removed before eating.

Anley Christianson, Ladysmith

Fish
1 teaspoon salt
1½ teaspoon vinegar
1½-2 teaspoons catsup

CANNED FISH

CLEAN, REMOVE SKINS AND CUT fish in chunks, pack in pint jars. For each 4 pints, mix salt, oil, vinegar, and catsup, and pour over the fish. Seal and pressure cook for 90 minutes.

Types of fish used are northern, bluegills, bullheads, but mostly whitefish.

Mrs. Charles Reichert, Haugen

Fish
1 teaspoon salt
4 tablespoons vegetable oil
4 tablespoons vinegar
4 tablespoons catsup

CANNED FISH

PLACE SALT, SALAD OIL, vinegar and catsup in a pint jar and shake well. Pack fish chunks in a quart jar. Add mixture and cook in pressure cooker for 1 hour and 15 minutes at 15 lbs. of pressure.

Mrs. Walter Passehl, Wausau

½ teaspoon salt
½ teaspoon salad oil
1½ teaspoons vinegar
1½ teaspoons catsup
Fish chunks (enough to fill 1 quart jar)
* This recipe is for 1 quart jar only

CANNED VENISON

TRIM FAT FROM MEAT and cut into bite-size pieces. Pack into pint jars. Add rest of ingredients.

Allow ¾ in. air space at top of jar. Pressure cook at 10# for 75 minutes for pints. Reduce pressure normally.

For quarts, double recipe and cook for 90 minutes.

Just reheat to eat. May be used as a sauce over bread or rice. Great for camping as unopened, it doesn't need refrigeration.

Laverne Wubben, Hazel Green

Venison
¼ teaspoon salt
¼-½ teaspoon black pepper
Ground beef suet—golfball-size pieces

CANNED VENISON

CUT VENISON IN SMALL CUBES or strips. Pack raw venison pieces in jars, leaving ¼ in. on top of jar. Add salt and pepper to taste in each jar.

Do not add any liquid. Seal with lids and screw band. Place jars in canner with cold water, making sure water covers the top of lids. Cook 4½ hours after water comes to a boil. Same time for quarts and pints.

Remove after cooking and let set until cool. Let stand 24 hours before using.

Mrs. Jan Teachout, Waupun

Venison
Salt and pepper to taste

VENISON SUBMARINE SANDWICH

EMPTY CONTENTS OF 1 QT. jar of canned venison into 10 in. pan. Pick out and discard the hardened suet. Heat the venison until it is boiling. Mix the flour and milk together. Add to the venison, stirring constantly until thickened. If it gets too thick, add a little water. Spoon onto the open sandwich buns. Top with mushrooms and, if you wish, onions. Cover with cheese. Microwave on medium high until heated through.

Sharon Prochaska, Green Bay

1 qt. canned venison
2 tablespoons flour
½ cup milk
Sandwich buns
Mushrooms
Cheese
Onions

VENISON HEAD CHEESE

CLEAN HEAD WELL AND CUT in 4 pieces. Soak overnight in ½ cup salt and 1 gallon water. Drain and rinse. Place all meat in large pot until meat is tender. Remove meat from bones and chop fine. Weigh meat, strain broth. Boil down broth to 4 cups for every 3 pounds of meat.

Add chopped meat to broth with rest of ingredients. Heat and simmer for 15 minutes. Pour in loaf pans and chill.

Mary DeLong, Chippewa Falls

Head of 1 deer
1 deer tongue
1 deer heart
4 pork hocks
½ cup salt
1 gallon water
1 tablespoon salt
1 tablespoon pepper
1 tablespoon accent
1 tablespoon onion flakes
1 tablespoon pepper flakes
1 cup vinegar

VENISON TRAIL TREATS

CUT VENISON INTO STRIPS ½ by ¼ in. thick. Add the remaining ingredients in a bowl and mix well. Pour liquid over meat strips and put in refrigerator overnight. Dry in oven until quite dry. Store in covered jar or sealed plastic bags.

Ken Tomaszewski, Janesville

3 lbs. lean venison
1 tablespoon salt
1 teaspoon onion powder
1 teaspoon garlic powder
1 teaspoon pepper
1/3 cup worcestershire sauce
¼ cup soy sauce

VENISON JERKY

MIX ALL SPICES TOGETHER. Soak meat in sauce for 5 hours (more for a stronger flavor) in refrigerator.

Dry in oven at 150° for 8-12 hours on rack or broiler.

Store in jars; keeps in freezer for longer periods of time.

Darlis Wilfer, Phelps

1½ to 2 lbs. venison steak strips
½ cup soy sauce
1 teaspoon onion salt
½ teaspoon garlic salt or powder
¼ teaspoon pepper
1 tablespoon worcestershire sauce
1 teaspoon Hickory smoke flavor

CORNED VENISON

CUT ABOUT 5 LBS. VENISON in 2-3 lb. pieces.

Dissolve ingredients in 1 gal. hot water. When cool, pour over meat in a crock, weight meat down, and leave in pickling 3-5 weeks.

Cook same as corned beef.

L. F. Krueger, Fond du Lac

5 lbs. venison
1 gal. hot water
1½ lbs. pure salt
½ lb. brown sugar
1 oz. cream of tartar
1 oz. baking soda
1 oz. pickling spices

VENISON JERKY

CUT MEAT INTO STRIPS 1/8 x ¼ in. thick, cross-grain for tender, or with grain for chewy. Marinate 24 hours in mixture. Remove from marinade and put on trays into dehydrator. Dry at 145° for 12 hours. Extra worcestershire sauce or A-1 Steak Sauce may be painted on meat when partly dry. Store in jar with lid for short term storage or in jar in freezer for long term storage.

I have made jerky out of venison, pheasant, goose, pigeon breast, beef, rabbit.

Laverne C. Wubben, Hazel Green

5 lb. meat
1 pt. soy sauce
1 pkg. meat marinade
½ tablespoon black pepper
10 drops tabasco sauce
1-2 pts. water
2 tablespoons liquid smoke
½ tablespoon garlic salt
4-6 oz. worcestershire sauce
Sprinkle of crushed red pepper

JERKY VENISON

CUT DEER MEAT ABOUT ¼ x 1½ in. and lay out on cookie sheets so that none overlaps. Let set for 2 days. Wipe off with paper towels.

Mix ingredients together and sprinkle lightly on meat. Then put the meat on oven racks until dry. Put cookie sheets in bottom of oven to catch any drippings.

Floyd W. Plank, Augusta

Venison
1 teaspoon red pepper
1 teaspoon black pepper
1½ teaspoon smoking powder
½ teaspoon salt

VENISON JERKY

CUT MEAT WITH GRAIN 1/8 to ¼ in. thick. Trim fat.
Lay strips of meat in sauce. Use oblong plastic cake-type pan. Do not use aluminum.
Keep layered meat in refrigerator at least 24 hours.
When baking, line bottom of oven with aluminum foil. Lay strips of meat directly across oven racks. Bake at 150° for 4 hours leaving oven door cracked 1 in. while baking.

Deb Heusi, Stratford

2-3 lbs. venison

Marinating Sauce

¼ cup worcestershire sauce
¼ cup soy sauce
¼ cup water
1 teaspoon tabasco sauce
½ teaspoon liquid smoke
½ teaspoon black pepper
¼ teaspoon garlic powder
1 teaspoon seasoned salt
1 teaspoon onion salt
1 teaspoon Accent

VEN JERKY

CUT 3-4 LBS. VENISON ROUND cut in strips (with the grain) about 3/8 in. x 1 in. Cure in brine for 45 minutes. Rinse in warm water and pat dry. Put in oven on foil so pieces don't touch each other and hold oven temperature at 100° for 5-6 hours.
Make brine by mixing all ingredients.

L. F. Krueger, Fond du Lac

3-4 lbs. venison

Brine

½ cup pure salt (not table)
3 cups water
3 tablespoons liquid smoke
2 teaspoons liquid garlic
3 tablespoons maplene
(3 tablespoons rum extract, optional)

VENISON JERKY

CUT VENISON WITH GRAIN 3/16 in. thick. Mix all ingredients and marinate in crock or plastic container for 24-48 hours, stirring occasionally. Remove and place on racks in smoker. Smoke using hardwood at no more than 90° until dry.

Paul Merfeld, La Crosse

5 lbs. lean venison

Marinade

5 oz. worcestershire sauce
5 oz. soy sauce
1 tablespoon garlic salt (optional)
1 tablespoon onion salt (optional)
1 tablespoon celery salt (optional)

SMOKED VENISON JERKY ALA PAUL

SLICE VENISON ROUND, FLANK, or brisket with the grain into ¼ in. strips after pounding it into ¼ in. thickness with the edge of a large plate or wooden meat mallet.
For every 1½ to 2 lbs. of venison, mix the listed ingredients. Let liquid sit and steep in refrigerator for 24 hours to blend.
Lay the venison strips in glass baking dish and pour the liquid over it. Marinate the meat for 4-6 hours turning at least twice.
Pat dry with paper towels and lay on a fine mesh rack in smoker. If meat is a little grey, the smoking process will color it beautifully.

Brenda and Paul Ross, Fremont

1½-2 lbs. venison
1/3 cup soy sauce
1 large garlic diced and crushed
1/8 teaspoon salt
1/8 teaspoon finely ground pepper
1½ teaspoons brown sugar
4 dashes tabasco sauce
1/3 cup burgundy wine

OLD FASHIONED GERMAN DRIED STAG (VENISON)

USE 10 LBS. BONED, DEFATTED, rolled, and tied venison round or brisket, and cut into chunks. Make mixture by combining ingredients, and divide the mixture in half and rub into the meat well all over until it seems unable to absorb any more.

Place the meat in a gal. crock or jar and refrigerate for 3 days. A juice called the "pickle" will automatically develop. Turn meat twice daily so all sides spend equal time in this juice.

After 3 days, remove meat and rub in half of the remaining salt mixture. Put back in same crock in the previous "pickle." Turn for 3 more days as before and on the 4th day rub in the last of the salt mixture and give it 3 more days in the "pickle."

At this point, you can remove the meat and hang it in the highest ceiling in your house for 1 week to 10 days until the surface is dry. Slice paper thin.

You can smoke it for 3 days over very low heat (90°) with a light smudge of apple or hickory sawdust into which you have crushed 1 bay leaf per 1 qt. of sawdust. Turn off heat and leave meat in smoker for 24-48 hours to dry.

Recipe by Agnes Scanlon,
Submitted by Brenda and Paul Ross, Fremont

10 lbs. venison

Salt mixture for each chunk of meat

1 cup household salt
½ cup + 1 teaspoon sugar
1 teaspoon saltpeter

PICKLED VENISON HEART

WASH AND TRIM HEARTS. Cut in bite-sized pieces Cook in salted water until tender.

Make brine by mixing all ingredients. Let sit in refrigerator for 3-4 days.

Gerald Lahner, Cau Claire

Venison hearts

Brine

1 cup vinegar
½ cup water
1 tablespoon sugar
1 onion, sliced
Salt and pepper to taste

FINALLY PERFECT PICKLED FISH

USE ABOUT 8 LBS. FISH (any kind). Dry fish and salt with canning salt mixture. Make sure both sides are evenly covered. Put in bowl and cool in fridge for 2 days, turning once each day. Rinse well and pat dry.

Combine all ingredients to make mixture. Cut fish in 1 in. pieces, pack in 1 gal. jar, and pour mixture over and refrigerate for 1 week.

Brenda and Paul Ross, Fremont

8 lbs. fish
Canning salt

Mixture

2 qts. white vinegar
4 cups sugar
1 box allspice
2 tablespoons pickling spice
4 large sliced onions (red onions look nice)
Pepper flakes or whole dried red peppers
1 cup Chablis wine

PICKLED FISH

FILLET AND SKIN FISH AND cut into chunks. (Use any fish except carp and suckers; they are too bony.)

Make brine by combining ingredients, and pour over fish, cover, and refrigerate for 48 hours.

Pickle fish by combining white vinegar, water, and pickling spices and bring to boil and simmer 10 minutes. Cool. (This is enough pickle for 4 one-quart jars.)

In pint jars, alternate sliced onion and fish, fill to about ½ in. of top and add 2 teaspoons sugar, 1 bay leaf, 1-2 dried hot red peppers. Put the cold pickle over the fish. Use a knife to get out all air, cap and refrigerate for 3 weeks.

L. F. Krueger, Fond du Lac

Fish

Brine

1 cup salt
1 cup sugar
1 gal. water

Pickle

1 qt. white vinegar
1 cup water
3 tablespoons pickling spices

Topping

Sliced onion
2 teaspoons sugar
1 bay leaf
1-2 dried hot red peppers

COOKED PICKLED FISH

FRY FISH IN BUTTER UNTIL golden. Place cooked fish in deep earthern bowl.

Make marinade by sauteing onions in oil. Add rest of ingredients and bring to boil. Pour over fish. Let stand for at least 24 hours. May be served as a cold appetizer or gently heated before serving.

Gib Dutton, Rochester, MN

Fish

Marinade

2 tablespoons oil
6 small sliced onions
1½ cups water
½ cup white wine vinegar
4 small carrots, sliced
4 hot peppers cut in 8ths
3 bay leaves
2 teaspoons salt
12 peppercorns
2 cloves garlic, crushed
1 tablespoon capers
6-8 pimento olives, sliced

VIRGINIA'S PICKLED FISH

BRING VINEGAR, water, salt and pickling spices to a boil. Drop cleaned fish in hot brine and let simmer 5 minutes or until fish are white, but not flaking. Cool, place in jars or crocks in layers with slices of raw onion. Let stand 2 to 3 weeks. Be sure to cover jars.

Yield: 6 pint jars.

Virginia Kraegenbrink, Menomonee Falls

30 pan fish
2 cups white vinegar
2 cups water
2 tablespoons pickling spices
3 large sliced onions

PERFECT PICKLED FISH

SKIN AND FILLET FISH, cut in bite sized pieces. Put in a bowl, crock or large jar. Cover with white vinegar. Add salt until mixture looks milky. Let stand for 10 days at room temperature.

Pour off vinegar and cover with fresh water, soak for two to four hours and taste. If too salty, soak longer in more fresh water.

Pack loosely in large jar with layers of onions and cover with the sauce of your choice.
Mrs. Len Johnson, Portage

SOUR CREAM SAUCE WITH PICKLED FISH

BLEND INGREDIENTS, stir and taste. Add more vinegar if desired. Pour over fish. Ready to serve in 4 to 5 days.
Mrs. Len Johnson, Portage

1 large can evaporated milk
3 - 4 tablespoons vinegar
3 tablespoons sugar
4 tablespoons mayonaise
1 large onion, diced

SWEET SOUR SAUCE WITH PICKLED FISH

BOIL UNTIL SUGAR IS well dissolved. Let stand until cold before pouring over fish or they will become soft. Cover and refrigerate for minimum of 12 hours.
Mrs. Len Johnson, Portage

1 cup white or cider vinegar
1 cup sugar
4 cloves
4 allspice
1 bay leaf
1 stick cinnamon

PICKLED FISH

CUT SMALL FISH INTO CHUNKS the size of herring. If using larger fish such as northerns, fillet and then cut into chunks so bones marinate.

Soak in salt brine 24 hours. (Strong enough to float an egg) Drain. Do not rinse. Cover with white vinegar and let stand 24 hours. Drain and make brine by combining ingredients and bring to boil. Let cool. Pack fish in jars adding sliced onions. Pour brine over fish and onions. Marinate in refrigerator for 1 week.

Marilyn Lemke, Watertown

Fish
Salt brine
Vinegar

Brine

2 cups white vinegar
1½ cups white port wine
1 cup sugar
½ cup water
1 tablespoon pickling spice

FISH LIKE HERRING

SOAK ANY FISH FILLETS IN a brine of 4 cups cold water and ½ cup canning salt for 1 day.

Drain brine off fish, do not rinse, cover with white vinegar and let set 24 hours. (Soak onions in a dish of mild salt water for 24 hours)

Drain fish and onions and make brine by combining ingredients and boil for 1 minute. When cool, add wine.

Pour over fish and onions. Let set 7 days.

Mrs. Rhea Sasse, Fremont

Fish fillets
4 cups cold water
½ cup canning salt
Vinegar

Brine

1 qt. white vinegar
1 qt. water
2 cups sugar
3 teaspoons pickling spice
8 small red peppers
½ cup sherry wine

PICKLED FISH

CUT FISH INTO PIECES and soak in 3 tablespoons of salt water overnight. Rinse fish, then make brine using the listed ingredients. Bring to a boil, place fish in brine in jars and add a slice of onion and seal. It makes about two pints. Goes good with soda crackers.

Todd Schauer, Abbotsford

3 - 4 cups fresh water fish
1 cup vinegar
½ cup water
2 tablespoons sugar
1 teaspoon mixed spices

CHARLIE'S SOUR FISH

USE 3 QTS. SLICED FISH. Skin and take the backbone out. Heat 1 qt. water and ¾ cup table salt. When cool, pour over fish so they are covered. Cover with a plate. Let set for 24 hours. Rinse with cold water.

Mix ingredients and boil (except wine). Allow to cool. When cold, add wine. Pour mixture over fish. Add sliced onions. Cover with a plate. Keep in cool place for 5 days. Put in jars. Keep chilled.

Darlis Wilfer, Phelps

3 qts. sliced fish
1 qt. water
¾ cup table salt

Mixture

1 qt. vinegar
1 cup sugar
1 tablespoon allspice
1 cup Rhine wine
Sliced onions

PICKLED FISH

CUT 1½ QTS. FISH FILLETS (almost any kind) cut in small, bite-size pieces. Put in salt brine (1 qt. water and ¾ cup salt), let stand in refrigerator 24 hours.

Rinse and cover with white vinegar and let set another 24 hours. Drain. Put fish in jars with sliced onions in between layers of fish.

Make brine by combining ingredients and boil a few minutes. Cool and pour over fish in jars. Refrigerate 1 week or 10 days before eating.

Iris Faude, Medford

1½ qts. fish fillets
1 qt. water
¾ cup salt
White vinegar
Sliced onions

Brine

1 cup sugar
1 cup water
1 cup white wine
2 cups white vinegar
1½ teaspoons pickling spice

PICKLED SUCKERS

FILLET FISH, REMOVE SKIN. Soak 24 hours in mixture of 1 cup salt and 6 cups water. Rinse. Soak 24 hours in vinegar. Rinse.

Make brine by combining ingredients. Simmer for 15 minutes. Add pickling spice. Layer fish and onions and pour brine over top. Ready in 12 hours.

Donald Dorner, Luxemburg

Fish
1 cup salt
6 cups water
Vinegar

Brine

2 cups vinegar
1 cup sugar
¼ cup 7-up
¼ cup white port wine
2 tablespoons pickling spice

PICKLED SUCKERS OR NORTHERNS

SOAK 3 LBS. FISH FILLETS in brine made of 4 cups water and 1 cup canning salt, for 48 hours. Refrigerate at all times.

Drain and rinse fish and soak again in vinegar to cover for 24 hours more. Drain and put in jars with layer of sliced onion.

Make pickling solution by combining all ingredients and bring to boil. Cool, and pour on fish. You may add ½ cup of white wine.

Refrigerate a week or 2 and eat!

Francis Lardinois, Green Bay

3 lbs. fish fillets

Brine

4 cups water
1 cup canning salt
Vinegar
Onion, sliced

Pickling solution

2 cups white vinegar
2 cups sugar
1 teaspoon whole cloves
2 teaspoons mustard seed
1 tablespoon whole allspice or pickling spice
1 teaspoon pepper
½ cup white wine (optional)

PICKLED SALMON

CLEAN SALMON, DEBONE AND CUT into strips. Soften 3 medium onions thinly sliced in hot water and drain well.

Mix all ingredients. In serving bowl, alternate layers of salmon, onions, and the marinade mixture. Let stand 24 hours.

Gib Dutton, Rochester, MN

Salmon
3 medium onions, sliced

Marinade
1 cup white wine vinegar
3 tablespoons olive oil
1 hot pepper, minced
3 cloves garlic, crushed
2 bay leaves
10 cloves
1 tablespoon capers
Pimento olives to taste

PICKLED FISH

CUT FISH IN SMALL BITE-SIZE pieces. Soak 48 hours in brine that will float an egg. Drain, soak 24 hours in white vinegar. Drain and discard vinegar. Make brine by combining ingredients and heat until sugar dissolves. Pour over fish and add sliced onions in layers with fish.

Let stand for 2 weeks in refrigerator or out of refrigerator for 2 days.

You must have enough syrup mixture to cover the amount of fish. You may use smelt, suckers, walleye, or northern.

Mrs. Elaine Heiar, Bloomington

Fish
Salt brine
White vinegar

Brine

4 cups sugar
4 cups white vinegar
¼ cup pickling spice
1 cup white sweet wine
Sliced onions

PICKLED SUCKERS

FILLET AND SKIN 5 QTS. of suckers. Cut to cracker size. This makes about 10-12 pints.

Put in crock with 3 cups pickling salt. Add vinegar to cover completely. Put plate on top and stir daily for 5 days.

Drain fish, soak in ice cold water for 2 hours, adding ice cubes.

Drain, pack in jars (pint size) add onions to taste. Pour brine over fish. Seal, and refrigerate.

Make brine by combining ingredients and boil only until sugar is dissolved. Let cool, and add to fish.

Dennis Mayer, Manitowoc

5 qts. suckers
3 cups pickling salt
Vinegar
Sliced onions

Brine
6 cups vinegar
4 cups sugar
2 cups white port wine
1 box whole mixed
pickling spices (1¼ oz.)

PICKLED FISH

CLEAN AND SKIN ANY GOOD eating fish. Remove bones and cut into pieces 1 in. wide and 2 in. long and ½ in. thick. Put into salt brine strong enough to float an egg, for 48 hours. Drain and cover with water and 1½ cups white vinegar for 24 hours. Drain and put fish and sliced onions in layers in gallon jar, then cover with brine.

Mix brine by heating 4 cups white vinegar and 3 cups sugar to dissolve sugar.

Cool and add 1½ cups sweet white wine. Add pickling spice (remove cinnamon sticks), cover, and refrigerate for 1 week.

Marlene Eder, Almena

Fish
Salt brine
Water
1½ cups white vinegar
Sliced onions

Brine
4 cups white vinegar
3 cups sugar
1½ cups sweet white wine
1/8 cup pickling spice

SMOKED CATFISH

BRINE # 1

MIX THE SALT, SUGAR, garlic and wine in a quart jar and let stand for 12 hours so flavors blend. Then add water and pour over fish.

2 cups fine salt
½ cup brown sugar
2 cloves minced garlic
1/3 cup white wine

BRINE #2

MIX INGREDIENTS together and let stand for 12 hours.

2 cups fine salt
1 cup brown sugar
2 cloves minced garlic
½ cup white wine
1 crushed bay leaf
Small pinch of mace

Brine 1½ inch thick catfish steaks (skin on) for 12 hours. Dry on racks in breezy shade for 2 hours until pellicle forms on skin. The steaks will look like they were lightly varnished.

Smoke at 350° for 3 hours with heavy smudge, turning once. When internal temperature reaches 185°, shut off heat source, open vents and let wood smudge out. Cook for 1 hour.

Brenda and Paul Ross, Fremont

PICKLED FISH

FILLET AND CUT FISH IN bite-size pieces. Soak in salt water for 24 hours. (5/8 cup salt to 1 qt. water) Drain. Soak in vinegar for 24 hours. Drain. Do not cook the fish.

Make brine by combining ingredients and boil for 5 minutes. Cool, and pour over fish. Layer fish, onions, and brine and refrigerate for 5 days.

Mrs. Richard Strauman, Prairie du Chien

Fish
Salt water
Vinegar

Brine

3 cups white vinegar
3 teaspoons pickling spices
1 cup sugar
1 cup water
½ cup white wine
Sliced onions for layering

PICKLED FISH

FILLET FISH, LEAVING FILLETS whole. Mix 1 cup salt to 10 cups water. Soak fish in refrigerator for 24 hours. Rinse and cover with vinegar and refrigerate for 24 hours. Pour off vinegar and cut fish into bite-sized pieces.

Make brine by combining ingredients. Bring to boil and then cool. Layer fish and sliced onions, and brine over top. Let stand 3 days before using.

Laverne Kutcher, Beaver Dam

Fish
1 cup salt
10 cups water
Vinegar

Brine

2 cups white vinegar
1 cup sugar
1 cup water
1 cup white port wine
1½ tablespoons pickling spices
Sliced onions for layering

PICKLED FISH

SOAK 2 QTS. BITE-SIZED FILLETS for 24 hours in salt brine strong enough to float an egg.

Drain, do not rinse, and then soak 24 hours in cider vinegar. Discard vinegar.

Layer fish, sliced onions, and 1 sliced lemon in large jar. Boil and cool the remaining ingredients and pour over fish. Let sit in refrigerator for 3-4 days.

Gerald Lahner, Eau Claire

2 qts. fish
Salt brine
Cider vinegar
Sliced onions
1 sliced lemon

Brine

2 cups white vinegar
1 cup water
Scant 2 tablespoons pickling spice
1 cup sugar
4 shots of muscatel wine

PICKLED FISH

FILLET FISH AND CUT INTO PIECES. Bring kettle of water to boil. Add fish and bring to boil again. Remove fish and drain immediately. Place fish in cold water to cool. Drain again. Place fish and sliced onions in layers in glass jar and cover with the solution. Combine all ingredients and pour over fish and refrigerate.

Ray Kreuzer, Muskego

Fish
Sliced onions

Solution

½ pint white vinegar
1 cup sugar
½ pint white port wine
2 tablespoons pickling spice

KAROLYN'S PICKLED FISH

CUT FISH INTO ½-IN. PIECES. Soak and refrigerate for 24 hours in salt brine. Drain. Cover fish with white vinegar and refrigerate for 24 hours. Drain, but do not rinse.

Boil the following until sugar dissolves; cool and add 1 cup sweet white wine.

Pack fish in glass jar, layer with onions, lemon, sliced orange, and pimento. Continue layering until jar is filled. Cover with cooled brine.

Keep refrigerated and covered with a tight lid.

Jane & Mike Grosvold, Holcombe

2 qts. fish
2 qts. water
2 tablespoons canning salt
White vinegar

Brine

2 cups white vinegar
1 cup water
¾ cup white sugar
2 tablespoons pickling spices
1 cup sweet white wine
Onion slices
Lemon slices
Orange slices
Pimento pieces

BLUEGILL HERRING

CLEAN 30 BLUEGILLS or any other small pan fish. Fillet or leave whole. Soak in PLAIN salt water brine (strong enough to float an egg) for 24 hours. Take fish out of salt brine and soak in white vinegar for 24 hours. Place something heavy on top of fish so they are all under the vinegar. (If there is not enough brine, double batch and if there is any left over, save it for the next batch).

Boil together: 1 cup white sugar; 2 cups white vinegar; 1 cup white port wine and 3 tablespoons pickling spices.

Place fish in layers with 3 or 4 sliced raw onions in glass jars or crocks (use no metal). Pour cooled brine over fish and onions. Cover and keep in refrigerator for 2 to 3 weeks. They are delicious!

Yield: 7 pint jars.

Virginia Kraegenbrink, Menomonee Falls

30 bluegills or other pan fish
Plain salt water brine
1 cup white sugar
2 cups white vinegar
1 cup white port wine
2 tablespoons pickling spices

NORTHERN HERRING

THIS IS OUR FAVORITE herring recipe. It's a lot cheaper than herring found in the store and it's a nice way to use northerns with the bones in.

Take a gallon glass jar and fill with water and enough salt to float an egg.

Cut northern up to sizes desired & put in a gallon jar. Refrigerate for 48 hours.

Drain fish and cover with 1½ cups white vinegar. Refrigerate for 24 hours.

Drain, remove and rinse fish. Replace in jar, alternating layers of fish with layers of onions. Heat the following mixture before adding to fish: 4 cups white vinegar; 1½ cups sugar; ¼ cup pickling spices and 1 cup white wine. Let stand for 10 days.

Robert Niehaus, West Bend

1 northern pike
5½ cups white vinegar
1½ cups sugar
¼ cup pickling spices
1 cup white wine

VENISON SAUSAGE

MIX GROUND VENISON WITH ground pork fat at 2-1 ratio. Sprinkle Morton's Sausage & Poultry Seasoning over meat and knead into the meat with fingers until seasoned at rate of 1 pkg. seasoning to 12 lbs. of meat. Stuff into pork casings as links or as rope sausage.

Laverne Wubben, Hazel Green

Ground venison
Ground pork fat
Morton's Sausage & Poultry Seasoning
Pork casings

SALAMI

MIX INGREDIENTS WELL. DIVIDE IN 2 parts. Roll in foil and boil in water for 1 hour. Cool. Pick holes on bottom of foil for draining. Return to refrigerator for 24 hours before cutting.

Berneice Dombek, Lyndon Station

3 lbs. ground venison
or beef or combination
1 teaspoon pepper
½ teaspoon garlic salt
½ teaspoon mustard seed
½ teaspoon mustard powder
1 cup water
3 tablespoons Morton's
Quick-Curing Salt

BOB'S SMOKED VENISON SAUSAGE

GRIND PORK AND VENISON. Mix. Combine salt, pepper, and rest of spices. Add flour, onion, and 2 cups water to meat. The water makes the sausage mix and stuff easier and will evaporate during the smoking process. Mix until the mustard seed is evenly distributed throughout the meat. Let stand at about 40 degrees for 24 hours. Stuff in 2 in. casings and hang in smokehouse. Bring temperature in smokehouse to 180° and hold until internal temperature of sausage reaches 150° (about 2 hours).

Reduce heat and smoke to taste. The best smoked flavor comes from a very cold smoke. It is not necessary to have a fire in the smoker all the time, just fire often enough to keep the sausage from freezing. Sausage will pick up a good smoked flavor simply from hanging in well-seasoned smokehouse.

Bob Thorpe, Aniwa

5 lbs. pork
10 lbs. venison
4 tablespoons salt
2 tablespoons pepper
4 teaspoons sage
4 tablespoons mustard seed
4 tablespoons commercial cure
(1 lb./100 lbs. meat)
1 heaping teaspoon garlic
2 cups whole wheat flour
1 onion grated or ground with meat

VENISON SAUSAGE

MIX TOGETHER ALL INGREDIENTS and refrigerate for 24 hours (covered). Form in 2 rolls and wrap tightly in foil. Bake on rack in pan for 1 hour at 350°. Cool in foil until able to handle. Remove from foil and re-wrap. Refrigerate.

Yvonne Boelter, Milwaukee

1 lb. ground venison
½ lb. ground beef
½ lb. ground pork
1 teaspoon course ground pepper
Scant tablespoon liquid smoke
1 cup water
2 tablespoons quick curing salt
½ teaspoon garlic powder
½ teaspoon marjoram
1 tablespoon mustard seed

SMOKED VENISON SUMMER SAUSAGE

THIS RECIPE IS CALCULATED for 10 lbs. of sausage. Chill meat (38° is perfect). Then grind through a 3/16 in. grinder plate. Place in a large plastic, wood, glass, or ceramic tub or crock.

Mix all ingredients by hand to blend spices evenly and chill in cooler for 2-3 days.

Stuff into 2¾ x 24 in. beef middles. These are usually available from a butcher. 3 x 28 in. fibrous casings may also be used. Make the sausages about 1 foot long and then tie them off. Be sure they are stuffed tightly.

After stuffing, hang so they do not touch each other and dry at room temperature for 5 hours. Transfer the hanger to smoker or smokehouse and smoke at 120° with a heavy smudge for 6-8 hours or until an internal temperature of 145° is reached.

Smoking longer (6-8 hours) will flavor the sausage more.

When smoking is completed to your satisfaction, remove and shower with tapwater until an internal temperature of 120° is reached.

Hang at room temperature in a draft free area for 2 days. Your house will smell as delicious as the oldtime meat markets did and you will have a delicious auburn summer sausage!

Brenda and Paul Ross, Fremont

8 lbs. lean elk meat or venison
2 lbs. fat pork trimmings

Mixture

1 tablespoon cracked black pepper
10 teaspoons household salt
3 tablespoons sugar
½ teaspoon saltpeter
1 tablespoon + 1 teaspoon coriander
1 teaspoon ground ginger
1 tablespoon ground mustard
1 teaspoon mustard seed
1 tablespoon garlic powder
2 cups rose wine

VENISON SAUSAGE PATTIES

USE 2 LBS. PORK FOR EVERY lb. of venison. For every 10 lbs. of mixed meat, evenly sprinkle the following ingredients: salt, pepper, and sage. Grind the meat twice, using a coarse setting first, then a fine setting. Form into patties and freeze.

It will keep for several months.

Lori Kramer, Wisconsin Rapids

2 lbs. pork for every lb. of venison
4 oz. salt
1 oz. pepper
½ oz. sage

VENISON SUMMER SAUSAGE

USE 2 LBS. GROUND VENISON (plain, we never add pork as many do, the natural small amount of tallow left on the deer as we skin it is enough moisture).

Mix all ingredients and then mix with the ground meat. Make into rolls of size you wish. Roll in foil with meat to shiny side. Refrigerate for 24 hours. Place on a rack over a pan to catch drippings. Insert fork through under side of foil to allow drainage as it bakes.

Bake for 1 hour and 15 minutes at 325°.

Marilyn Benish, Yuba

2 lbs. ground venison
1½ teaspoons liquid smoke
1 cup water
1 tablespoon mustard seed
½ teaspoon onion powder
1/8 teaspoon garlic powder
3 tablespoons Morton's Tender Quick Meat Cure

BEER AND MOLASSES SMOKED FISH

CUT 2-3 LARGE FISH IN HALF lengthwise, but don't scale. Combine together all ingredients and mix well. Place fish in crock and pour brine over top, keeping the fish under the surface of the brine. Store in refrigerator for 24 hours, stirring after 12 hours to ensure proper penetration into fish. Smoke with your favorite apple or hickory wood.

Mark Holzmann, Mount Calvary

2-3 large fish

Brine

4 cups water
¾ cup salt
1 12 oz. bottle beer
½ cup dark molasses
1 teaspoon pepper
½ teaspoon whole cloves
Pinch of chili powder

HINZ' WORLD FAMOUS SMOKED FISH SPREAD

LET CREAM CHEESE WARM TO room temperature. Finely chop the smoked fish and onion. Add remaining ingredients. Mix thoroughly with hand and form ball. Chill. Serve with crackers. Excellent to handle those large quantities of leftover smoked salmon and trout.

Michael A. Hinz, Sheboygan

8-12 oz. smoked fish
8 oz. cream cheese, softened
1½ teaspoon lemon juice
1 tablespoon horseradish
½ teaspoon Accent Flavor Enhancer
1 small onion

SMOKED FISH SPREAD

MIX ALL INGREDIENTS. Salt and pepper to taste.

Jerry Wick, Milwaukee

1½ lbs. smoked fish
1 cup mayonnaise or salad dressing
2 tablespoons finely chopped sweet pickles
1 tablespoon dry mustard
Dash worcestershire sauce
Salt and pepper to taste

SMOKED FISH SPREAD

COMBINE ALL INGREDIENTS and blend in food processor.

Mrs. George Mass, Lac du Flambeau

9 oz. smoked fish, deboned
½ cup plus 2 tablespoons sour cream
4 oz. cream cheese (at room temperature)
1 tablespoon fresh lemon juice
11 tablespoons butter
2 tablespoons chopped dillweed
2 tablespoons minced scallion

VENISON MINCEMEAT

COVER DEER NECK WITH WATER, add tablespoon or so of salt and simmer until the meat falls away from bone. (It should take about 2 hours depending upon size.)

Add suet and apples to venison and put through meat grinder or processor; don't chop them too fine.

Add this ground-up mixture and the white sugar to the cider and bring it to a boil. Then cook it for half an hour. Stir constantly. Add rest of ingredients and bring to boil. Cool. Mix in brandy and rum to taste and pack in sterilized jars. It makes great pie.

G. D. Winter, Shawano

Deer neck
Beef suet (1/3 to ½ of the weight of venison)
Apples, peeled and cored
White sugar (same weight as the venison)
1 qt. of apple cider
1 tablespoon ground cloves
1 tablespoon grated nutmeg
1 tablespoon cinnamon
1 teaspoon powdered mace
1 teaspoon allspice
2 boxes black raisins
Brown sugar (about ½ as much as the white sugar)
Candied orange and/or lemon peel

MINCEMEAT

GRIND MEAT, SUET, APPLES, raisins, oranges, and lemons. Add all other ingredients and simmer 2-3 hours. It may either be canned, used immediately, or frozen for later use.

Berneice Dombek, Lyndon Station

6 cups venison
2 cups suet (beef)
10 cups apples
4 cups sugar
2 cups syrup
6 cups raisins
2 oranges
2 lemons
1 tablespoon salt
2 tablespoons cinnamon
2 tablespoons nutmeg
2 tablespoons allspice
1 tablespoon cloves
1 qt. cider or fruit juice